THE EVERYTHING

Dog Obedience Book

Dear Reader,

Congratulations! You're trying to be a responsible dog owner. You know how I know that? Because you obviously care enough about your dog's care and behavior to pick up this book.

Dog ownership is a big responsibility and a lot of work, especially if you have a puppy or adolescent. No matter what kind of dog you have—big or little, purebred or mixed, puppy or adult—this book will teach you how to build a healthy relationship with him (or her!), teach him just about anything, solve common behavior problems, and live with him to both prevent property damage and fulfill his needs for mental and physical activity. If you don't have a dog yet, or for your next dog, you'll find information about selecting your next best friend.

I feel very fortunate to have spent my entire life in the company of dogs, and especially lucky to be able to love what I do and do what I love for a living. I hope this book helps you make the most of your life with your dog.

Happy Tails!

Jennifer Bridwell

The EVERYTHING® Series

Editorial

Publisher	Gary M. Krebs
Director of Product Development	Paula Munier
Managing Editor	Laura M. Daly
Associate Copy Chief	Sheila Zwiebel
Acquisitions Editor	Kerry Smith
Development Editor	Meredith O'Hayre
Associate Production Editor	Casey Ebert

Production

Director of Manufacturing	Susan Beale
Production Project Manager	Michelle Roy Kelly
Prepress	Erick DaCosta
	Matt LeBlanc
Interior Layout	Heather Barrett
	Brewster Brownville
	Colleen Cunningham
	Jennifer Oliveira
Cover Design	Erin Alexander
	Stephanie Chrusz
	Frank Rivera

THE
EVERYTHING®
DOG OBEDIENCE BOOK

From bad dog to good dog—a step-by-step guide to curbing misbehavior

Jennifer Bridwell

Adams Media
Avon, Massachusetts

This book is dedicated to my most ardent supporter, CFO, and best friend, my "Mommie Dearest," and to the memory of Midas, who took the first steps on this journey with me in 1982.

An Everything® Series Book.
Everything® and everything.com® are registered trademarks of F+W Publications, Inc.

Published by Adams Media, an F+W Publications Company
57 Littlefield Street, Avon, MA 02322 U.S.A.
www.adamsmedia.com

ISBN 10: 1-59869-257-7
ISBN 13: 978-1-59869-257-0

Printed in the United States of America.

J   I   H   G   F   E   D   C   B

Library of Congress Cataloging-in-Publication Data

Bridwell, Jennifer.
The Everything dog obedience book / Jennifer Bridwell.
p. cm. — (An Everything series book)
ISBN-13: 978-1-59869-257-0 (pbk.)
ISBN-10: 1-59869-257-7 (pbk.)
1. Dogs—Training. 2. Dogs—Behavior. I. Title.
SF431.B755 2007
636.7'0887—dc22   2007010847

This publication is designed to provide accurate and authoritative information with regard to the subject matter covered. It is sold with the understanding that the publisher is not engaged in rendering legal, accounting, or other professional advice. If legal advice or other expert assistance is required, the services of a competent professional person should be sought.

—From a *Declaration of Principles* jointly adopted by a Committee of the American Bar Association and a Committee of Publishers and Associations

Many of the designations used by manufacturers and sellers to distinguish their products are claimed as trademarks. Where those designations appear in this book and Adams Media was aware of a trademark claim, the designations have been printed with initial capital letters.

All interior photographs taken by Brandee McBride-LaCava

This book is available at quantity discounts for bulk purchases.
For information, please call 1-800-289-0963.

Contents

THE EVERYTHING DOG OBEDIENCE BOOK

Acknowledgments

I am so grateful to the thousands of people and dogs I've worked with in classes and private lessons over the years—you've taught me as much as I've taught you!

I deeply appreciate the generosity with which Freddie Merritt, DVM; Cindy Ice, DVM; Toni Thompson; Marianna Beard; and the late and sorely missed Patty Ruzzo both shared and encouraged knowledge with grace and humor.

Thanks to Carol Walsh, for trusting me with your "baby" and not freaking out when I made it my own! Amanda Wendt and Chris List, my team at The Canine Connection Dog Training, thanks for helping me keep all the plates spinning. It's been an eventful couple of years; you'll never know how much I appreciate you and your support.

To Neville, for keeping the home fires burning, and for walking the dogs on Sundays!

Top Ten Things to Know about Training Your Dog

1. It's never too early or too late in your dog's life to start training.

2. You are training your dog all the time, whether you're trying to or not.

3. Your dog doesn't know English (or any other verbal language).

4. Being nice to your dog isn't the same thing as being permissive.

5. Your dog isn't born knowing it's wrong to chew your shoes.

6. If you treat your dog like a person, he's going to treat you like a dog.

7. Love isn't enough to create a well-behaved dog. He needs exercise, discipline, affection, training, and socialization.

8. Giving your dog people food won't turn him into a beggar.

9. The smartest dogs aren't necessarily the easiest to train.

10. Your dog is not a person in a dog suit!

Introduction

▶ AS LONG AS there have been humans on the planet, there have been dogs in our lives, from peaceful but separate coexistence when dogs were little more than the scavenging cleanup crew for our trash piles outside the cave, to the present trend of designer dogs and extravagant care of the most coddled "fur-babies." Our relationships with dogs have changed a lot over time, and not always for the best.

As our relationships with dogs have changed, so have the methods used to train them. The method pendulum has swung from punishment-based pop-and-jerk methods, to a no-corrections, cookie-power approach, based on methods used to train marine mammals. The problem is, you can't leave your dog in the tank and go home; he lives in the "tank" with you. The truth is, there is no one perfect method that is going to work for every dog, every owner, or every problem. And that's okay; we're all individuals, and we shouldn't expect a one-size-fits-all, cookie-cutter approach to work for anything but, well, for making cookies! In general, you're pretty safe recognizing and rewarding the stuff you like, and ignoring or correcting the stuff you don't. *The Everything Dog Obedience Book®* will help you find the balance of methods that work best for you and your dog.

Unfortunately, many people wait until their dog has a behavior problem to start training. In fact, what people would call dog problems are really people problems, either because the behavior is totally normal for the dog (although perhaps exhibited in an inappropriate way) or because the person somehow caused the dog's behavior, usually by rewarding the wrong things early in the relationship.

The important thing to remember is that your dog is always going to think, feel, act, and react like a dog, no matter how much you try to treat him like a furry person. As long as you take his normal dog needs into consideration and make sure he has productive outlets for them, and give him clear boundaries and leadership he can rely on, your dog really can become your best friend. Like life, the relationship you develop with your dog is a journey, not a destination—enjoy it!

Chapter 1

The Right Dog for You

Finding your perfect companion may not be the easiest task you'll ever undertake, but it may certainly be one of the most rewarding. Pedigree or mixed breed, puppy or adult dog, you can find the ideal prospect to mold into the dog of your dreams with a little research and patience. Unfortunately, great dogs don't usually come out of the box that way—nope, they have owners who took the time and energy to understand and train them.

What Dogs Want You to Know

Dogs need a lot more than just love and affection to become good pets. Understanding who they are, including their normal behaviors and their physical, emotional, and mental needs, is a vital part of a happy and fulfilling life with dogs.

The Lap Wolf

Dogs want you to know that they're not furry people. They're not, even though most of them tolerate, even enjoy, being treated like people. What's not to love? Being one the people means comfy places to rest, yummy stuff to eat, and attention on demand…wait a minute! They've got it better than people! All the benefits with none of the responsibilities—what a deal!

For the most part, treating dogs like people is fine as long as you don't expect them to act like people in return. They simply don't and can't think or act like people. It doesn't make them any less wonderful for being who and what they are, but the truth is, from the 260-pound mastiff down to the 4-pound Yorkie, they all have the heart of a wolf beating inside them.

Speaking the Language

Dogs also want you to know that until you teach them the meaning of a word, they don't know what it means, even if you repeat it many times, loudly. Unlike people, they're just not verbal animals, and they don't know any word until it has been associated with its meaning many times. For them, any language is a foreign one, so expecting them to understand and respond to commands they've never been taught is not only unrealistic, it's also unfair. While you're teaching your dog to understand your language, the next several chapters will help you learn your dog's.

Have Realistic Expectations

Now that you have an idea what you're getting into, let's really get into the nitty-gritty. It is going to take time, dedication, and persistence on your part to help your dog be well behaved.

The Dog's Motto

Without guidance, dogs tend to act like dogs. "If it smells good, eat it; if it feels good, do it; if it smells bad, roll in it" seems to be their basic motto for life. Knowing what to expect means you can nip unwanted behavior in the bud and provide appropriate outlets for both your dog's energy and his normal doggie behaviors.

Two Steps Forward, One Step Back

During the training process, there is a normal cycle of progression and regression. Think back to when you learned a new skill, like driving a car with a manual transmission or playing a musical instrument. For a while, you made steady progress, and then all of a sudden, you were all thumbs and stalled the car at a light or hit a sour note. It's no different with dogs. At some point during training, you're going to give a command that you're sure your dog knows, and he's going to look at you like he's never heard the word before. When and why regression happens is not as important as how you handle it. Expecting normal regression prepares you to deal with it and help your dog through any confusion. You and your dog will both make mistakes along the way and that's ok; find the lesson in each one.

FACT

There are several theories about why learning regression happens. One of the most popular theories is that regression occurs when the brain is transferring information from short-term to long-term memory. Whatever the reason, take advantage of it for what it is—a training opportunity.

Assess Your Lifestyle

Your lifestyle is the most important consideration in choosing your ideal canine companion. If the dog's care and training doesn't fit into your lifestyle, then the relationship is simply not going to work, and will end up with both of you being miserable and not enjoying each other's company.

Looks Aren't Everything

Choosing your dog based primarily on how she looks makes about as much sense as choosing your spouse that way. Let go of any preconceived notions you have about certain breeds that you've gotten from movies or TV, and be honest with yourself. If your idea of a perfect weekend is spending two days under the covers watching old movies, then an energetic and active dog isn't an ideal match. Work all day, stay out late, and sleep in? A puppy probably isn't a good idea at this point in your life.

The Tough Questions

Before you start searching for your new dog, ask yourself some tough questions:

- Why do I want a dog now?
- How many hours will the dog be alone each day?
- Am I active or sedentary?
- How much time can I realistically devote to daily basic care like training, exercising, and brushing my dog?
- How much living space do I have?
- Are there children prominently in my life?
- Can I afford the costs involved with owning a dog?
- Who will end up as primary caretaker of the dog, and does that person want a dog?

Now that you're thinking about how your lifestyle affects your choice, you're ready to start doing research to find the right dog for you. You may have even decided that this isn't the right time to add a dog to your life. If you're not sure, do a little research project for a month. Most people who own dogs are more than happy to talk about them. Ask people you meet with a dog how the dog is to live with—how much money, time, and energy they spend taking care of the dog, and what they like most and least about dog ownership. Take notes and re-evaluate your decision.

Where to Get Your Dog

Where you get your dog will depend greatly on what kind of dogs your research has led you to put on your shortlist. There are lots of different ways to find your new pet, from searching the Internet to finding a dog in the street. Other than actually finding a dog and keeping her, you are probably going to have several options from which to choose her, including breeders, shelters, and rescue groups.

Breeders

If you're looking for a purebred puppy or a competition prospect, you'll want to start with a breeder. Most breeders occasionally have adolescent or adult dogs available as well. There are many great, responsible breeders out there who do everything in their power to improve their breed. Unfortunately, for every wonderful breeder in the world, there are several that aren't so great. Through lack of knowledge, misguided intentions, or plain greed, they just want to produce puppies to sell. Because there are so many common genetic health problems in purebred dogs, it is very important to get your purebred puppy from a breeder who does health testing of the parents before breeding them. Along with the major registries like the American Kennel Club and the United Kennel Club (see Appendix B for contact info), every breed has a parent club, which sets the standard for both the breed and the members of the club (the breeders), often including a code of ethics that members must follow with the care, breeding, and placement of their dogs. Getting your purebred dog from a responsible breeder improves your chances of getting a healthy, happy dog that appears and behaves normally for his breed.

How to Find and Select a Breeder

Finding a breeder is easy. You can find literally thousands of them in the back of any dog magazine, the classified section of your local paper, bulletin boards around town, or on the Internet. However, just because someone has managed to produce puppies doesn't mean that he or she is a good source from which to purchase your dog. Finding a great breeder who cares about the long-term well-being of both the puppy and you is a little tougher, but is easy enough with a little research and time. In addition to the American Kennel Club, breed parent clubs, and other national and international dog clubs, most areas have local all-breed kennel clubs and individual-breed clubs. These clubs are usually great resources of both information and support. You can also pick the brains of your local veterinarians, groomers, and trainers. Dog professionals usually know or have listings for both breeders and local dog clubs, and they may even share a little insight into some of the breeds that you're considering.

Rescues and Shelters

Whether you're looking for a purebred or a mixed breed, puppy or adult, rescue organizations and shelters can also be great places to find your new companion. Almost every breed has its own rescue organization—and some have one or more in each state or region. In addition, you can often find purebreds—most often adolescents—in shelters.

Many shelters and rescue organizations list their available dogs on *www .petfinder.com*, which can save you a bit of legwork. Most shelters welcome visitors but may have certain requirements, so it's best to call before you go.

The Problem With Pet Stores

Pet stores, especially the few independently owned ones left, are wonderful sources of quality food, supplies, and information for puppies. However, they're not good places to actually purchase a puppy. The overwhelming majority of puppies for sale in pet stores are factory farmed in puppy mills by "breeders" whose only motive is to produce as many puppies as possible as quickly as possible, with little or no regard for the health or welfare of the puppies or the parents. Because the puppy mills breed with no regard to the parent's suitability for breeding (i.e., whether the dog closely matches the breed standard, and whether the dog has no temperament faults and has been tested to be free of hereditary medical defects), the puppies produced are often ticking time bombs of medical and behavioral problems.

Unfortunately, the problems don't stop when the puppies are born. They miss the vital handling and socialization that a responsible breeder would provide them during their first few formative weeks. Then comes the trip to the pet sore. The journey itself is traumatic, sometimes with a stop for several days at an overcrowded puppy warehouse. Finally, the puppy makes it to the pet store, only to be isolated in a sterile environment with no enrichment. If he's lucky enough to be really cute, then people might handle him multiple times a day. Then again, some people have no business handling puppies, and he could just as easily be frightened by an unpleasant experience.

Pet-store puppies are notoriously difficult to housebreak because they have been forced to eat, sleep, pee, and poop in the same confined area. This goes against the natural desire for cleanliness that puppies learn when they are three to five weeks old. The longer the puppy stays in the pet store, the more difficult the housebreaking and socialization process will be.

Finally, pet stores that sell puppies capitalize on impulse purchases. Buying a puppy on impulse is never a good idea. Raising a puppy is a huge commitment of time, energy, and money after the purchase of the puppy. Puppies purchased on impulse commonly end up in shelters because their owners failed to realize the responsibility and work required.

Choosing the Right Type of Dog for You

Now that you've taken the time to analyze your lifestyle, you should have some idea of the personality type you're looking for. Are you looking for a busy, active dog, or one that wants to curl up with you by the fire while you read? Once you've decided on the activity level you can live with without losing your mind, it's time to start narrowing down your possibilities.

What Age Is the Right Age?

The first thing you'll want to decide is whether to look for a puppy, adolescent, adult, or senior dog. There are pros and cons to each choice. A young puppy doesn't have any of the bad habits that an older dog might, but it's practically a full-time job to housebreak, manage, and train a puppy. An adolescent or older dog may come with some baggage or bad habits that you have to undo, but they may already be housebroken or partially trained, or have a more practical energy level for your lifestyle. Don't let the cuteness factor be your guide when deciding what age your new dog should be. Millions of puppies are in shelters because people couldn't resist the little fuzzballs, until the novelty wore off and the reality of puppy parenting set in.

Purebred or Mixed Breed?

Your next step is to decide whether you want a purebred dog or a mixed breed. With purebred dogs, there is a written breed standard describing the physical attributes of the breed, like size, color, and coat type; so you can assume that most dogs of that breed will (at least roughly) look like the breed they are. Additionally, you can get some idea of the normal personality traits and activity level that breed is likely to have. However, not every dog reads as the breed's standard, and an individual may deviate from the norm slightly or greatly. If you're thinking about a purebred dog, it's a good idea to go to a couple of dog shows so you can get an idea of what the breed you're considering is really like, and what their maintenance needs are.

Be patient. Finding the right dog can take time. Researching several breeds, visiting several breeders, shelters, or both—maybe multiple times—can be a little frustrating, but, again, getting a puppy or dog on impulse is never a good idea. You're going to be living with this dog for hopefully fifteen years or more, so take a little time to find a great prospect.

Some of the best dogs in the world are mixed or random bred dogs. Mixed-breed dogs come in all shapes, sizes, and coat types. Sometimes the breeds in the mix are obvious—or you know who the parents are—and sometimes it's a mystery. If you're searching for a puppy, this can be a bit of a gamble if you have specific size or personality traits you're looking for.

Adopting the Special-needs or Geriatric Dog

There are angels among us. They are the ones who have the time, patience, and fortitude to adopt a special-needs dog. These dogs may have behavioral or medical issues that make them less-than-ideal candidates for most people. Maybe they're just old and need more in the way of care than their previous owners were able to provide. If you're looking for a long-term project and have the emotional, physical, and financial means, by all means consider adopting one of these dogs. Shelter Alliance and Resources for Animals with Handicaps, (SARAH, Inc, see Appendix A for more info) is one of several organizations that specializes in rescuing, rehabilitating, and placing special-needs dogs.

Picking Out Your Perfect Prospect

Now that you've decided what kind of dog you're looking for and have some idea of where you're going to get your new family member, it's finally time for the fun part—meeting and playing with puppies and dogs!

The Pick of the Litter

If possible, plan on visiting each litter you're choosing from several times, from the time the puppies are about five weeks old until they're ready to come home (usually between eight and twelve weeks) so you have some idea of the general temperament and energy level of the puppies before you make your final selection. Some breeders will make the selection for you, placing the puppies in the homes that they feel will be most successful for all concerned. If you are getting your puppy from a breeder, this is the time to ask about health testing that was done on the puppies' parents prior to breeding (do your research for the breed you've selected and find out what genetic health problems are common). You should also meet the puppies' parents—at least their mother—if possible. If you don't like the temperament of the parents, continue your search with another breeder. If you have your choice of puppies, you'll want to observe and handle them as a group and individually. The pushy, pick-me type of puppy may seem almost irresistible, but may not be the best choice if your personality isn't as strong as the puppy's. The breeder or caretaker of the litter is an invaluable source of information about the puppies' individual personalities. Use their observations to help you choose the best match for your personality and lifestyle. There are also some simple tests you can do with the puppies individually to help you make your decision:

- **Have the breeder place the puppy in a quiet room with you** (they can observe, but shouldn't interact with the puppy). Does the puppy come right to you? Jump up on you? Paw or mouth you? Ignore you? What if you call her?
- **Get up and walk around the room a bit, encouraging the puppy to follow if necessary.** Does the puppy follow willingly? Get in your way by tripping you or jumping on you? Go the other way? Not move from the original place?
- **Pick up the puppy and gently restrain her.** Does she accept restraint willingly? Struggle a little? Struggle a lot? Fight frantically, including biting and growling?
- **Get down on the floor with the puppy.** One at a time, pick up and handle each foot and lightly pinch the webbing between the toes with your fingertips (no nails, please!) for a few seconds. Do the same with each ear, looking inside the ears and again, lightly pinching the ear leather. Gently pull the puppy's tail and lightly grab him by his scruff (the loose skin at the back of the neck). Did the puppy accept handling calmly? Did he struggle to get away? Did he cry? Did he fight furiously?
- **Put the puppy down and stroke him a couple of time from his ears down to his tail.** Does he stay with you, snuggling up for more attention? Does he go away, but come back with little or no encouragement? Does he go away and stay away? Does he seem to hold resentment about the last test?
- **Take one of the puppy's toys** (a crumpled ball of paper works in a pinch) and toss it a few feet from the puppy. Does she go get it and bring it back? Does she chase it but lose interest? Does she get it and run away with it? Does she ignore it completely? If she ran away with it, what does she do when you follow her and try to get it back?
- **Take an old metal pot or pan and drop it a few feet from the puppy.** In another minute or so, open an automatic umbrella a few feet from the puppy. Does the puppy startle, but then investigate the novelties within a few seconds? Does he cautiously circle them but never make contact? Does he jump right on them, maybe even mouthing them? Does he head for the hills in a panic?

Ideally, perform these tests on the litters you're evaluating two or three times from the ages of six to ten weeks to get the clearest picture of the puppies' basic temperaments. In general, most pet homes are looking for a "yes" to the first question in most or all of the tests above. Pushier or more dominant puppies are fine as working dogs or for experienced dog owners or competition homes, but they can be a little (or a lot) too much to live with for the average person who works and wants a life other than entertaining a dog.

FACT

Registration with the AKC or any other registry in no way represents or corresponds to the quality of the dog. It only proves that the dog's parents were registered as purebreds, and that the dog is also registered as a purebred. It is used as a selling tool with dogs, because many people mistakenly assume that registration "with papers" means the dog is good quality.

On the other hand, if you're looking for a dog to run your daily mile with you, a Pekingese isn't a great choice, unless you're planning on carrying her. Overly submissive or fearful dogs aren't usually easy to live with either, as they can be crippled by their fears and neuroses. A puppy that is calm, friendly, and confident is just easier to live with than one who isn't. Of course, picking out that potentially perfect puppy is just the beginning— there's a lot to do before you bring him home!

Selecting the Adolescent or Adult Dog

Adolescent and young adult dogs are often in need of new homes because of some behavioral issue that their previous owner couldn't live with. Many of these issues are relatively easy to solve and were actually caused or exacerbated by the owners in question, but you do need to be aware that you're not dealing with a blank slate and may have some bad habits to undo. Ask the current caretaker of the dog about the dog's behavioral strengths and weaknesses. You'll want to know how the dog is when having his nails trimmed; how he acts when he has food, bones, or toys (in other words, is he overly protective?); and if he's ever threatened or put his teeth on people. You'll also be interested in whether he's mellow and laid back, or excitable and nervous. If you're getting your dog from a shelter, find out if the staff will allow you to interact with him through the fence before meeting. If you can play with him a little, find out the answers to these questions:

- Does he seem happy to see you?
- If you put your hand flat on the fence, does he snuggle up?
- Ask the staff for a handful of dog food and toss half of it on the floor between you and the dog. While he's eating, kneel down. Does he continue eating happily? Does he get stiff? Growl or worse?
- After he's done eating, give the fence a little kick and give a little yell: "Hey!" Does he startle but come right back happily? Does he cower, run away, or back away growling? Does he react with aggression, growling, barking, or jumping on the fence?
- Make up to him with a sweet voice and a couple of pieces of dog food. Does he forgive you or hold a grudge?

If any dog you're considering responds to any of the tests in anything less than a friendly manner, keep looking. If he's friendly, ask for a leash and take him for a little walk. Even walking inside the facility for twenty minutes is enough for you to get some idea of whether you can live with his personality and energy level. Untrained is one thing, but indifferent or aggressive probably aren't among your top picks. If there are other family members or pets, they should also be introduced to the candidate. Pets should be introduced in a neutral environment to reduce stress.

ALERT!

It can be tough emotionally to visit a shelter. You may feel you can save all the dogs you see. It's a sad fact that some dogs just don't have what it takes to become good pets. There are too many nice dogs languishing in shelters to risk injury to yourself or others with a dog that can't be helped.

Before You Bring Your New Dog Home

Congratulations, you've finally picked out the right dog for you! Now it's time to prepare yourself and your environment for the arrival of your new best friend.

Getting Ready for the New Arrival

Before your dog comes home, you may want to take at least a couple of days off to sleep in (especially if you're getting a puppy) and gather supplies. It's so much easier to have them before you need them, rather than wait until the dog is in the house to realize what you need but don't have. The section "Tools of the Trade" in the next chapter will help you figure out what supplies you'll need. You may also want to plan your dog's arrival around a vacation so you can adjust to your new routine without worrying about keeping a tight schedule. You should stick as closely to your normal schedule as possible, including the times when your puppy will be crated when you go back to your normal activities.

Before you get your dog, you will want to have a safe way to transport your dog to his new home. A crate is the safest option for any age dog, but a puppy or small dog can be held on the lap of someone in the back seat for a short trip (have towels handy in case of accidents on the way home). Seat belts are available for the restraint of larger dogs. For the safety of the dog and everyone else on the road, the dog should not ride on the driver's lap. You should also plan on having at least several days' worth of whatever food your new dog is currently eating on hand to avoid adding digestive upsets to what will already be a stressful time.

Home at Last!

When you first get home, give your dog a few quiet minutes to relieve herself before bringing her in the house to meet her new family. Let her explore the immediate area and meet each family member on her own time without everybody grabbing at her. Everyone is bound to be excited, but try not to overwhelm her with everyone in the neighborhood coming over to meet her the day you bring her home. Give her a few days to settle in while you both adjust to your new routines.

Expect a few sleepless nights. This is a whole new life for your dog, with none of the things that are familiar to her to give her comfort. Crating her in your bedroom at night is a good idea. Letting her out of her crate to sleep in your bed because she's crying isn't. Grit your teeth and hang in there. Some dogs are soothed by a wind-up clock ticking right outside the crate, and it wouldn't hurt to give her a couple of big fluffy toys to cuddle up with. It helps to make sure she's tired out and recently pottied before you put her in the crate for the night. If you do have to take her out in the middle of the night to relieve herself—chances are you will for a few weeks—don't play with her or give her treats. Give her a few minutes to do what she needs to do, and then put her right back in the crate. Don't forget to take lots of pictures so you don't forget her first days home.

Chapter 2

Starting Out on the Right Paw

The first few months your dog is home are critical. They set the tone and pattern for what your relationship will be for the dog's lifetime. That may sound a little bit intimidating, but starting out right is relatively easy with a little discipline and consistency on your part. Before you bring your dog home, take a few minutes to visualize him two years from now. How do you want him to behave? For the next two years, remember you are training him whether you intend to or not.

Leaving the Past Behind

One of the great things about dogs is that they live in the moment. Good or bad, whatever background they come from, they are ready to leave it behind. Some of them may need a little help in overcoming learned fears or in changing bad habits, but they don't lie around dwelling on anything that happened before. Whatever your dog's past is, there is nothing that you can do to take it away or make up for it, so all you can do is move forward.

Let It Go

While letting go of the past is easy for dogs, it often isn't so easy for people. Sometimes new owners focus on the dogs' past, making excuses for the dog's behavior and attributing every mistake to a history of abuse, real or imagined. They can actually keep the dog from progressing because they're so wrapped up in coddling the "victim." While coddling might make the caretaker feel better, it doesn't help the dog at all.

Other people might be holding on to their own past, or memories of past dogs, and expect the new dog to behave in the same way as the previous dog did, especially if they are the same breed. Even worse is expecting the new dog to know the same rules and commands the other dog knew.

Tools of the Trade: Everything You Need to Contain and Control Your Dog

There is an abundance of tools at your disposal to help keep your dog safe and out of trouble. Depending on the circumstances, you might use a combination of crates, gates, tethers, draglines, and leashes to keep your dog under control—and that's just indoors! This section will focus on the supplies you need to interrupt and prevent mischief.

The Basics

You'll need to gather some supplies to get started out right.

- **Crate:** at least one; consider getting a second crate for car travel.
- **Collar:** at least one well-fitting plain collar; maybe get special training collars later.
- **Leashes:** at least one 6-foot leash (longer lengths are helpful), possibly a retractable. Do yourself a favor and buy a leash that feels good in your hand, rather than what fits your dog or matches his collar.
- **Gate(s).**
- **Draglines:** at least one 6-8 foot and at least one 25-50 foot.
- **Aversives:** at least six of each type you use (noise, water, or taste). You'll get more details about aversives later in this chapter.
- **A fence,** or at least a plan for how you will contain your dog outside.
- **Food and water dishes:** stainless steel is best.
- **Food:** If you know what your dog is eating now, get enough to feed him for at least a couple of weeks so any change can be done gradually.
- **Toys:** Time and experience will teach you what your dog likes, so start with a few different types
- **Chewing items:** again, experiment with a variety (you'll get more detail about this in Chapter 8).
- **Soft treats for training.**
- **An appointment** with your veterinarian within a few days of bringing your dog home.

Aversives and Deterrents for Misbehavior

There are several things that you can use to help your dog realize the error of his ways when he makes poor choices. You want to use something that is aversive—that is, something your dog doesn't like and will work to avoid—but isn't harmful. What you use will depend on your dog's individual personality. Just like people, what one loves, another can't stand, so you'll have to experiment a bit to figure out what is most effective for your dog. Commonly used aversives include noisemakers, like throw chains or shaker bottles (½ gallon or gallon–sized plastic milk jugs with ten pennies inside and the top taped shut). Squirt guns or spray bottles with stream settings can also be used to interrupt or deter your dog from unwanted behavior, as long as your dog isn't one that thinks a stream of water is something to play with! For certain behaviors, particularly unwanted "mouthy" behaviors like play-biting, inappropriate chewing or excessive barking, you will want to use something that tastes bad to your dog. You might use one of the readily available possibilities like Bitter Apple, vinegar, Tabasco, or human breath spray. Whatever aversives you use, have plenty of them handy wherever you hang out with your dog. You don't want to have to go find something; you want it to be there when you need it.

Once you've assembled all your supplies, yippee! You're ready to bring your dog home!

Indoor Containment/Confinement

Indoor confinement options will help you housebreak your dog, as well as help prevent property damage from inappropriate chewing. You will probably want to crate your dog when you're out of the house and when you're home but can't pay attention to what your dog is doing. Gates can be used both to keep your dog in the same room with you and to keep him out of off-limits areas. Finally, tethers and draglines can help you control your dog by limiting his options and keeping him close to you. Upcoming chapters will give you ideas for how to use these management devices to your best advantage.

Crates

A sturdy crate is your best friend (other than your dog, of course) and the easiest way to keep your dog from being destructive. When it comes to house-breaking, a crate is practically an essential. Crates come in a few basic types. The most common are plastic airline crates and wire crates. Which type you choose will depend on your budget, décor, and to some extent, your dog.

If you don't want to have to buy successively larger crates as your dog gets bigger, get the size that will fit him as an adult. Wire crates usually have panels that can be used to adjust the size of the crate. To determine what size crate to get, figure out how much space your dog needs to stand up, lie down, and turn around, without too much room to spare. If your budget allows, you might consider getting two or three crates, so your dog has a safe place to be in your car or in a second room, like your bedroom at night.

Gates

Gates are an easy way to give your dog a little more space without giving him the run of the house. Use gates to control space, keeping your dog in and out of specific areas you designate. Gates come in a wide variety of sizes, functions, and prices. From the simplest, old-fashioned, expandable baby gate you can get at your local box store for around $10, to a more elaborate gate with a door that opens when you step on a lever, there is a size and type to suit practically any need and budget. If you have an open floor plan, you may have to get creative with your gating choices. You can easily make custom gates from PVC lattice fence panels available at most major home-improvement stores. The panels come in several sizes, but the 4" × 8" sections are probably the most versatile. Attach them together with cable ties or cut them for a custom fit.

FACT

Houdini Dog, master of escape, was able to break out of ordinary airline and wire crates! Specialty crates, made from welded sheets of aluminum, can contain even the most determined escape artists. See Appendix A for suppliers.

Tethers and Draglines

Tethers and draglines are tools to help you keep your dog under control when you are in the same room with him. Tethers are short (2–4 feet) and are used to keep the dog in one specific area. One end is attached to your dog's collar, and the other end is attached to something stationary—an eyehook in the baseboard, a sturdy piece of furniture, or you (see Appendix A for sources of chew-proof tethers, or you can make your own from vinyl-coated steel cable available from your home-improvement store). While you're buying tethers or the material to make them, pick up some leash snaps and some of the soft and strong nylon mountain-climbing rope to make your draglines (and tethers, if you're not using the steel cable). All of these supplies are usually on the same aisle. You will want enough of the rope to make several draglines—6 to 8 foot lengths for inside, and 25 to 50 foot lengths for outside. After securely attaching the leash snap to one end, tie a couple of knots along the length and at the other end (so it doesn't slide out from under your foot if and when you need to step on it). Draglines are an easy way to give your dog a little more supervised freedom while enabling you to get control of him quickly.

Outdoor Containment

If you have a yard and want to allow your dog access to it, you'll need a way to keep him in the yard. You have some basic choices when it comes to outside containment options for your dog, including solid fences; invisible or electronic fences; portable kennels; and tether, runner, or trolley systems. Depending on your budget, your dog, area restrictions, and how you use your yard, you may want to use more than one containment option to keep your dog safe.

ESSENTIAL

If your dog digs under the fence, try burying chicken wire, metal hardware cloth, or concrete landscape pavers about a foot deep all along the fence line to provide an underground barrier. Dog climbs over? You can try putting an additional foot or so of fencing along the top of the existing fence angled in toward the yard. For determined escape artists a backup invisible fence may be necessary.

Solid Fences Versus Invisible Fences

Traditional solid fences are possibly the most reliable way to keep your dog in your yard and relatively safe. The main disadvantage to them is that they are expensive. Also, some determined dogs will climb over them or dig under them (although there are things you can do to deter both of these behaviors).

Many areas have restrictions on what type or height fence you can have, which may not be suitable for your dog. Some areas don't allow visible fences at all. For this reason, you may want to consider an invisible or electronic fence.

ALERT!

No matter what kind of containment you use, until your dog is reasonably trained, he shouldn't be spending unsupervised time in the yard. You want him to reliably come to you when you call, and to know where he's supposed to potty, play, and dig before you allow him the option of making up his own mind.

Invisible fences have the advantage of being relatively inexpensive (at least compared to traditional fencing), and are generally acceptable by even the pickiest of homeowners' associations. They also have several disadvantages that should be carefully considered. The primary disadvantage is that they don't keep dogs or other animals from coming into your yard to harass your dog, which may be mildly annoying or downright dangerous. In addition, some dogs are too sensitive for them, and will either react with extreme fear or avoidance, sometimes refusing to leave the house or porch. Also, some dogs have been known to develop aggression problems because they connect the shock with the presence of people or other dogs outside the boundary. Finally, some dogs have such a high pain tolerance that they don't mind the shock and will cross the boundary without hesitation to tour the neighborhood. Invisible fences do make excellent backup fences for diggers and climbers, and some companies offer indoor versions as well.

Portable Kennels

Portable kennels come in a variety of shapes and sizes to accommodate practically any dog or area. Not to be confused with crates, portable kennels are usually outdoor structures (although some people use them in garages or basements) ranging in size from about 4 feet wide by 6 feet long, to just about as big as you want to make them. The actual portability of them depends on the finished size of course, but they all come apart and set up relatively easily if you want to change their location. They have the advantage of being large enough for a sleeping area (with a dog house, if you like) a play area, and a potty area. Portable kennels can be used either as your dog's main exercise and play area in the yard, to contain him if the rest of the yard is in use, or to visually and physically designate a potty area in your yard. They usually come with an attachable roof, so are generally a very secure option for containing your dog safely.

For now, you'll want to use a plain buckle or quick-lock collar for your dog. You should just be able to get two fingers under the collar. If your dog can back out of her collar, use a martingale or half-check collar (see Appendix A for sources of these collars). Other collars may be used during training and will be discussed in detail in Chapter 12. Never leave any type of choke collar on your unsupervised dog.

Tethers, Runners, and Trolley Systems

Tethers, runners, and trolley systems have the advantage of being the least expensive of outdoor containment options. Like electronic fences, they don't stop other animals from bothering your dog, and they have several other disadvantages as well. Safety is the major concern, as dogs can and will wrap themselves around trees or other stationary objects, possibly choking themselves or injuring their limbs if they get caught in the line, not to mention tripping any unsuspecting human that walks by. They also tend to increase frustration as the dog repeatedly hits the end of the line in an attempt to get to something or someone out of their reach. This frustration can result in aggression in an otherwise nice dog. For safety reasons, these options are best used only with supervision. The overhead trolley system is the least problematic if it works for your living area.

Introducing Your New Dog to the Family

Introducing your dog to her new human family is a time of joy, but it can also be overwhelming and stressful. The first meeting establishes a tone. Set your dog and the training process up for success with careful planning.

The First Meeting

Take it slow and let the dog approach and meet each person on her own time to minimize stress. If you have enough people, sit on the floor in a ring, and just let her approach and snuggle as she pleases, rather than passing her around like a football. If you need to pick her up, squat to get her rather than leaning and looming over her, which can be very intimidating. Meetings between your dog and children should be very closely supervised, and the dog should be on leash for the safety of all concerned. Let her get settled in for at least several days before you have all your friends and neighbors over to meet her.

Keep It Happy

Introductions should always be positive experiences. If the dog is scared or stressed, back off and try again later. If she's overly confident and pushy, avoid rewarding behavior like jumping up—she should only get attention for "four on the floor" or sitting.

Introductions to Other Pets

If you have other pets that she'll be living with, it's best to introduce them on neutral territory if possible. Most pets can learn to coexist peacefully, and some like or even love each other, but you can smooth the road by helping the first meetings go well. All dogs involved in meeting other pets should drag a leash or dragline so you can get control of the situation quickly and safely (without having to grab the collar) if necessary. Don't panic if there are mild scuffles or episodes of one dog humping the other. Try to give them some time to work it out, intervening only if there is an outright fight or if one dog bullies the other, or ignores protest or submission signals from the other dog. Most scuffles are bluff and posture, and generally, the more noise you hear, the less there is to worry about. Keep a spray bottle or high-power squirt gun handy, just in case. Meetings between dogs and cats or other pets are sometimes best done through a gate or crate to start. Switching the pets' bedding, (so the dog gets the cat's, and vice versa) is often helpful in creating an environment of acceptance. Feeding them for good behavior in each other's presence and preventing your dog from chasing your cats are other ways to help make the transition period easier.

What Are You Rewarding?

The behaviors you reward, even unintentionally, will be repeated, whether you actually like the behavior or not.

It's very easy to let puppies get away with behavior that you won't find acceptable later on, simply because they are small and cute. The same is true with a rescue dog. You may want to let a dog settle in for several weeks before setting any behavior boundaries for fear of damaging his ego. While you think you're being nice, he's probably thinking "Aha! A pushover! Let me see what I can get away with!"

Whatever Works

Dogs have a "whatever works" policy when it comes to getting things they want. If something works, they tend to stick with it. Over time, they develop habits and become more persistent when they don't get immediate results. For the next several months, you want to be very conscious of the behaviors you are rewarding, so you don't unintentionally help your dog acquire bad habits, like jumping up or barking for attention or to come out of his crate. Until you're in the habit of expecting and rewarding good behavior from your dog, take a moment to think about whether your reaction to his behavior will cause that behavior to be repeated or avoided in the future.

What Do You Want Your Dog to Do Again?

Reward the stuff you like! It's so simple, really. Just catch your dog doing something right, and let her know you like it with praise, treats, or both (more about using treats effectively in upcoming chapters). If she's doing something you don't like, try to ignore her and wait her out until she offers something you do like, or at least can live with, and reward her for that. If she's allowed to "win" or get what she wants with obnoxious behavior because you think it'll be easier to just let her have her way "this time," think again. You will actually teach her to be more persistent, making each battle last longer and longer. You don't have to be the strongest or loudest dog in the fight; you just have to be the last dog in the fight the first few times she tries if you expect her to understand that things are going to be your way. It doesn't require you to be harsh; just be patient and firm in your resolve. If you've already lost a few battles, you can still win the war, but you may have to add some corrections to help get behavior you can reward.

ALERT!

If your dog is barking, don't bark along with him! Yelling "shut up" might make you feel a little better for a second, but it's not usually very effective. The same is true for using your hands to push a jumping dog off. From the dog's point of view, negative attention is better than nothing!

Laying Down the Law

It's time to decide what the rules of your dog's life are going to be. Sure, you can let the dog decide, but chances are you won't be very happy with the choices he makes.

Sticking to Your Rules

It's up to you to make the rules. Whatever they are, you can be sure that if you don't stick to them, your dog won't either. Unfortunately, when it comes to well-behaved dogs, wishing doesn't make it so, and no one has come up with any Lassie pills yet. Remember the beginning of this chapter, when you were visualizing your dog two years from now? So ask yourself:

- Is my dog allowed on the furniture? If so, which furniture? Whenever he wants, or only by invitation?

- Is he allowed to jump on people? Certain people or everybody?
- Where does he sleep?
- How does he behave when I'm eating?
- How does he behave when I have guests?
- What does he do when someone comes to the door? What if someone leaves a door open?
- What does he do when I call him? When I want to put his collar or leash on? If I need to take something away from him?

Visualize him again now. Do you have a different picture of him?

Getting the Dog You Deserve

There is a little joke among dog trainers—after two years, everybody gets the dog he deserves. It's not entirely true, of course, because genetics and life can intervene with even the best-laid plans. But, for the most part, you are in control of whether your vision of your dog will become reality. Whatever the rules are going to be for him as an adult dog, those should be the rules now. Nothing could be more unfair than changing all the rules just when your dog thinks he has it all figured out.

ESSENTIAL

It's so easy to spoil a new dog. Let's face it, an eight-week-old puppy can poop on your foot, and it's almost cute. Not so with an eight-month-old! Not allowing the cuteness factor and feelings of guilt or pity to override common sense are two of the biggest obstacles you have to overcome to become an effective leader your dog can count on.

Deterring Misbehavior

Much of what people think of as misbehavior is actually normal, healthy behavior that has gone awry. Maybe the dog chose an inappropriate target when she picked up the remote control instead of one of her toys when she had the need to chew. Or perhaps she picked a bad time or place to urinate, like on the dining room floor during dinner.

Prevention

Until you're sure your dog understands the rules of house, don't give her the freedom to make bad choices. Use a combination of supervision and confinement to prevent her from making, and by default getting rewarded for, poor choices. Chapter 4 explains how to use confinement options like crates, gates, and tethers to help prevent misbehavior.

FACT

Providing your dog with appropriate outlets for her normal behaviors and keeping her busy with regular mental and physical exercise are great ways to keep her from misbehaving out of boredom and frustration from excess energy.

For now, unless your dog is safely confined, you can assume that if you don't see him, something bad is happening. Property damage is occurring, whether it's a possession being chewed or a rug being pooped on. Know what he's up to!

Deterrents

In addition to prevention, you'll probably also have to make use of deterrent (or aversive) devices like shaker bottles, spray bottles, or squirt guns to help you interrupt behavior you don't like. It's not enough just to stop her from chewing the remote; you also have to redirect her to more acceptable forms of entertainment. As often as possible, you want to use deterrents in a sneak attack, connecting the unwanted behavior with a negative consequence, like a shaker bottle falling from the sky, or a blast from the squirt gun. After the correction, you get to be the sympathetic good guy, showing her what is okay. If you have to go looking for a deterrent, it's too late, so keep plenty of them handy. It doesn't take most dogs long to figure out that every time they grab the remote, or your sunglasses, or the houseplant, something bad happens. Ideally, time the correction when your dog is just grabbing the forbidden treasure, rather than when she's contentedly chewing it up.

The Four Keys to a Great Dog

So you're living with your dog at last. You already know that you're training him all the time, but did you know that helping your dog become well behaved is really a four-pronged approach?

A Holistic Approach

In the next four chapters, you'll learn how to build a healthy relationship of leadership positively. You'll also find out how to manage both your dog and the environment to utilize his energy without damage or loss of your prized possessions. In addition you'll discover simple ways to teach your dog to do practically anything. And finally, you'll discover and how to socialize him to people, dogs, other animals, and new experiences safely.

Your Newest Best Friend

Relationship, management, training, and socialization are the four keys to your great dog. Together, they instill your dog with a desire to learn new things, and build a relationship of trust and teamwork. You owe it to yourself and your dog to spend some time understanding and appreciating him for who and what he is—your newest best friend.

Chapter 3

The Leader of the Pack

3

Unlike people, dogs don't understand democracy. When it comes to what is acceptable behavior, they don't even get to vote. As far as they're concerned, you either serve, or you are served. Their behavior is more or less controlled by the alpha, the highest-ranking member of the pack. They may occasionally attempt to negotiate the terms to get access to things they want. But for the most part, they are quite content to accept the laws of the land, provided they're clearly and consistently explained and enforced.

Why Leadership Matters

Leadership is the be all and end all of your partnership with your dog. From your dog's point of view, your relationship determines how she behaves toward you and whether or not she listens to you and responds reliably to your instructions, especially in distracting or stressful situations.

I'll Be Right With You

There are going to be many times in your dog's life when you ask her to do something she'd rather not do, or at least would rather not do right now (otherwise known as the infamous "I'll be right with you, right after I do this other more interesting thing first" phenomenon). Your relationship with her will be the deciding factor in whether she not only hears your command, but also listens and responds to it—no matter what. To put this in perspective, think about how many (probably quite a few) things in your life that you'd rather not do, but you do them anyway out of responsibility to some higher authority (like a boss).

A Shy Dog's Dream

If you have a shy or fearful dog, you may think babying him and not demanding much of him will make him feel better. It might make you feel better, but it's not doing him much good. In fact, it's probably reinforcing his fearful behavior. It's amazing how much a shy and fearful dog can blossom with calm, confident leadership. You can almost hear them breathe a sigh of relief "Whew! Thank goodness someone took control—I was afraid I was going to have to do it!"

Most dogs don't want to be in charge. If nobody else steps up to take the job, they'll do it out of necessity, because someone has to be in charge. But for a shy dog, being forced into a position of leadership creates tremendous stress and can cause fear aggression. It takes an enormous amount of pressure off of them when they know they can count on someone else to make the big decisions.

The Pushy or Demanding Dog

Pushy, confident dogs also need leadership, but for different reasons. Unlike their shy counterparts, they can demand that they get the attention they believe they deserve. Because of their enthusiasm, zest, and flash, this personality makes a great show dog or working partner, but it can be a lot to live with. Sometimes this type of dog is dominant by nature, but being rewarded for pushy, dominant behavior causes most dominance problems.

Little dogs need leadership too! It is incredibly easy to let a tiny dog get away with something you'd never think of ignoring in a larger dog. Without leadership, little dogs often develop a Napoleon complex, assuming that everyone on the planet is there to serve them. Some rule with an iron paw, and think nothing of disciplining (biting) their lowly subjects for the slightest affront to their delicate egos.

Sometimes the pushy behaviors aren't even recognized as such at the time because they appear to the owner to be affection and are rewarded regularly. Does your dog nudge or paw you to demand petting or to get you to throw a toy? Bark at you when you're on the phone? Are you giving in to his demands? Over time, this gradually increases your dog's rank, at least in his own mind. Before long, he might test whether you're in charge of other things, like if you are "allowed" to cut his toenails or take a toy from him or move him off the couch. It's easy to figure out why these dogs need leadership.

Alpha Is a State of Mind

Every team needs a captain. Did you ever notice how the captains of sports teams aren't necessarily the biggest or physically strongest members of the teams? They may not even be the best players. They usually do share at least one common trait, though. That trait is leadership ability. They're also likely to be calm, confident, and assertive.

You Too Can Be a Good Leader

If you're not a natural team captain, don't panic. You just have to fake it until you make it. Behave your way to success and act like a good leader. Acting like a good leader means that you set standards, and expect and insist that they are met. It means remaining calm and taking charge of situations that might cause your dog to misbehave or panic. If you get frustrated and hysterical in response to your dog's hysteria or out-of-control behavior, no one is in control, and the leadership position is up for grabs. If this happens repeatedly, your dog may decide that you're not worthy of the leadership spot.

Control your breathing! If you hold your breath in stressful situations (and most people do), you hold on to tension, which telegraphs directly to your dog. Consciously force yourself to take regular, even breaths; you and your dog will both feel better!

Don't Forget to Breathe!

You may need to force yourself to take a deep breath (don't forget to let it out!) and tell yourself "I am in control of this situation," but your calm, confident energy will instill your dog with confidence and trust. With a little practice, not only will your dog believe you're the leader, but also you might even start believing it yourself!

Sweat the Small Stuff (and the Big Stuff Will Take Care of Itself)

With dogs, leadership usually isn't taken with violence. In truth, it's really not so much taken as it is given. It depends on lots of little day-to-day interactions, rather than big brawls over big issues.

Who Controls the "Good Stuff"

For dogs, it's not about who is strongest or meanest; it's about who can get and control the valuable resources. For the health of the whole pack, there has to be teamwork and cooperation, so it wouldn't be beneficial to have the leader beating everybody else up. Most disagreements between dogs are settled with a combination of eye contact and body language, with a little bluff and posture thrown in. If the resource in question is really valuable and worth protecting, the scuffle could escalate into an actual fight, but most often one dog gives up, or submits, before that happens. Whenever possible, you want to avoid these battles altogether by teaching your dog right from the beginning that you are in control of all of the "good stuff" in his life, whether it's food, petting, or access to a cushy spot on the couch. If he wants it, you can make him earn it, establishing leadership positively, without confrontation.

No Free Lunch!

Until your position of leadership is clearly defined, put your dog on a nothing-in-life-is-free program, making him earn access to all of the stuff he likes by performing a simple task for you. Teach him to do things that make your life easier, like sitting to have his leash put on when you're getting ready to take him for a walk. (Chapter 10 will help you teach your dog to sit). His enthusiasm is cute, but it's frustrating trying to snap a leash on a small moving target. And if he's already out of control before you even get the leash on, how is he going to behave on the walk? Does he jump when you're preparing his food or putting it down, making you spill it everywhere? Teach him to sit and wait until you release him to eat. (Chapter 13 helps you teach your dog to wait politely for privileges). Do this every time you feed him. Now you're in control of his very survival every day, so you must be the leader. When he knows who controls all the little things in his life, he's much less likely to question or challenge who controls the big things.

This Land Is My Land

Control of territory is a vital element of leadership. Territory means both the real territory, like your house and yard, and the immediate territory, including the space your dog is occupying right now. It's all yours—feel powerful? As Master of Your Domain, you'll grant your dog access to new parts of your territory gradually (and under supervision) based on his ability to control himself. It's not a hotel or a playground; it's your home. Until he shows that he respects it, giving him free run of it is like letting a class full of preschoolers loose in it. Unless you like it messy, it's probably not a good idea.

This Space Is My Space

The personal space that you occupy, and the space your dog occupies, is another important aspect of territory up for control. You want to regularly remind your dog that occupying a space doesn't mean he owns it. By teaching him to move out of your way, rather than your getting out of his, or walking around him, or stepping over him, you are subtly but powerfully reminding him who is in charge. You can easily teach him to yield space to you by shuffling into him, your feet close to the ground, and praising him when he moves out of your way. You can also use this technique to intercept him if he's jumping, a major infringement on your personal space. If you didn't invite him to, don't allow him to lie on you, or cover parts of your body with parts of his, which implies ownership. You own him, not the other way around. Never, even if it seems funny at the time, allow him to push a person out of, and then occupy, their spot, especially if it's the person's bed.

Teach your dog to yield space to you on command by pairing a command with your shuffle. Don't know what command to use? Try "Excuse me" or "Move." Don't forget to praise!

Love Is Given, Respect Is Earned

Without a doubt, your dog loves you. One of the most wonderful traits dog have is that they give their love freely, without reservation or condition.

Love (Not) For Sale

Dogs really don't care if you're rich or poor, or whether you give them the best food or whatever was on sale, or even if you care enough about them to take them to the vet or the groomer. They love you just the same. But here's the thing: because they give their love so freely, it's not for sale. They won't love you more if you give them more treats, or expensive toys. They won't love you more if you don't set any guidelines for their behavior and let them do whatever they want. In fact, the opposite is true.

I'm Awesome!

As wonderful as dogs are, they're opportunistic (and to be honest, ungrateful) creatures by nature with a what's-in-it-for-me? philosophy. They don't appreciate much of the nice stuff people do for them.

Dogs don't sit around thinking, "I have an awesome person. She gives me whatever I want, whenever I want it, so I'm going to be a really good dog." No, it's more like, "Wow, isn't this great, I get to do whatever I want, I'm a really awesome dog." If you cater to your dog's every whim and desire, he won't take it as a measure of your love, and feel the need to repay you the next time you ask him to do something. Instead, he'll take it as evidence of your servitude. This doesn't cause too much trouble when the issue at hand is an extra cookie, but when it gets to real issues, like whether or not to come when you call, love isn't enough; you have to have respect.

Where Do I Stand?

Over the next several months, every little interaction you have with your dog tells him something about your relationship and where he stands in the hierarchy of your pack—or basically whether he should treat you with respect or disdain. If you set reasonable guidelines for his behavior, and then consistently, gently, and firmly insist he abide by them, you will have not only his respect, but also his utter adoration and devotion.

Say What You Mean, Mean What You Say

Consistency is a major factor in all aspects of raising and training your dog. The importance of being consistent is really brought to your attention when you start actually giving your dog commands.

Less Is More

Since people are verbal, we tend to chatter—a lot. Dogs aren't at all verbal, so if your command is hidden in babble, you make it really tough for your dog to understand what you want. Sure, she may look at you adoringly while you prattle on, "Do you wanna sit, Snookums? Sit for mommy, precious... Who's a good girl? C'mon and sit," but how is she supposed to pick out what she's actually supposed to do? Talking to your dog while you're hanging out on the couch with her after a long day is one thing, but when it comes to giving commands, say what you mean.

It's a Command, Not a Suggestion

You want to teach her to listen to you, not train yourself that you have to shout or give multiple commands to get her to listen. Your tone should be firm, but your volume should be conversational. If you have to yell or repeat basic commands, you're not in control, and your dog knows it. Leaders give their commands calmly, and expect them to be complied with.

Try the K.I.S.S. method of giving commands—Keep It Short and Simple. You can use your dog's name to get her attention, but your command itself should be only one or two words.

Do You Really Mean It?

Meaning what you say is just as important as saying what you mean. If it's not important to you that your commands are complied with, how can it be important to your dog? He doesn't know that it's important until you teach him that it is.

He's not necessarily being defiant or disobedient if he ignores a command. He just might not know the meaning of the command in that context (more about that later), or he might not know that he has to do it every time, even if something distracts him. You might want to give him the benefit of the doubt that he didn't hear you and want to repeat the command. He almost always heard you, but didn't understand that it wasn't optional. It's his job to listen, and it's your job to teach him to listen by helping him be correct every time you give him a command.

Chapter 5 will teach you how to teach your dog the meaning of all the words in his behavior vocabulary in a fun and positive way. Once your dog understands the meaning of the words, and until he's has the habit of complying with your first command, set yourself up for success by doing two simple things:

1. Don't give him any command you are not in the position to enforce.
2. Enforce every command you give, even when it's not convenient for you.

Getting Reliability

You can help your dog become reliable by consistently rewarding her for correct responses to your commands and gently insisting upon compliance when she makes a mistake. It won't take her long to realize that whether she complies, or you make her, your command will be followed. This makes life much easier and less stressful for her, because she never has to wonder who is in charge or whether she should follow instructions.

The Foundation for Training

Whether you want a dog that excels in obedience competition or just a great family pet, your relationship with your dog is the foundation for all of the training that you'll be doing with him.

Will Work For Cookies

Your relationship is the difference between creating a dog with a desire to work for you, instead of a dog that wears a "will work for food" sign, or worse, a dog that only performs out of fear. Nothing is more annoying than a dog who only responds to a command when a bribe is dangled in front of his nose.

ALERT!

It's not just what you say, it's how you say it. Don't have a discussion with your dog about a command, or pose it as a question. Say it once like you mean it. Praise should be enthusiastic and sincere; you want to see a tail or butt wagging!

A Solid Foundation

You can help build a solid foundation for training by providing your dog with clear, consistent boundaries and guidelines. When he can expect predictable consequences for his behavior, it's in his own best interest to make the right choices and be rewarded for them, rather than being corrected (or at least not rewarded) for poor choices. A healthy relationship is the cornerstone on which to build your great dog.

Chapter 4

Managing Your Dog for Success

Managing your dog is the second critical part of the training process. Successful management starts with physically controlling your dog so he can't practice unwanted behavior. Good management also includes controlling the environment, so the lure of attractive but forbidden items isn't overwhelming for him. The final piece of the management puzzle is keeping his energy directed in positive ways by providing enough mental and physical exercise for his needs.

Controlling Your Dog

Controlling your dog is the first part of your management plan. Young dogs (and some older ones) rarely make wise choices if left to their own devices—they do what feels good at the moment.

It's All a Test

When you first bring your dog home, she is constantly testing, and with her behavior, asking the question "What happens if I do this?" She learns what works and what doesn't based on the immediate consequences of her actions. When she gets away with chewing something inappropriate or urinating behind the couch, she has already gotten her positive reinforcement. She had a need, and it was fulfilled. Voila—the seed of a bad habit!

FACT

More than 80 percent of dogs in shelters were surrendered because of behavior problems like chewing and inappropriate elimination in the house. Nearly 100 percent of the surrenders could have been avoided with good planning and management.

By simply controlling your dog and not allowing her the opportunity to practice her vices, you can prevent her from developing a multitude of bad habits. You have two primary options for controlling your dog: supervision or confinement.

Supervision

Supervision means that your dog is in close proximity to you. Until he's keeping himself out of trouble and responding reliably to commands, he should have a dragline attached to his collar so that you can get control of him and enforce commands quickly without a prolonged and hysterical chase around the dining-room table.

If you're involved in an activity that is too engrossing to pay attention to your dog while you pursue it, like surfing the Internet or reading the paper, tether him to you or near you. There's a limited amount of damage he can do six feet away from you. If you feel confident that you can let him have a little freedom, have plenty of your aversives handy so that you can interrupt him when he's thinking about taking off with the throw pillow, rather than when he's shredding it with abandon.

If you find evidence of a doggie misdeed but didn't catch her in the act, roll up a newspaper and smack yourself in the butt. Repeat "I wasn't watching my puppy" five times and promise yourself not to give her the chance to make the same mistake again.

Confinement

Along with supervision, confinement is a necessary management tool. For many, if not most dogs, the crate is the easiest, most affordable, and most practical confinement choice. In addition to the obvious uses of keeping your dog out of trouble when you're not home and helping with housebreaking, your dog's crate can help you manage him when you are home as well. In the beginning, and maybe for a while, depending on your dog, you may have to crate him even for brief trips to the bathroom or to answer the phone. Some dogs just can't handle the freedom to make their own choices, so hang in there and give him the management he needs until he's ready for the privilege of more freedom.

Expanding Boundaries

Based on his success (or lack thereof) in his current area, expand his options and boundaries a little at a time. By increasing his freedom gradually, you can catch any problem behavior before it becomes a solid habit. Especially during adolescence, you should expect periods of regression, so don't get discouraged if you occasionally have to put him back under "lockdown" for a few weeks and start over on his boundary-expansion program.

Listen to Your Dog

Your dog will tell you when he's ready for more freedom. The way he'll tell you is that he won't make any mistakes or have any accidents in his current area for a period of at least three weeks. Like fine wine, a good dog can't be rushed! Be patient and wait until he's ready before you start broadening his horizons. If he makes a mistake in his new area, revert back to the last setup that he was successful with. Wait two or three weeks and try again.

ALERT!

Your dog's crate should be used to keep him out of trouble, not to punish him for getting into it. Punishments should always occur at the same time the unwanted behavior does for your dog to make the connection. Crates are a fact of your dog's life. You want him to like being in there.

Controlling the Environment

If your housekeeping style is more obsessive-compulsive than freestyle, you have it made when it comes to controlling your environment.

Pick It Up!

Just picking up all of the bits and pieces that you might usually leave lying around during your dog's early exploration will go a long way to preventing both destruction and the habit of destruction. Personal items like kids' toys, shoes, and dirty laundry are especially attractive targets of destruction, as are items your dog can shred, like newspaper and toilet paper. Unless your idea of the perfect full-time job is picking up tiny bits of shredded tissues or sewing the eyes back on your kid's stuffed animals (if you're lucky, and not soothing your child because the puppy chewed the head off her favorite doll), you'll be well served to control your dog's environment.

Puppyproofing

If you have a puppy or adolescent dog in your house, it's time to puppy-proof and put the priceless family heirlooms away for a while, or at least out of your puppy's reach. Candy dish on the coffee table? Not now. Scavengers that they are, untrained dogs will naturally explore trashcans, tables, and countertops for food. They don't know that these activities aren't acceptable in a human household until you teach them. As far as they're concerned, unguarded food is free for the taking, and who can resist a free meal? Even one successful counter-surfing venture is enough for some dogs to never forget without some serious intervention. Avoiding the problem by making sure food and trash are securely stored is imperative for your dog's behavior and health.

Is your puppy teaching you tricks? If she's stealing household items, and you're running around waving your arms and screaming after her, she's just taught you to play "Look at what I can make my owner do!" Dogs think this chase game is great and will repeat it as long as you keep "playing." Avoid the game altogether and keep attractive but forbidden items out of reach.

Give Your Dog a Job

If your dog were living in the wild, she'd have a job. Every day, she would spend the majority of her time and energy out scavenging and hunting, and probably would end up with just enough food to do it again the next day.

Frustration and Boredom

Like most people today, pet dogs tend to be overfed and underexercised. Add in selective breeding, creating dogs that are bred to hunt or do other work virtually all day. We bring them home, leave them alone with nothing to do all day, and then expect them to lie quietly by our feet as we watch TV at night. It's no mystery why our dogs are bouncing off the walls: they're bored, frustrated, and need a job.

Creative Job Hunting

If you don't give your dog a job, she'll have to create her own, and you probably aren't going to be overjoyed with her choices, which might include classics like Redecorating the House, Digging Your Own Pool, or Keeping the Evil Delivery Men Away. The jobs you find for your dog might be very simple, like making her work for her food or other things she likes. They could also be very elaborate, like teaching her to pick up all of her (or the kids') toys.

Do Something!

Just giving dogs simple tasks to perform throughout the day makes some of them happy, while others need more physical jobs. Regular obedience training is a job every dog can do and will benefit from. For a truly happy and fulfilled dog, find out what your dog was bred to do and do it (more information on breed-specific activities is in Chapter 20). Take your dog hiking or swimming. Have a good game of Frisbee. Whether for eventual competition or just for fun, find a dog-training school and train your dog in a more distracting environment. Even better, one that offers therapy-dog training, agility, rally, or tracking can help you keep your dog happy, busy and out of trouble indefinitely. The point is, do something!

All evidence to the contrary, your dog really isn't trying to drive you crazy, but all that energy has to go somewhere. Put on your sneakers and take her for a twenty-minute walk at a brisk pace. You'll both be panting before you head for home.

Are You Proactive or Reactive?

Everybody wants a well-behaved dog, but not everybody wants to take the time and effort to help their dog become one. Your puppy isn't going to raise herself to be a good dog, so you'll have to do it. If you intend to keep her for her whole life, instead of giving her away or to a shelter, or euthanizing her when her care becomes inconvenient or you just can't take her behavior anymore, then you are going to have to be proactive, by taking action to prevent misbehavior, rather than just reacting to it.

Proactive Management

Proactive management consists of anticipating the normal things that dogs do. If you know that she tends to get excited and jump on people when they come to the door, don't wait for her to jump all over the pizza guy to try to get her dragline on. Let her drag it if you're home, or put it on before the doorbell rings, or at least before you open the door. If she's already stolen food off the counter a few times, don't leave it there to keep rewarding her and strengthening the habit. Hole digger? Don't leave her unattended in the yard. If she goes nuts every evening at 6:45, tearing off like her tail is on fire, grabbing anything in her path—even if it's a human ankle—then take her out for a game of fetch or for a run at 6:30. If she's hyperactive and acting crazy, she's trying to tell you that she's bored and frustrated and needs to burn off some energy.

Proactive Training

It's important to train proactively as well. Do you remember Chicken Little and "the sky is falling"? If you know your dog has a weakness for grabbing anything that isn't nailed down, keep several aversives, like shaker bottles, handy so you can ambush him with a barrage of several bottles falling around him to teach him that taking items that don't belong to him isn't a safe activity. Immediately direct him to something that is okay. If he has behaviors you don't like, it's not enough just to teach him what not to do. You have to replace the unwanted behavior with a new, more acceptable, and preferably mutually exclusive behavior. A great example of this is jumping up. He can't very well be sitting and jumping up, so teach him to sit to greet people (Chapter 10 will help you teach your dog to sit).

The Dog in Your Dog

Your dog has come to you with a certain set of behaviors that are normal for him and completely foreign to you. You can't train who he is out of him, but you can teach him to engage in his normal behaviors in ways that are acceptable to you. He doesn't just want to chew; he needs to chew. Provide him with a variety of chewing options and pay attention to what he actually chews on. Just because someone sells it as a chew toy doesn't mean he's going to like it (see Chapter 8 for different ideas). If he likes to dig holes, give him a legal spot to dig with a defined corner of his own, or a kiddie pool half-filled with play sand with treats and toys buried in it. Teach him to take care of his personal hygiene issues off your couch or bed—nobody needs to see that!

Tired Dog, Happy Owner

To raise your dog while keeping your prized possessions—not to mention your sanity—intact, you are going to have to find ways to wear out your dog on a regular basis. It's not rocket science. Sleeping dogs don't leave paths of destruction and chaos. They're not barking at you or pawing you for attention while you're talking on the phone, watching TV, or working on the computer.

Wear That Puppy Out!

Luckily, you have a ton of options when it comes to exercising your dog:

- Swimming
- Taking an obedience or agility class
- Fetch
- Frisbee
- Hiking
- Playing with other dogs (all parties well socialized)
- Food-scattering or treat-dispensing toys
- Long, fast walks—not meandering strolls
- The Find-It game

Find something, anything, you both enjoy, and participate. Get a doggie playgroup together a couple of times a week. Alternate yards for variety, and start, interrupt, and end each play session with a brief training session for fun and variety.

Take a Proper Walk

Although walking just isn't enough to satisfy most dogs' energy, it can help take the edge off. Done properly, with your dog walking nicely at your side, not out in front of you, or sniffing a tree, or dragging you down the street, it can even strengthen your relationship. Walking helps, but pottying should be done first, and then the walk, for at least twenty minutes, should be at a brisk pace. If you must stop for potty breaks, stop walking altogether for a couple of minutes. When you're ready to start walking again, move out like you're on a mission. The faster you move, the more interesting you will be. All of these options require a little effort on your part, but your great dog is worth it.

The Find-It Game—Fun Indoors or Out

Find It is a game you can play with anything that your dog likes and will work for access to. Food, whether it's your dog's whole meal or just one or two special treats, is a great choice for the objects to be found in this game, as are favorite toys and even your dog's favorite people. Start the game so that your dog wins early and often by letting him watch you "hide" the food or other object just a few feet away. Either have someone restrain him or tether him until he's able to hold a sit-stay while you hide his treasures. Go back to him and release him with an enthusiastic "Find it!" Make a big deal about it when he finds the goodies, tell him how smart he is, and start over, moving the target a little farther away. Keep going until you can go around a corner or hide things in less-obvious locations.

Did you know many zoos use environmental enrichment to feed the animals for their mental and emotional health? By hiding food around enclosures or freezing it into blocks, the animals have to work for their food, preventing many common emotional problems like compulsive and repetitive spinning, pacing, and self-mutilation.

Low-effort Ways to Keep Your Dog Busy

You work all day. Maybe you have a second job, or go to school, or take care of your family, too. The last thing you want to think about or do after a long day is entertaining your dog. You know you have to figure something out because there's just so much time she can spend in the crate, and she's bursting at the seams and acting out in aggravation. There are quite a few things you can do to keep her occupied and help her burn off a little steam at the same time.

There are a variety of food dispensing toys to keep your dog gainfully occupied.

Nature's Way

Since your dog's daily job in nature would be finding food for that day's survival, put her to work at dinnertime. Don't just dump a scoop of kibble in the bowl; scatter the kibble around the kitchen floor, the porch, or the yard, and let her spend half an hour doing what normally takes a minute or two. She'll use her nose, brain, and some physical energy finding every last kibble. If the idea of dog food all over your kitchen floor is too much for you to bear, give her a Buster Cube or one of the large treat balls designed to dispense kibbles a few at a time as she bats and nudges it around the house or yard. A really food-motivated dog will work for hours to get every last kibble.

Make Crate Time Entertaining

Want to give her something fun to do in the crate? Try a stuffed Kong toy. Buy a size larger than is recommended for your dog's breed or size on the package. Stuff it with a variety of goodies to keep her occupied and satisfied. Rotate what you put in the toy to keep her interested. Try making a mixture of canned and dry dog food, stuff it tightly in the toy, and put it in the freezer. Make several so you always have a frozen pooch pacifier on hand. A little peanut butter or liverwurst can be added to the mixture for variety. Or, you can put a small chunk of hot dog or cheddar cheese (something smelly) in the small end, fill up the rest with regular dry dog food, and use a big biscuit as a stopper in the large end—it's the treat that keeps on giving. If she's occupied with working for her meals for an hour or more each day, at least that's an hour that she's not chewing the sofa.

FACT

What you spend in toys, you save in couches! If you can use an egg timer to measure the time it takes your dog to destroy a toy, don't despair. Keep a few heavy-duty toys around to direct him to, but once or twice a week, give him a toy he can destroy. As long as he doesn't eat the stuffing, it's a mentally healthy activity for him.

Outdoor Fun and Entertainment

If you have some kind of fence or outdoor containment for your dog, chances are she'll be spending a decent amount of time there. Hopefully you won't give her too much unsupervised time out there before she's trained, but if you do, you may be surprised at some of the hobbies she takes up. Thinking about new siding for the house? Great, she's already started the demolition. Air conditioner needs new insulation? No? Oh well, it does now. And surely there's buried treasure in one of those holes she dug. Well, what did you think she was going to do out there all by herself?

Avoiding Boredom

Your first plan of action is obvious: Don't leave her outside unattended for long enough to get bored. If you're out in the yard with her, you can direct her to an appropriate activity, whether it's digging a hole in her digging pit, chasing goldfish in a kiddie pool, or herding a giant indestructible ball around the yard.

ALERT!

For safety's sake, kids and dogs should never be left together in a yard unsupervised. Even a dog half a child's size can easily knock the child down unintentionally, or worse. It's just not worth the risk to take chances.

If you need to leave her for a few minutes, make sure she has something really interesting, like a treat dispensing toy or a raw marrowbone, to keep her attention. It's rare dog that will exercise and entertain herself in a yard for any length of time without engaging in some behavior that's unacceptable to her people. Excessive barking, destructive chewing, digging… dogs left alone in yards do tend to act a lot like dogs!

Chapter 5

Ready, Set, Train!

Dog training is part art and part science. Before you start teaching your dog commands, take a few minutes to learn the basics of learning theory. You may wonder why you should care about learning theory when all you want to do is train your dog. Once you know it and start applying it to your training plan, you'll find it helps you understand your dog a little better—or at least why he does some of the things he does.

5

How Your Dog Learns

Like every other animal on the planet, your dog learns from the consequences, both good and bad, of his actions. If something good happens, your dog is likely to repeat that action, expecting a similar result. On the contrary, if something your dog doesn't like occurs as a result of his action, that behavior is more likely to be avoided in the future.

The Training Process

You'll be using operant conditioning to train your dog. With operant conditioning, you'll help your dog make the connection between particular behaviors and their consequences. While you want to be as nice to your dog as possible during training, it is probable that you'll need to employ a variety of both positive and negative consequences. Into each life—even a dog's—a little rain must fall.

The Technical Stuff

While it's not important that you remember and use the correct scientific terms when you train your dog, it is helpful to understand what they mean and what role each plays in training your dog. There are four possible consequences each time your dog performs a behavior:

1. Something Good Happens = Positive Reinforcer
2. Something Bad Happens = Positive Punisher
3. Something Good Is Removed = Negative Punisher
4. Something Bad Is Removed = Negative Reinforcer

The terms *good* and *bad* are subjective and relative, depending on the dog. What's great to one dog, like a squirt from a spray bottle, is torture to another. Some dogs love to have their ears stroked; others can't stand it. Let your dog tell you what she likes and what she doesn't.

In operant conditioning terms, positive has nothing to do with whether your dog will like it. It just means that something is added. In contrast, negative always means something is taken away, not that something "bad" will happen.

Punishment and Reinforcement

The terms *punishment* and *reinforcement* have concrete meanings as well. By definition, punishment must effect a decrease in an unwanted behavior (either the frequency or the intensity) or it's not a punishment (it's nagging, but more about that in a minute). In contrast, reinforcement always must effect an increase in a desired behavior. Even praise and petting aren't always positive reinforcement. If the behavior you want isn't increasing because of it, it's just affection—not that there's anything wrong with that!

Operant Conditioning in Action

Let's say you're trying to teach your dog to behave politely at feeding time, so you've decided to teach him to sit for his dinner. From the perspective of each of the four possibilities:

Positive Reinforcement: You tell him to sit, he does, and you give him his food
Negative Reinforcement: You tell him to sit, put pressure on his collar until he sits, and when he does, you take the pressure off
Positive Punishment: You tell him to sit and swat him on the butt when he doesn't (no, that's not a recommendation—just an example!)
Negative Punishment: You tell him to sit, and take the food away when he doesn't

In this example, the reinforcements are meant to increase the frequency of him sitting on command, while the punishments are meant to decrease the frequency of not sitting on command.

ESSENTIAL

Remember the hot/cold game you played as a kid? Think how hard the game would have been if you only got half of the information—if you were only told you were getting cold or colder. Your dog needs lots of immediate feedback about both what you like and what you don't.

You'll be using both reinforcers and punishers in your balanced training plan, although the lines between them may blur a bit at times.

Primary and Conditioned Reinforcers

Reinforcers can be primary, or hard-wired, like food or social contact. Practically anything that your dog likes and will work to get is a primary reinforcer. Secondary, or conditioned reinforcers, are reinforcers that your dog (or you, for that matter) has learned to like because of its association with a primary reinforcer. Your paycheck is a perfect example of a secondary or conditioned reinforcer—if you didn't associate it with money in the bank, you wouldn't be so excited to get this otherwise worthless scrap of paper every Friday, would you?

ESSENTIAL

If your dog goes running to the cabinet where you keep the dog biscuits every time you say "cookies," then you already have a secondary reinforcer. Your dog has connected the conditioned reinforcer "cookies" to a primary reinforcer—food. See, you're training already!

Using a Conditioned Reinforcer

Even before you establish which first behavior you want to encourage, you want to establish a conditioned reinforcer (CR). For training purposes, you want to establish a specific CR so that you can isolate and mark a behavior (or piece of one) for primary reinforcement. It's basically the bridge between the behavior you want and the dog's reward. It lets her know she did something right, and is going to be rewarded for it.

Establish a Conditioned Reinforcer

Establishing a CR is easy. Simply decide what you want your CR to be, and pair it with a primary reinforcer until your dog makes an obvious connection between them. It might take only a few repetitions for some dogs to learn that their CR means good stuff for them, while others may need more practice. Most dogs figure it out in only a few brief sessions of multiple repetitions.

To get started, take your dog and some tasty treats somewhere with a low distraction level. You are not asking or expecting anything of your dog at this point. Just click or say your CR, and then give your dog a treat. Repeat 5–10 times per session. This is often called loading or charging the CR. Make sure you use your CR, whatever it is, before you make a move to give your dog a treat. Remember, your dog is visual, not verbal, and you want your intended CR to tell your dog the treat is coming, not the motion of your hands. When you see your dog visibly startle or respond in a positive way when she hears her CR, it's time to move on and work on specific behaviors!

FACT

Clickers, which are small plastic and metal noisemakers, are popularly used as CR, but many people use a verbal CR like "Yes!," "Great!," Or "Bingo!" The word or sound you use isn't at all important, but using it consistently and correctly is.

Getting the Behavior You Want on Command

There are four things you have to do get your dog to perform a behavior on command reliably:

1. Get the dog to perform the desired behavior.
2. Name the behavior.
3. Reinforce the dog for performing the behavior on command.
4. Help the dog be correct if he doesn't perform the behavior on command (not necessarily punishment; just help him be correct)

Notice how you want to get the dog to perform the behavior before you name it. This is important for a couple of reasons, not the least of which is to keep you from repeating commands before you've taught them, thereby diluting them or making them irrelevant to your dog.

Getting Your Dog to Perform the Behavior

You have several options to choose from to get your dog to perform the behavior—shaping, luring, and physical modeling. You'll probably use a combination of all three, sometimes for the same behavior. Shaping requires the use of a conditioned reinforcer, but no matter which method you use to get the behavior, it helps to have a well-established conditioned reinforcer so you can let your dog know the moment she's done the right thing.

Shaping essentially means waiting for your dog to offer at least part of a behavior, noting that he's done something correctly with a CR, rewarding the incomplete behavior, and then gradually raising the criteria for reward until the dog is offering a complete behavior. If you have the patience to break behaviors into their smallest pieces and do lots of repetitions, you can teach your dog to do even complex combinations of behaviors using only shaping, but you may have to ignore a lot of other offered behaviors in the process.

ALERT!

Make sure you're not marking and rewarding unwanted behaviors like pawing at you or the treats, jumping up, or barking at you, any or all of which may happen in the early stages of training. If your timing is bad and you consistently mark these extra behaviors as part of the behavior you're trying to encourage, your dog may think they are part of the required behavior. In training terms, this is called a superstitious behavior.

Luring involves using a treat to literally lead your dog by the nose into the position or behavior you want. When the dog gets into the desired position, you use your CR/treat to let him know that's what you wanted.

Physical modeling means you move your dog's body into the desired position. You may use modeling both to teach your dog behaviors, and to enforce behaviors after teaching them by another method. You can use your CR or reward to indicate desired modeled behaviors in the teaching phase.

In the lowest-effort method for owners, capturing simply means catching your dog in the act of doing something you like. As she does whatever the behavior du jour is, you name the behavior, and provide a CR/treat. Unless you're just hanging out watching your dog all the time, waiting for her to offer behaviors you can name and reward, this method is best used as a supplement to other methods.

Shape a Simple Behavior

To shape the behavior "circle to the right," start the session by charging your CR. Then, ignoring anything else your dog does, wait for her to just turn her head to the right, and offer a CR/treat for that several times. When you can see that she's purposely turning her head to the right to get the CR, raise your criteria so she has to turn her head farther for the CR/treat. Reward that behavior several (3–5) times. Raise your criteria again so she has to take a step to the right for the CR/treat, then several steps to the right, and so on, until you have her going in a complete circle. It may take several short training sessions to get it. Start every training session by charging your CR and starting at the beginning of your behavior sequence, the head turn. Raise your criteria as quickly as she shows you she remembers what has been rewarded. Keep quiet other than your CR (use tape over your mouth and use a clicker, if necessary!).

Don't lie to your dog! Every time your dog hears his CR, a treat must follow it. Do vary the amount of time that passes before he gets the treat from one second to several. Eventually you'll be able to note a behavior you like anywhere and take him to get a treat, rather than having to have treats on you all the time.

Using Treats Effectively

There is a great deal of controversy regarding the use of treats in the dog-training process. You certainly don't want to have to carry a bag of treats around for the rest of your dog's life to get him to listen, but you do want training to be an enjoyable and positive experience for yourself and for him.

Motivation

There is no doubt that the use of treats in training greatly increases the dogs' motivation to learn new things. They are an obvious choice to use as a reward with a CR, because of their intrinsic value as a primary reinforcer. Since you can vary the size, number, and value (how much the dog likes one), they're an ideal choice to strengthen a behavior with multiple rewarded repetitions. The problem with using treats is that they can become a crutch—for people and dogs—if they're not used properly.

Praise and Affection

You may think your dog should work for praise alone. While praise certainly is an important part of training, most dogs just aren't motivated enough by it for it to be an effective reinforcer. The same is true with petting. Your dog gets showered with so much praise and petting just for being that those things really don't have special value. Anything, including affection, loses value when it's too freely available. Special toys or games are a valuable training tool to help your dog stay tuned in to you, and as a supplement or alternate for treats for some behaviors.

Dog Treats or People Food?

It's really a personal choice as to what kind of treats to use. For training treats, you want to use something soft that you can cut or break into tiny pieces, like a quarter of your pinkie nail, but that won't crumble into dust when you break it or feed it to your dog. You want your dog to be able to eat the treat without chewing it or chasing crumbs on the floor. You want him to swallow it quickly and look right back to you for the next repetition or command.

Treats—the Good, the Bad, and the Nasty

Human food lends itself well to making great dog treats—string cheese, hot dogs, deli meat, any kind of leftover meat, pieces of carrot or apple— whatever you have on hand and your dog likes. Dogs should never be given anything that contains onions, chocolate, or anything heavily spiced or salted. Low-fat options are the best choice for the majority of your treats.

Afraid your dog will beg if you use people food instead of dog treats? Your dog doesn't need to eat people food even one time to know that it's food. It's the context in which you feed your dog that will cause or prevent begging.

Like some people, some dogs have sensitive digestions and don't respond well to dietary changes, so use what' s best for your dog. Dog treats, even those labeled as training treats, usually don't make great treats for training. In addition to being expensive, they tend to crumble, and many of them are made with ingredients that are tasty but useless to your dog.

Schedules of Reinforcement

When you first start teaching your dog a new behavior, you'll be using a fixed schedule of reinforcement at a 1:1 ratio. That's a fancy way to say that for every correct response your dog gives, she'll be rewarded. Very quickly, as soon as your dog is performing the behavior easily (about the same time you start naming the behavior; more about naming the behavior in Chapters 9 through 16), you'll want to move to a variable schedule of reinforcement. To put it simply, you'll wait to get several correct responses before offering the CR or reward. So, you might want to see two behaviors (or repetitions of the same behavior) before you CR or reward, then three, then one, then four, and so on, so your dog can't predict which behavior or repetition will get the CR, which makes her try harder to get it.

The Power of the Unexpected

The most powerful schedule of reinforcement that keeps dogs working hard for the treats is a random schedule. This schedule works on the same principle as a slot machine. If you got a quarter for every quarter you put in, after a while you'd get bored. And, if one time you didn't get a quarter, you'd get frustrated and angry quickly, maybe taking out your frustration on the machine that always pays off. No, you keep putting that quarter in because you might get a big payoff, and it could happen at any time, so you'd better stay there and keep playing so you don't miss your chance to win. This is exactly the attitude you want to foster in your dog—that training is a game he wants to keep playing.

Rewarding the Best

A random schedule is the way to build that desire, but you have to make sure you're rewarding your dog often enough to keep him motivated. Since you're not rewarding every effort when you are on a random schedule, make sure the efforts that do get rewarded are the best examples of that behavior—the fastest response, the straightest sit—whatever your criteria for that exercise at perfection is, reward the closest approximation of it.

Weaning Off Treats

Chances are, you'll continue to give your dog treats for the duration of her life, whether they're for training purposes or just because she's cute. Preventing yourself and your dog from relying on treats as a crutch to get behavior is easy, if you can discipline yourself to remove them as a lure and switch to a variable and then random schedule of reinforcement as quickly as possible with each behavior.

But We Always Do It with a Treat!

At some point during the process of switching your dog from a food-lured behavior to a hand-lured one, or from a fixed to a variable or random reinforcement schedule, your dog is going to say "Unh, unh, I can't do it without the treat." Your response must be "Oh, yes you can, and I'm going to help you." Gently insist that she does what you asked, even if you have to physically place her into the correct position. Still praise her when she gets into the correct position, but no reward if you had to do the work to get her there—if you have to give somebody a treat for it, give it to yourself (another good reason to use people food for dog training!). The very worst thing to do if your dog refuses a command is to bring out a treat to "help." If you do, not only is your dog training you to use treats as a bribe instead of as a reward, but you're also training your dog that if she doesn't do the requested behavior, she'll get a treat.

How to Use Corrections Fairly Instead of Nagging

Corrections, punishments, constructive criticism. Whatever you want to call it, at some point you will have to help your dog understand that he's made an error and has to correct it.

Correcting or Nagging?

There is a delicate balance to be achieved between using the least amount of force necessary to get the job done, and using an effective correction for the situation. By definition, an effective correction will reduce the frequency or intensity of the unwanted behavior in a few repetitions. If you have to keep repeating the same correction or punishment, you're not reducing the unwanted behavior, you're nagging. Nagging teaches your dog (spouse, kids) to tune you out.

The corrections you use will depend on the situation, the offense, what you have handy, and your dog. For a soft dog, or a minor infraction, you might use a simple verbal correction, like a guttural "Aacckk!" when your dog is getting ready to put her feet on someone, or a little pressure on her collar if she "forgets" to sit when you tell her to. For something more serious, or dangerous to your dog or others, like chewing electrical cords, you want to use something that your dog will remember and try to avoid happening again, like a rain of shaker bottles falling around her.

Catch Your Dog in the Act

For any correction to be effective, it has to be timed with the action it's correcting. Your dog doesn't know that you are mad that she urinated on the floor half an hour ago; she knows you're mad because there is pee on the floor now. After-the-fact punishments only cause confusion, distrust, and fear. The moment your dog makes the right choice, the reinforcement she receives should far outweigh the correction she got, whether it's praise, attention, treats, or a combination. Being right should be an obviously better choice for your dog than being wrong.

Since dogs don't have verbal language, they don't understand what "no" means unless you teach them. What they do understand is tone. A low, growly, guttural sound is something most dogs understand naturally to mean "Stop that!."

Physical Corrections

Whether it's physically restraining or positioning your dog if he's made an error or ignored a command, or holding him by his scruff if he gets into a puppy play-biting frenzy, there will no doubt be times when you will have to physically correct your dog. A physical correction is never to get back at your dog in retaliation for something he's done; it's just to help him become correct. Physical corrections should never be applied in anger or frustration. As a matter of fact, if you're frustrated and angry, it's not a good time to work with your dog at all. If you hit or kick your dog to punish him, it's not correction; it's aggression. Don't be surprised if you get aggression or fear in return if you do resort to such measures.

Timing

Timing is a critical part of successful dog training. There are several intertwined ways that good timing can significantly improve the success of your training program.

Timing Reinforcement

Your timing in delivering reinforcement is absolutely critical to your dog's understanding of each exercise. As far as your dog is concerned, what you reward is what she'll repeat, not what you meant to reward. Let's say you're trying to get your dog to look at you on command (last section of this chapter explains how you can accomplish this). You've charged your CR, and you're waiting for your dog to look at you. She does, but before you can CR, she looks at your hand. You CR when she's looking at your hand, thinking she'll know you meant it for the eye contact. She won't, but the behavior of watching your hand has gotten a little stronger if you want to put that on cue (command).

Teach yourself good timing so you can use CRs effectively. Take a tennis ball and bounce it on a flat, level floor. Every time the ball hits the floor, CR (say "yes," click, whatever your CR is). No ball? Watch somebody walking—in person or on TV—and CR every time his left foot hits the ground.

Timing Corrections

Just as important as timing reinforcements or rewards correctly, the timing of corrections is vital if you want them to have any effect on the behavior you're trying to modify. Dogs not having language means you can't explain that the reason you're yelling at your dog at 5 P.M. is because he got into the trash at 10 A.M. During training sessions, you'll want to pay close attention to your dog. If you do, you'll begin to notice that you can anticipate when she's about to make a mistake, like break a stay, for instance. If you can catch her when she's thinking about breaking, rather than when she's halfway across the room, your correction is much more meaningful and you can use much less force to get the job done.

Other Aspects of Timing

From another perspective, there are two other elements of timing that affect training. They are:

- The duration of your training sessions
- The time of day your training sessions take place.

Aside from the lifestyle training you'll be doing as a matter of course, you'll also want to have some separate formal sessions. The duration of your training sessions should be very short, anywhere from a minute or two to fifteen or twenty at the most. You always want to quit while your dog still wants to play.

ESSENTIAL

Hanging out watching TV at night? It's amazing how much training you can get done in a commercial break. It's the perfect amount of time to work on one or two exercises and leave your dog wanting more.

The time of day that you have your training sessions is important, too. You want to have them when your dog is motivated to work, like before mealtimes, but not overexcited, like after being in the crate for eight hours.

Consistency

In training, lack of consistency will come back to bite you in several ways. Inconsistency in commands causes confusion, like if you try to make one command have several meanings. For example, don't try to have the word "Down" mean lie down, get off the couch, and get off you. How is your dog supposed to know what you mean if you're not clear? In contrast, one meaning shouldn't have several commands, like "sit" one time and "siddown" another. Make things as easy for your dog to figure out by saying what you mean. You may have seen some dogs appear almost hyperactive in their response to commands, throwing several behaviors out in a row, hoping to find the right one. These dogs are usually loaded with stress and confusion about what their owners actually want.

Clear Expectations

Consistent expectations, both in your general idea of how your dog should behave and in how he responds to commands, are also important. If you're not sure how he's supposed to behave, how is he going to figure it out? If you just react to what he does, rather than letting him know right from the beginning what's okay and what's not, you are always a little behind. Know what you expect from him when you give a command, and be consistent in making sure it happens until it's his habit to respond reliably. For example, if you expect him to respond to a single, quiet "sit" command, then that's what you enforce from the beginning. Mean what you say.

Predictable Consequences

On the matter of enforcement, be consistent in the consequences he receives for behaviors you like and the ones you don't. Your dog should always know when he's right even if it's just a smile and a hearty "Good boy!" When he does make a mistake—and he will—something has to happen to correct the error and reduce the chance that it will happen again in the future. It might be simply turning and walking away from the dog if he's not paying attention on leash, or a blast from a squirt gun as he's moving in on the plate of nachos on the coffee table. When he consistently gets predictable consequences for his behavior, deciding between right and wrong is easy.

Repetition

Repetition will come into play in your training program in several different ways as well.

Practice Makes Perfect

Repetition implies practice. Just like getting to Carnegie Hall, your dog needs practice, and lots of it, to become well trained. Particularly when modifying unwanted behaviors, you have to make sure your dog is practicing her replacement behavior (sit instead of jump, for instance) regularly for her to form a new, more acceptable habit. If she doesn't get to practice, the behavior you want won't be there when you need it. Chapters 9 through 16 give suggestions for how many repetitions to do, but five repetitions per session is a reasonable number to aim for.

Generalization

Your dog will need lots of repetition of each exercise in different situations before she truly understands the command. Dogs are very context specific. For example, if you train the sit-stay in your kitchen every day, she'll be very good at the sit-stay… in your kitchen. It is likely that she'll have no idea that the sit-stay she does in the kitchen has anything to do with what you're asking her to do when you're trying to write your check at the vet's office—until you teach her. To help her generalize a command, or understand that sit-stay means sit-stay, wherever you happen to be, you'll have to work on it in different environments until she shows you she understands it by responding reliably. You will find out how to help your dog generalize and become reliable at the end of this chapter.

The Training Game

Although how your dog behaves is serious business, and you are serious about him behaving appropriately, training doesn't have to be a dull and serious chore. Approach the teaching of your commands as a game. Right away, this fosters a positive attitude in your dog toward learning new things, and creates a desire to work for you. There is a simple training game you can play with your dog to get your training started. Along with being fun and easy, it teaches you how to use your CR and shape a basic behavior. As a bonus, it builds the relationship between you and your dog, and lays the foundation for other exercises.

Eye Contact

Along with teaching your dog that paying attention to you pays off for her, eye contact is the foundation for several other commands. It is essential as part of your leadership program, and is an absolute necessity for modification of fear or aggression. Here are the steps to take:

1. **To start, take your (at least mildly) hungry dog and a bunch of tiny, yummy treats to a low-distraction room.** With a handful of treats in each hand, charge your CR—click or say your CR word ("Yes!") and give your dog a treat—5 or 6 times, alternating which hand you use to give your dog the treat.

2. **Hang your arms and hands naturally at your sides in between repetitions, keeping your hands still with the treats safely in your fist.** After you have CR/treated 5 to 6 times, just wait patiently (and quietly!) while you watch your dog's eyes. Most dogs will try looking at your hands, maybe licking or pawing at your hands, perhaps barking at you—whatever your dog does to try to get the treats, ignore it and keep your hands still. In pretty short order, most dogs will at last glance up at you, as if to say, "What's the holdup, where's the next treat?"

3. **The moment your dog makes eye contact with you, CR/treat.** Repeat 5 to 10 times.

After the first few times your dog gets CR/treated, you may see the light bulb go off as your dog figures out what is actually being rewarded. You'll know he's figuring it out when he gives up all the extra behaviors he was trying to get the treats. Quit the session after a success and while your dog still wants to play. If he never makes eye contact during your session, you can try making the tiniest noise to get him to look up at you—a soft kiss, tongue click, or whistle is usually enough. CR/treat even though you had to help. Repeat a couple of times, and then give him another chance to do it on his own. It can seem like a long time when you're waiting, but do try to wait at least 20–30 seconds before helping. If he wanders away, keep him on his dragline and step on it to keep him fairly close to you. Have at least two to three eye contact training sessions a day until you can barely give him the treat before he's throwing his eye contact back to you. For most dogs this happens in the matter of a few sessions.

Bloodhound Daisy watches Andrea's eyes, not the food in her hands.

Put It on Command

Now that your dog knows what the deal is, you're ready to name the command.

ESSENTIAL

As soon as your dog is readily offering eye contact, raise your criteria by making sure you're not CR/treating any extra behaviors that you don't want to be part of eye contact, like whining. If your dog is doing something extra that is acceptable for polite behavior, like sitting with eye contact, by all means, CR/treat.

Start your session as usual, charging your CR, and CR/treating voluntary eye contact 5 times, alternating hands. As soon as you've given him the fifth treat, insert your eye contact command (*Look* and *Watch* are popular choices—you can call it anything you want as long as you are consistent). Basically, you are just slipping your command in before he does what you know he's going to do. Repeat 5 times, using your command right after the previous treat and before he looks back to you. Continue having at least two to three sessions a day using your command. After a few days, test it around the house by giving the command, and CR/treat when your dog responds correctly. Only give the command once. If he looks, he gets a CR/treat. If not, he missed his chance for reinforcement this time. Don't let him teach you to beg him for his attention!

Make It More Challenging

Now that you have named the command, it's time to make the exercise more challenging by adding duration and distraction. Work on each challenge separately. To add duration, start your session the way you normally do, but after a few repetitions, wait for your dog to maintain eye contact for a few seconds before you CR/treat. Add duration by doubling the time required for your dog to maintain eye contact for several repetitions, and then make it easier again. So you might do your repetitions like this:

- 1 second
- 2 seconds
- 4 seconds
- 8 seconds
- 2 seconds

Quit for that round, and give your dog a few minutes to think about it before you start your next session with:

- 2 seconds
- 4 seconds
- 8 seconds
- 15 seconds
- 4 seconds

When your dog is committed to holding eye contact with you, it's time to add distraction. Start by holding your arms straight out from your sides at the shoulder (so you look like a "T"). If your new position isn't distracting enough, wiggle your fingers. CR/treat for watching *you*, not your fingers. When he's good at that, alternate dropping treats from your outstretched hands (be ready to step on the treat if your dog dives for it—his only opportunity for reinforcement comes from eye contact). When you can't get him to fall for the falling treats, take your show on the road. Start right outside the door, then at the mailbox, then at the corner, and so on, gradually increasing the distraction level. Recruit helpers to distract him by walking in a circle around you. Have them start at whatever distance your dog can maintain eye contact and have them move gradually closer until they're practically touching you. When he can handle that, add some distance again, but have them carry, then squeak, a toy.

Daisy ignores Jordan's offer of a toy to pay attention to Andrea.

Winning the Training Game

It's easy to win the training game by setting your dog and yourself up for success. The way you'll get each behavior will vary, but if you are consistent, you can teach your dog to do virtually anything reliably. To help your dog win the game, build on success rather than trying to undo failure by making sure he is solid at one level before progressing to the next, but raise your criteria often. If he gets confused or the distraction is too much for him to overcome, back up to the last step where he was successful. Remember to switch to first a variable, then random schedule of reinforcement when your dog is competent at each level.

You're really winning the game when you can integrate training seamlessly into your lifestyle. Practice is vital to your success. Find ways to make your life with your dog easier, like teaching her to sit and give you eye contact as a way to ask permission for access to privileges. If necessary, wake up 10 or 15 minutes earlier a couple of times a week to have a little uninterrupted time with her. Out for a walk? Stop every 5 minutes for a brief training break, choosing a different exercise to work on during each break. Interrupt play sessions with a single command, like "Down," make sure it happens, and go back to playing. Over time, your dog will start to respond faster so she can get back to playtime. Spend two or three minutes before her mealtimes working on a command she's struggling with. She'll be extra motivated to comply.

Getting the idea? Be creative and figure out what works for you, your dog, and your life!

Chapter 6

Socializing Your Dog

Dogs that are well socialized and trained have freedom. They can accompany their owners practically anywhere and be relaxed and well behaved. They can stay in the same room with guests at a party and not be a nuisance. Socialization is a lifelong commitment and involves a lot more than just playing with the neighbor's dog every once in a while. From the time he's a puppy, and throughout his life, your dog will need continued exposure to different people, animals, and experiences to be a calm, confident, adaptable companion you can count on.

Critical Times for Socialization

The first two years of your dog's life largely determine his behavior and attitude toward people, dogs, other animals, and new sensory experiences for the remainder of his life. Puppy or not, you will need to plan on actively socializing your dog from the time you bring him home throughout his life. Lack of early socialization can cause lifelong fear issues and aggression. If your dog is already past the puppy stage, there's still hope, but your job will be harder and your dog may be more resistant to change.

ALERT!

Puppies should not be removed from their litters permanently until they are at least 7 weeks old (8 weeks old by law in many states). Their mothers and littermates have important lessons to teach them about rules, getting along with others, and controlling themselves. Puppies removed from their litters before 7 weeks, and orphaned or singleton puppies have reduced bite inhibition and lowered ability to get along with other dogs if not handled and socialized carefully and regularly.

Developmental Stages

Your dog will go through several developmental stages over the first two years of his life, each of which contribute to the dog you end up with. Although learning takes place in virtually all of them, some are more crucial than others in the final basic temperament of your dog:

Neonatal: 1 to 14 days after birth. The puppy is totally dependent on his mother, has very little sensory awareness, and very little learning takes place. Through regular mild physical stress (like placing puppy's foot on a wet washcloth for a moment), a breeder can improve the puppy's later adaptability and even increase the size of the puppy's brain.

Transitional: 15 to 22 days after birth. The puppy's eyes and ears open, he gets awareness of his surroundings, and he starts to control bodily functions. Breeders can improve brain development by enriching puppies' environment.

Primary Socialization: 3 to 5 weeks after birth. This is a time of rapid physical and motor-skill development. The puppy learns all the behaviors that make him a dog—body posturing, accepting discipline from his mother, barking, and bite inhibition. breeder should begin socialization to new people, sounds, sights, and textures.

Secondary Socialization: 5 to 12 weeks after birth. This is the most critical developmental period for behavior. The puppy imprints on people and forms lifelong positive and negative associations about people, dogs, animals, sights, and sounds. The puppy will be much less accepting of new things after this period.

Juvenile: 3 to 6 months. The puppy learns survival skills, what works and what doesn't. Habits of behavior are born.

Adolescent: 6 months to 2 years. The testing phase. Social hierarchy becomes very important; resolving leadership is job number one.

If you have a puppy, you'll never get this time back—stop reading right now and get your puppy out to meet someone new, then come back in and continue reading.

Critical and Sensitive Periods

In addition to the developmental stages that dogs go through on their way to adulthood, they are also affected by several critical or sensitive periods (sometimes called fear periods) in the first two years. Not as predictable in their onset or duration as the developmental stages, these periods can last anywhere from a few days to a few weeks and occur several times in the dog's puppyhood and adolescence, often overlapping with the developmental stages. The fear periods are characterized by the dog's loss of confidence and hyper-reactivity to otherwise innocuous events, while other stages are notable for the puppy's behavioral development.

The Fear Imprint Stage

The first critical period, the fear imprint stage, occurs between 8 and 11 weeks old, right in the middle of the secondary socialization period. Traumatic events during this time tend to leave a lasting impression. Puppies should be exposed to a wide variety of people, animals, sights, sounds, and events in a fun way at this time.

Puppies exposed to an ever-changing variety of stimuli positively at 7 to 12 weeks usually form permanent positive associations with them, while puppies who aren't exposed to such differences are often never able to accept them comfortably. They may show avoidance, fear, or even aggression to whatever they aren't used to.

The Flight Instinct Stage

The second stage, the flight instinct stage, occurs between 4 and 8 months. For most puppy owners, the honeymoon is over. Suddenly that sweet little bundle of fluff is ignoring you when you call—and was that a growl you heard when you saw your neighbor's dog? This is the time for resolving relationship problems while they're brewing. If you've already started training, this is when you can expect regression. If you haven't started, what are you waiting for?

The Second Fear Period

Overlapping this stage, from 6 to 14 months, is the second fear period. During this stage, habits of behavior are being formed. Calm, assertive leadership is essential. Puppies may show fear or apprehension in new situations. It is imperative to avoid reinforcing fearful behavior by "poor babying" what would otherwise be temporary shyness. Without extensive socialization at this stage, some dogs may never be able to comfortably accept new dogs, people, or situations.

Socializing with People

Making sure your dog is well socialized with people is the single most important thing you'll do for her in her life. The truth is, she can eat every shoe you own, pee on every carpet, and drag you down the street when you walk her, and while you would be happier if she didn't do these things, not one of them will cost you your house if she does them. If she's fearful and aggressive with people, however, and threatens or bites someone, or several someones, the chances for her living a long and happy life are seriously reduced.

100 People by 100 Days

The first three months of your dog's life are the most formative for what will be her adult temperament. Your goal is for your puppy to meet a hundred new people by the time she's a hundred days old. You may have a little makeup work to do if the breeder didn't start socializing your puppy, but it's not as hard as it sounds.

FACT

Large and giant breeds will often go through a final testing and sensitive period between 18 and 24 months. If training and socialization is lax, it is not unusual for aggression or fear issues to appear in previously social dogs during this time.

Invite at least five new people a week to come to your house to meet your puppy. They can come as a group or one or two at a time. Take your puppy to your job on your day off and introduce him to all your coworkers (if you have a dog-friendly environment). Go to the vet's office when you don't have an appointment (call ahead to make sure they don't have a potentially infectious dog before you go), and have all of the staff members who are available give him a treat and a cuddle. Enroll in a puppy preschool class. Call the local assisted living center and see if it's okay to bring him there to meet some of the residents.

It's easy to find a hundred people if you try. Everyone who handles your puppy should handle him gently, but make sure they don't encourage behavior you won't want later, like jumping up, mouthing, or rough play and wrestling. Include people of all sizes, shapes, and colors. Don't forget people with facial hair, glasses, hats, accents, wheelchairs, canes, crutches, strollers, walkers, umbrellas, bicycles—if there is a person attached, your puppy should meet them!

Socializing the Juvenile

"Independence" and "curiosity" are the watchwords of the three- to six-month-old juvenile. During this time, puppies practically grow wings as they explore their world, often with their mouths. By this time your puppy has pretty much formed her opinions about people, dogs, vacuum cleaners, the vet, and almost everything else she experienced during her first hundred days. She is much more likely to be suspicious of new people and situations during this stage if she wasn't socialized well previously.

During this time, socialization should be positive and calm with people. She should never be forced to allow someone she is fearful of touch her. Take several trips to the groomer and vet to get kisses and cookies, so she remembers them as places where good things happen, rather than bad places that only cut toenails and give shots. Since her vaccinations will be complete by this time, take her anywhere you're allowed—pet stores, dog parks, art festivals—anywhere there is likely to be a crowd. Bring along some treats and make a rule that no one is allowed to pet her if she isn't sitting—and stick to it. By the end of the outing, you have a dog that not only thinks people are pretty cool, but also thinks that sitting is pretty cool, too. Be prepared for her age-related independent streak to get the best of her, as she ignores you, forgets to do the right thing, or becomes selectively deaf in response to your commands. This is an excellent age to enroll your puppy in obedience classes if you haven't already done so. In-home socialization should continue, with the emphasis on her polite behavior with guests.

Socializing the Adolescent

Socializing the seven- to twenty-four-month-old takes on new meaning as breed and inherited temperament tendencies surface. You can't force a naturally aloof dog to love everyone, but you can teach him that the presence of people means good things will happen for him, which can do a lot to improve his attitude. Knowing where he stands in the pack order is very important to him at this age, and he may run for higher office if given the opportunity. Fear periods coincide with growth spurts, so be extra careful during those times to ensure that his interactions with people are positive. Socializing the more outgoing dog is a matter of making sure she remains calm and polite during her interactions with people.

Consistency in rules is important, as well-meaning but clueless people can reward the very behaviors you are trying to prevent. This would be a good time to take the social dog along to your child's sports event, if allowed, but be prepared to remove her for a few minutes if the excitement of so many potential playmates is too much for her level of training and self-control.

Trying to figure out what's okay to let her get away with in her interactions with people? Try this guide: Would it be okay if she did the same thing to a toddler or a great-grandmother? If it's not okay with them, it's not okay. You can always teach her to put her feet up on someone (on command) if you want to, after she stops trying it on her own.

A Never-ending Process

Even if you live like a hermit, your dog will have to have contact with people outside his pack at some point in his life. Repair or delivery people will come to your house, and your dog will have to go to the vet, the groomer, or the kennel. Continued socialization with people through adulthood is essential for maintaining canine social skills.

Socializing with Dogs

Making sure that your dog is well socialized to other dogs requires time and effort, but the payoff makes the expenditure well worth it. You won't have to worry about your dog behaving aggressively when you encounter other dogs on walks, you can let another dog play with and tire your dog out and save you the trouble, and maybe you'll even make a friend at the dog park who will take care of your dog instead of you leaving him at the kennel the next time you go on vacation.

Socializing the Puppy

Socializing the young puppy is important, but you do have to be careful about exposing your puppy's delicate immune system to potentially fatal communicable diseases. Your puppy's dog socialization began in her litter at 3 weeks, but it has to continue for her to learn to communicate well with her own species. Socialization to other dogs for puppies under 12 weeks is best done under very controlled circumstances where unvaccinated or unhealthy dogs are unlikely to be present.

Already have a dog? Hopefully your current dog is already dog friendly and has a healthy follower relationship with you. If so, have the two dogs meet on neutral territory, with leashes on and lots of treats for good behavior. If not, consult a professional trainer to help ease the transition.

Avoid areas where stray or feral dogs roam, and high dog-traffic areas like dog parks, even if no dogs are present when you're there. Your puppy shouldn't socialize with dogs who visit those areas until vaccinations are complete. The dogs that your puppy does socialize with should be trusted to be friendly to your puppy during this formative time. Females who have raised litters are often good choices because they know just the perfect balance of affection and discipline to apply. Playing with other puppies continues your puppy's education in bite inhibition and other important social skills.

The Older Puppy

Starting around 16 weeks, or when your puppy's vaccinations are complete, you can begin socializing her to dogs of all sizes, colors, and coat types. Even dogs with different ear sets and tail postures are to be considered different enough to seek out socialization opportunities. Dogs' play with each other tends to involve a lot of chasing, wrestling, play-biting, barking, and growling. This can be unnerving for many new or first-time dog owners.

If in doubt, take your puppy to a doggie daycare or a socialization class at your local obedience school (or go by yourself), and watch how dogs play with each other until you're comfortable. You want to keep your puppy safe, but you don't want to make her neurotic by being overprotective.

Of course, if a dog doesn't play well with your puppy, remove your dog from the situation for her safety. Always ask the other dog's owner if your puppy can meet their dog before allowing her to, but take their answer with a grain of salt. Sometimes people will rationalize their own dog's aggressive behavior as play. You can always let your puppy drag a leash or dragline until you're sure her potential playmate is suitable—and it's not a bad idea from a training standpoint.

On-leash Interactions

On-leash socialization can be an issue of contention for many dogs, usually because their owners do all the wrong things. You can increase the possibility of pleasant on-leash meetings just by keeping your leash loose instead of keeping tension on it. If things get snarly, simply turn and walk away—your dog will have no choice but to come with you.

If your dog hasn't been well socialized up to the age of six months, it is usually a much more difficult (sometimes impossible) process to teach her to accept new dogs. While she doesn't have to enjoy the presence of other dogs, you can teach her that she is safe in the presence of them and that you are in control of the situation. There is no excuse for allowing an unsocialized dog to take a the-best-defense-is-a-good-offense attitude with every dog she encounters.

Socializing with Other Animals

Even if your dog is your only pet, he'll encounter a variety of other animals in his life—some routinely, like other dogs, cats, and the local wildlife; and some rarely, if ever, like livestock. Taking the time to expose your dog at an early age to a variety of animals of all sizes and shapes will greatly improve the chances of him accepting the presence of even the "strangest" animal as nothing to worry about later in life. Whether your dog will be living with other pets or you just have the occasional encounter with the neighborhood fauna, you want your dog to be under control and unafraid.

Safe Interspecies Interaction

Your primary objective in socializing your dog with your other pets is keeping all parties safe and comfortable in each other's presence. Keep in mind that dogs are predators, and most other household pets could easily be considered prey. To keep everybody safe, use a combination of management, training, and supervised socialization. It may be helpful to have pets first smell, then see each other from behind a barrier—maybe even from a distance at first—making sure that good things like praise, petting, and special treats are given for calm, nonreactive behavior. Dogs should be prevented from chasing housemates, but the housemates should also be prevented from panicking and running away, inciting the dog's chase instinct. Since scent is such a strong means of information exchange for animals, as mentioned previously, switching their bedding is often helpful during the socialization process. With time, and by building on success, most animals can learn to at least tolerate each other, if not live in total harmony.

The Great Outdoors

Socializing your dog to animals outside your home is something that needs to be done early and often if you expect her to accept those animals as nonthreatening later. If she will spend time around horses, sheep, chickens, or any other livestock, it is imperative that she be introduced to them as early as possible—before 12 weeks is best. She should be kept leashed for safety until she learns some self-control around these animals. Animals that your dog might see, but won't be allowed to interact with, like deer, squirrels, and neighborhood cats, should be dealt with calmly. Teach her to give you eye contact when you encounter such attractive nuisances. The trick is to get her attention when she first notices the "prey" rather than when the chase is on. This will both increase your chance of success and will diffuse the fear of the animal your dog wants to chase. Animals that aren't running away aren't as much fun to chase.

Accepting New Experiences and Sounds

Your dog doesn't just need to be exposed to people and animals to be sure of himself. He needs experience with all kinds of sights, sounds, and surfaces. The best breeders start this process when puppies are just a few weeks old. They know that mild stress at an early age improves adaptability and coping skills later on.

How You Can Help

Puppies can't be raised in a vacuum, protected from anything and everything that might stress or frighten them. You don't want to traumatize or terrify your puppy; you just want to teach him to deal with unusual or slightly scary experiences without having a meltdown.

By cheerleading him through scary experiences, rather than trying to soothe him through them, you will help build his confidence and your relationship. Don't feel sorry for him; help him work out his fears. Exude confidence yourself, and walk right up to whatever he's afraid of with a cheery "Silly puppy! There's nothing to be afraid of!" Give him some treats when he's calm. Avoid cooing at him. "It's ok, good boy, it's ok" might sound soothing to you, but to your dog it sounds like praise—"Good boy, you're right to be afraid,"—actually reinforcing his fear.

Conquering Big or Scary Stuff

Garbage trucks, traffic noises, vacuum cleaners, planes, trains, and motorcycles are just a few of the things your dog might experience just in the first weeks he's home. His exposure at first should be at a distance so that he can function without fear, gradually moving closer.

It's a delicate balance, but you want to challenge your dog without overwhelming him. Obedience and puppy classes that include some work on agility contact obstacles are great for building confidence and teamwork.

There will be times (usually in the second fear period) when your dog reacts fearfully to something he's passed a hundred times before and never noticed, like the toilet brush or a neighbor's recycle bin. If it's not a big deal to you, it's less likely to be a big deal to him. Help him work through it cheerfully and move on.

Socialization Cautions

While socialization is vital to your dog's happiness and good behavior, there are some potential pitfalls to be aware of. The benefits of a socialized dog far outweigh the risks, but you do have to be aware of them.

Health and Safety

Just like when kids socialize at the playground, there is the possibility for illness or injury when your dog socializes with other dogs. The large majority of dog-dog interactions are peaceful, provided people don't try to dictate how the dogs interact. Occasionally, personality conflicts between dogs arise, or an irresponsible person lets their dog bully other dogs. Like people, not every dog in the world is going to get along with every other dog, and some dogs are outright dangerous. If in doubt, keep moving and look for another playmate.

Risk of Injury

Even if everybody gets along, dogs can get injured just by playing. In addition, there is the chance of your dog becoming infected with a communicable disease from socializing with other dogs. Unvaccinated puppies should not interact with dogs that have the potential to be carrying disease. There is no guarantee, as even vaccinated dogs can fail to form an immune response and be infected or become carriers of disease even if they don't appear sick.

Animals Are Animals

It's not just your dog's health and safety you have to be concerned about. If you have other household pets, never forget that your dog is an animal first, and any interactions with smaller animals should be attempted only under close and careful supervision. Also realize that interactions with smaller animals are never 100 percent safe. There are some animals that are just never going to get along. In these instances, careful management or even finding a different home for one of the pets may be necessary for the safety of everyone concerned.

Behavioral Issues

Dogs tend to act more like dogs when they're with other dogs. Until your dog is trained reliably, don't undo your hard work by giving your dog commands you can't enforce when he's playing. Give him a CR or treat any time he checks in with you, and then let him go play again. If he's fearful, either temporarily in association with a sensitive period, or genetically, he should never be forced to interact with anyone or anything that triggers the fear response. Use desensitization and counterconditioning to improve his opinion of whatever triggers his fear. Good timing is essential, as you can just as easily teach your dog to be more afraid if your timing is off, and you mark and reward fearful behavior instead of marking calm or confident behavior. If your dog has severe fear or aggression, consult a professional trainer or behaviorist to help you get started.

Chapter 7

Housebreaking

If you want absolutely nothing else from your dog, you want her to know where and when it's appropriate to eliminate. It may come as a surprise to you that dogs don't instinctively know or prefer to eliminate outside. What they do instinctively know is to keep their eating and sleeping area clean. You can use this knowledge to your advantage when housebreaking your dog. Although it won't happen overnight, your dog can be housebroken in a very short time with good management and consistency.

A Consistent Schedule

Your first job when housebreaking your new dog is to establish a consistent schedule. Dogs are creatures of routine and habit. A consistent schedule will help your dog become housebroken by providing a predictable routine.

Housebreaking the Puppy

For the very young (under 3 months) puppy, the schedule is all about observation. Your puppy doesn't have the physical ability to "hold it" at this age. When he's gotta go, he's gotta go right now, so no, you don't have time to put real shoes or a coat on. Don't give your young puppy even a moment to make a mistake—he has to be supervised every waking moment. You are safe to assume that any time your puppy stops doing anything—eating, sleeping, playing, chewing—he will have to pee within minutes, if not sooner. Whatever he's doing, if he stops, he has to go. Eating and chewing set off a bit of a chain reaction in young puppies, so you can figure that he'll probably need to poop within a few minutes of stopping either of these activities. Pay attention and take notes if necessary so you'll learn to recognize his signs that tell you he's getting ready to go. His signs might include sniffing the floor, circling, pacing, whining, staring at you, or sneezing. As soon as you see him starting to give you a sign, ask him, "Do you want to go out?" Carry or escort him to the door, repeating your "Go out" phrase a few times.

Accompany him to his potty area every time, both to praise and reward him for going in the right place, and so you can make sure he actually goes. This is a novel environment for him, so he may temporarily forget why he's there. Keep him on leash, but don't take him for a walk. Just take him to where you want him to eliminate and wait. Be as boring as you can possibly be. Ignore his attempts to play and explore; just wait and watch for up to ten minutes. If and when he goes, have a party, with lots of smiles, praise, and even a few treats. Allow him a few minutes of play or exploration as a reward for going quickly. If he doesn't go, bring him back inside, but keep him under very close supervision, either tethered to you or in his crate, for twenty minutes or so, then try again.

Sample Schedule for Puppies Under Six Months

- **6 A.M**—Potty time (Some puppies will just need to pee; others will have to do everything). Supervised play until breakfast.
- **6:30**—Breakfast (in crate if you need to shower or accomplish anything).
- **6:45**—Potty. After potty, supervised play until crating.
- **7:45**—Crate (one last pee before crating is a good idea, especially for young puppies).
- **11**—Potty, play.
- **11:30**—Lunch.
- **11:45**—Potty, supervised play until crating.
- **12:30**—Crate.
- **3**—Potty, then supervised play or back in crate until dinner.
- **5:15**—Potty.
- **5:30**—Dinner.
- **5:50**—Potty, play, potty, crate, potty, play, etc. until bedtime.
- **7**—Take away water (give ice chips or water a sip at a time if necessary).
- **10:45**—Potty.
- **11**—Bedtime.

Toy breeds can take longer to get physical control, and therefore to housebreak. It takes patience and careful supervision to prevent accidents (which with toy dogs are easy to miss until the evidence is found), but it can be done. You may have to use some creativity, including the possibility of some indoor alternatives (discussed in the last section of this chapter).

Most 8–12 week old puppies won't make it through the night without at least one potty trip. This should be as uneventful as possible. Just let your puppy potty and then put her right back in the crate, with no treats or playtime.

During the day, most puppies can be crated for about an hour for every month they are old. You may need to enlist the help of a friend, neighbor, or dog walker to make sure your puppy gets out often enough if you work outside of the home. Physical control comes in leaps, not steps. You'll just notice one day that your puppy can wait until after breakfast to go out that first time, or suddenly can wake up from a nap and not have to pee immediately. Adjust the schedule as your puppy physically matures.

Adolescent/Adult Dog Schedule

By the time they're seven or eight months old, most dogs can be pretty much housebroken, which means that except in the case of illness or extreme disruption of their normal schedules, they don't have accidents. None. Nada. Zip. The lack of accidents isn't because the dogs are perfect. It's perfect prevention building a habit of perfect housebreaking. Healthy adolescent and adult dogs usually have the physical ability to hold it for six to eight hours, although some of them may not know they can or understand why they should. They learn those skills from their owners, who, through excellent management, set their dogs up for success.

You can prevent your puppy from learning to "hold it" by taking him out too frequently. After he's 12 weeks old, try to stick to scheduled potty times, and crate him or tether him to you in between scheduled trips to prevent mistakes.

Weaning Off the Extra Trips

After seven months, most dogs will be eating twice a day, and will need to eliminate three to five times a day. If you've been using your "Go out" phrase for a while, you should notice some response from your dog—getting excited, running to the door, etc.—when you ask. Experiment with your schedule as your dog gets the idea of holding it and asking to go out. If someone is around to supervise, skip the midmorning and midafternoon potty breaks, and see if your dog can get by on three or four potty trips per day.

Supervision and Confinement as Housebreaking Aids

Your dog is not going to housebreak himself. To prevent accidents, and to help him learn to hold it, diligent supervision and confinement are absolutely essential elements of successful housebreaking.

No Freedom to Make Mistakes

Supervision means that your dog doesn't have the opportunity to go in some hidden location—behind the couch, down the hall, or in another room. If he's out of his crate, and until he is reasonably reliable or asking to go out when he needs to, he has to be where someone responsible can see him and interrupt him if he's about to make a mistake. Use draglines, tethers, and gates to keep him where you can see him.

For most dogs, confinement means crating. Particularly for young puppies or dogs just starting the housebreaking process, as mentioned previously, it is important that the crate is just big enough for him to stand up, turn around, and lie down, without a lot of room to spare. Don't give him enough room to sleep at one end of the crate and pee at the other.

Tire your dog out and make sure he has pottied before crating him. He'll be more likely to go in and relax for a longer period of time than if you stuff him in there when he's full of energy—and more!

If you have a toy breed or can't get your puppy out often enough, you might consider confining your dog in a larger area, like a bathroom or a folding puppy exercise pen with his crate (open) and one of the indoor potty options discussed at the end of this chapter.

Accepting the Crate

Natural den lovers, most dogs accept the crate quite readily. You can ease the process by making sure good things happen for your dog in there. Feed her in the crate sometimes, or give her special treats or chewies, like stuffed kongs, when she's crated. Leave the crate door open when she's not in it, and keep the crate in a high-traffic area of your house; the hardest thing for her is to be isolated. Whether you've been gone five seconds or five hours, only let her out of the crate if she's calm and quiet.

Teach her to go in her crate on command, like "Kennel up" or "Go to your room," by throwing a treat in there and using your command as she enters. Praise and give her a couple of extra treats if she stays in. When you're first teaching the command, let her out quickly, anywhere from a few seconds to a few minutes. After a week or so of her associating your command with her going in and getting treats, try using your command before you throw the treats in (you can still use the hand motion). Praise and reward her when she goes in the crate on command.

QUESTION?

Should your dog have a nice comfy bed in his crate?
It depends. If he doesn't chew his bedding or use it to absorb urine in his crate, then by all means, give him a bed. Don't give him several chances to destroy or urinate on his bed. If he doesn't use the bed for its intended purpose, don't give him one for several weeks, and then try again.

Teaching an Elimination Command

You're late for work. It's raining, snowing, or brutally hot. You don't want to wait half an hour for your dog to potty; you want him to go, and go now. Teaching your dog to eliminate on command is a way for you to make your life with your dog a little easier.

Going to the Potty on Command

Before you start, decide what command(s) you're going to use. You can use one command for both, or teach separate commands. "Hurry up," "Do your business," and "Get busy" are popular choices, but as always, the words you use aren't important. Using them consistently is. Plan on taking two to four weeks of consistent reinforcement to teach your dog his new command.

When you take your dog to his potty area, be nothing more than an observant post. Don't talk to him, or your neighbor, or let your dog entice you into taking him for a walk before he potties. The moment you see your dog assume the position, repeat your command several times, calmly and quietly (you don't want to distract him from his task) "Hurry up, Gooood Hurry up, Hurry up." After he finishes, give him praise and a treat, then give him some playtime or take him for a walk. Repeat the process for at least a week every time you take him to his potty area before you test your command. To test it, take him to his potty area and give him his command once. If he starts looking for a spot and produces right away, give him praise and a treat like he's the best dog in the world (well, he is, isn't he?). If he doesn't start looking for a spot, just continue as you were for another week before testing again.

Why Not Take a Walk to Potty?

If the object of your walk is for your dog to potty, rather than to exercise and spend quality time with her, then you'll probably end the walk as soon as she goes. This teaches her to hold it so she can prolong the walk. Let's say you walk her until you're tired, whether she's gone or not, and head for home. By the time you're back in house, she either has no reason to, or can't, hold it anymore and does exactly what you were trying to prevent. By making the walk part of the reward for pottying, you can encourage her to potty quickly and in the right place.

What to Do When Accidents Happen

Accidents are bound to happen now and then. Maybe your puppy had a little dietary indiscretion. Or, perish the thought, her schedule was neglected, or nobody noticed that she was asking to go out. Whatever the reason, you want to handle the situation properly to reduce the chance that it'll happen again.

Catch'Em in the Act

In order for your dog to learn from his mistake, you absolutely must catch him in the act of making it. He will not understand that you're mad at him for something he did several minutes ago, let alone several hours ago. If you do see him starting to go, interrupt him with a loud "Aacckk!" or give one of your shake bottles a toss. Get him right to his potty area and wait a few minutes for him to finish what he started inside. Praise lavishly when he goes outside. Make sure his next several successes are rewarded.

If you find a puddle or a pile, don't rub his nose in it or scream at him. He'll only get that you don't like finding messes, not that you don't want him to make them. Even though he might look guilty the next time there is a mess, he won't connect the mess with the act.

E ALERT!

After-the-fact punishments are never a good idea. They do nothing to solve the problem, but they do create stress and confusion. Some dogs get so worried about messes that they'll start cleaning them up by eating the evidence. This can quickly evolve into a disgusting habit that can be very difficult to break.

Cleaning Up

Clean up any messes as quickly as possible, before stains and odors have a chance to soak in and become difficult, if not impossible, to remove. You can demonstrate that you're disappointed and repulsed when you find a mess, but you don't want your dog to think that you're his personal cleaning crew, so put him in his crate while you clean up.

Start by picking up any solid waste, and blotting up as much liquid as you can. Follow that with a thorough soaking with an enzymatic cleaner, like Nature's Miracle or Out!, designed specifically for this purpose. You may have to soak and blot several times, especially if you didn't find the spot immediately.

FACT

Don't use household ammonia to clean up accidents. Ammonia is a component of urine, and its scent can actually draw a dog back to urinating in the same spot repeatedly. If you don't have enzymatic cleaner, you can liberally apply baking soda to absorb liquid and odor. Vacuum when it's dry, and soak the area with a mixture of white vinegar and club soda. Repeat until the spot is clean, and leave a towel over the spot until it's completely dry.

How to Tell Something Is Wrong

If, despite your best efforts, consistent schedule, and excellent management, your dog is still having accidents, you have to consider the possibility that there is a physical cause.

Medical Issues

There are a variety of medical conditions that can make the housebreaking process slower or more difficult. Any dog that is having frequent accidents despite diligent housebreaking efforts should have a thorough medical exam, including blood work, fecal analysis, and urinalysis. Some conditions are common, and easily treated, like intestinal parasites or urinary-tract infections. Others are much more serious, or even life threatening, like diabetes, impaction, or parvo. If in doubt, check it out!

When to Seek Professional Help

If your dog has been having frequent accidents for an extended period of time, it's time to seek veterinary assistance. Here's how you know when a problem requires medical intervention:

- Your dog is obviously leaking urine, or you find a puddle when she gets up from sleeping.
- She is urinating very frequently, in small amounts.
- She strains, but nothing comes out, or she appears to be in pain or vocalizes when she strains.
- You see undigested food in her feces, or she seems to poop more than she eats.
- There is mucous in her poop, her poop is a strange color (yellow, maroon, or black), or it has a foul smell.
- She's drinking and peeing more than normal.
- She has diarrhea and is vomiting (get to the vet now!).
- Any sudden change that lasts more than a couple of days.

What to Do If Your Dog Is a Submissive Wetter

Submissive urination is a common problem and can be very frustrating for dog owners to deal with. It often appears just before puberty, and usually goes away with a little maturity if it's dealt with properly.

Do's and Don'ts

Do keep greetings and departures calm. If she's hysterical when greeting people, wait for her to completely give up trying to get attention before even making eye contact with her. Start with just a little chest scratch and a few calm words of praise. If she starts to lose it, walk away until she's calm again. Give her something else to do, like making her sit, sprinkle a few treats on the floor, or give her a toy to hold so she's already a bit preoccupied when greeting. Do make sure she's been out to pee before greeting visitors.

Don't yell at her, or strike her, or punish her in any way other than removing attention if she starts to leak. Since submissive urination is, by definition, a submissive gesture, yelling or punishments usually result in a dog who has to repeat the gesture to get the message across.

The Chronic Leaker

Some breeds, cocker spaniels for example, are infamous for their lifelong submissive urination issues. This problem seems to have a genetic base, and as such, management, along with training, is in order. Along with the do's and don'ts for the average submissive wetter, you may have to resort to belly bands or doggie diapers to at least prevent the mess (and keep your frustration in check) if your dog is unable to control herself.

Housebreaking Adult Dogs

Housebreaking adult dogs can be more challenging than housebreaking puppies, but it doesn't have to be. The trick is to treat them just like they are puppies, which means not giving them chances to make mistakes (confinement and supervision are your friends!) and keeping them on a consistent eating and eliminating schedule until they are accident-free in the house for at least six weeks.

The Crate Soiler

Occasionally, dogs will urinate or defecate in their crates. Usually, it's a rare or temporary problem brought on by illness or neglect of their normal schedule. Sometimes, unfortunately, it's because the dog has learned not to mind being dirty. This is not a normal state for dogs, and is usually brought on by the dog being forced to eat, sleep, and eliminate in the same area for a prolonged period, like a six-month-old puppy in a pet store that has spent four months in the same cage. If your dog regularly eliminates in the crate, there are some things you can try:

- Remove all bedding from the crate, so there is no way for your dog to hide (or hide from) his mess.

- Feed him in the crate by scattering the food all over the crate floor instead of from a dish.
- Change the type of crate you use (from airline style to wire, or vice versa).
- Practice good supervision instead of crating whenever possible.
- Consider other containment options, indoor alternatives, and doggie daycare.

Indoor Alternatives

Although it's not really practical for larger dogs, there are a few indoor potty area options that are worth considering for small dogs and puppies. Newspaper and puppy pads are common indoor options, and dog litter boxes are swiftly gaining popularity. While newspaper is certainly the least expensive of the indoor options, it's also the least containable, and the messiest. Pads are reasonably inexpensive, and have a waterproof backing to protect the floor underneath. The problem with both newspapers and pads is that it's common for dogs to squat on the corner, depositing pee or poop on the floor next to them. Litter boxes and litter are more expensive than newspaper or pads, but the space is clearly defined, so after acclimation, misses are much less common. Unfortunately, some dogs are more interested in playing with or eating the litter than going in it.

Whatever method you want to try, it is very helpful to clearly define the space by enclosing the papers, pads, or litter in an exercise pen or litter box (the litter-box police won't come and get you if you put papers or pads in your litter box instead of litter!). The process is the same for indoor housebreaking as it is for outside training; accompany your dog to the potty area every time so you can praise and reward for her eliminating in the proper place.

It is possible to housebreak your dog outside, and use the indoor alternative of your choice as a backup, but it takes a little more time and effort on your part, and may confuse your dog a bit in the process. For most people and dogs, it's best to pick one method and stick with it.

Chapter 8

Chewing, Mouthing, and Play-biting

Dogs use their teeth for much more than eating. Their mouths and teeth are the closest equivalent they have to hands, and are used for exploration, play, and communication. To keep their jaws and teeth in good working condition, dogs must regularly exercise their mouths with vigorous chewing. Your job is to teach your dog when, where, and on what (or whom) it's acceptable to chew, and to prevent, interrupt, or redirect him from using his teeth inappropriately.

Preventing Property Damage from Chewing

Chewing fulfills multiple physical, mental, and emotional needs in your dog. He doesn't just want to chew; he has to chew, and he will chew virtually anything in his path to satisfy his urge, even though what he chooses to chew on might be completely inexplicable to you.

Puppy Chewing

When they're teething, and as part of their natural exploration, puppies spend much of their time picking up, mouthing, and chewing practically anything in their path. To keep your puppy from leaving a trail of destruction, there are several things you can do:

- Practice proactive management of both your puppy and the environment. Make sure your puppy doesn't have unsupervised access to your valuable stuff, keep your stuff safely away from your puppy, or both.
- Keep attractive chewing items available to your puppy at all times.
- Tire your puppy out on a regular basis; sleeping puppies don't chew.
- Interrupt and redirect your puppy to appropriate chewing items. It's not enough to just tell her what's not okay to chew and hope that she figures the rest out for herself.

Puppies start losing their baby teeth around 14–16 weeks, and teething continues through the fifth month. During this time, it is helpful to give your puppy no-sodium chicken broth ice cubes, frozen stuffed Kong toys, or frozen marrowbones to chew. They help the pup shed baby teeth and soothe sore gums at the same time. As an alternative for soft chewers, soak a washcloth in chicken broth, wring it out, and freeze it for a frozen chew (under supervision only!).

Adolescent Chewing—Where the Real Damage Happens

Adolescence is the time when most destructive chewing takes place. Once your puppy is through the teething stage and all her adult teeth are in, the real chewing begins as she sets her teeth and strengthens her jaws for what would have been a lifetime of hunting and scavenging for survival. Just because your dog lives in a human household, where her food is delivered to her bowl with no jaw power required, doesn't mean that the hard-wired need to keep the survival machine tuned up goes away. On the contrary, she needs to have access to appropriate chewing items even more than a feral dog would because she's not using her jaws in her daily survival activities. Also, because of the adolescent dog's high energy level in comparison to other life stages, too little exercise generally leads to destructive chewing. All that energy has to go somewhere!

As always, management of your dog and the environment is crucial to your success in preventing property damage. Your dog will continue to chew to relieve boredom, frustration, and stress (and just because it feels good) for her entire life. If you can prevent bad chewing habits and establish good ones when she's young, it is probable that she'll never even consider chewing inappropriate items as an adult.

Interruption and Redirection of Your Dog's Chewing

To teach your dog good chewing habits when she's not crated, you need to be there to let her know it's not okay to chew on some things, like shoes, chairs, and sofas, but that it is okay to chew on other things, like her toys, rawhides, and marrowbones. If you're not around to direct her, she's going to experiment and chew on whatever looks, smells, and feels good at the moment.

Timing Is Everything

The best time to interrupt your dog from chewing inappropriate items is before he starts, when he's thinking about grabbing something he shouldn't. The surprise of a shaker bottle landing right next to him every time he's reaching for a shoe might be enough to convince him that shoes just aren't safe to chew; you want him to think bad things happen just when you *think* about chewing them. The beauty is, you get to be his savior ("Poor puppy! What happened?") as you occupy him with something else. Of course, every dog is different, so his object of desire and your intervention technique may vary. As often as possible, the intervention should occur before or as he picks up a forbidden item.

If you walk in on him when he's already chewing something he's not allowed to, startle him with one of your aversives (even a magazine tossed in his direction might work in a pinch), and immediately redirect him. If you find the remains of something he chewed, it's too late. He's already gotten his reward just by getting away with it, and there's nothing you can do to take that memory away. What you can do is manage him and the environment so he can't repeat it.

ESSENTIAL

If you catch your dog chewing something illegal, try to restrain yourself from charging your dog and swooping in to snatch the forbidden treasure from him. You will certainly startle him, and maybe even frighten him, but probably not into dropping his booty. Instead, he'll probably become protective of his stolen treasure and will run away with it, threaten you to keep it, or both, setting up a vicious cycle of stealing.

Don't Do This! Don't Do That! And Don't Do That, Either!

You can't just keep telling your dog what not to do. Dogs don't understand what not to do at all. However, they can understand doing something else instead of what they're doing now. If your dog is in a major chewing phase (it waxes and wanes a bit through adolescence), do stop her from chewing inappropriately, but always follow up with redirecting her energy and focus, if not her chewing. She really isn't trying to drive you batty, but if she's constantly grabbing household items to chew, then she has needs (chewing and exercise, especially) that aren't being addressed properly.

Suitable Chewing Items for Your Dog

Every dog, like every person, is an individual. They each have their own likes and dislikes and chewing styles. Some are power chewers, and others are more delicate. With the wide array of chewing items available at your local grocery and pet store, it shouldn't be too difficult to find something suitable for your dog to chew that will satisfy his likes and his chewing style.

FACT

Power chewers come in all sizes. Dogs bred to use their jaws for their jobs, like the bull breeds, fighting breeds, and retrievers—Boston terriers, bulldogs, Staffordshire terriers, Labradors, and golden retrievers, to name a few—tend to need to chew more and be more powerful chewers than other breeds.

Consumables

Some chews, like rawhides, pig ears, Booda bones, and bully sticks are combination of a chew and a treat. Dogs should always be supervised when they have consumable chews due to the dangers that some of them present. It's generally a good idea to get at least one size larger than what is recommended for your dog, to reduce the likelihood of your dog breaking off and swallowing, or perhaps choking on, a piece that is too large. Some chews, like pig ears and rawhides, soften and swell as the dog chews and they have been known to get stuck in dogs' mouths, throats, and digestive tracts. A good rule of thumb is if your dog is consuming more than 1 inch per hour of the chew, than it's either the wrong size or the wrong strength for your dog.

Durable Goods

Durable chews are the items that you want to have available to your dog all the time. For soft chewers, a rawhide can be a durable chew, but Nylabones, hard rubber chews, and raw or sterilized marrowbones are more suitable as a durable chew for an average or strong chewer. Some have the added benefit of being dental devices, with nubs, grooves, or ridges that can be used with or without dog toothpaste. The hard rubber toys come in practically endless varieties, including designs that hold treats or biscuits to make them more appealing. They can be tossed in the dishwasher to keep them clean between uses.

ALERT!

Any natural animal chews you purchase for your dog, like rawhides, bully sticks, moo tubes, and the like, should be made (not just packaged) in the USA or Canada. Most of the Asian and South American processors use toxic chemicals in the production of dog treats and chews.

Pica: Chewing and Eating the Inedible

Pica, or eating nonfood items like rocks, wood, drywall, socks, and coins, usually starts with chewing the items. A dangerous, even deadly habit, pica can cause damage to the mouth and teeth, illness from ingesting toxic substances, and intestinal blockage, just to name a few of the possible ill effects.

Why Do They Do That?

Dogs with pica issues engage in the behavior for several different reasons. It usually starts innocently enough, with the unsupervised dog picking up an inappropriate item out of boredom or normal puppy exploration. Because no one is around to interrupt and redirect him to something appropriate and safe, he settles in for a nice chew and maybe even eats part or all of the contraband. In other words, it seems to be a successful turn of events for the dog, who is now much more likely to repeat the same behavior in the future. Most dogs who chew or eat random or indiscriminate items are just plain bored, frustrated, stressed or underexercised.

Some dogs with pica actually have an obsessive-compulsive disorder. With this type of dog, there is usually one particular item, like rocks, that they are compelled to chew. This is also the case with anxiety disorders, in which chewing rocks (or whatever the pica object is) seems to satisfy the same need that thumbsucking and nail biting do in people. We can't allow dogs to self-medicate in this fashion due to the potential for illness, injury, or death.

Protect Your Dog From Himself

Well, it's apparent that your dog isn't going to take his own health and safety into consideration when deciding what to chew on, so you're going to have to make the decision for him. Obviously, good management is imperative to prevent your dog from being successful in acquiring, chewing, or eating unsuitable stuff. Since so many dogs start the behavior just because they're bored or have too much energy for their activity level, finding them a job or two and regularly exercising them to the point of tiredness is sometimes enough to fix the problem. Of course, providing appropriate and attractive chewing alternatives is important. Treat-dispensing toys, balls, or cubes are especially helpful in this regard.

FACT

At one time, it was theorized that dogs that eat rocks have a mineral deficiency or digestive disorder. Research has never been able to substantiate the theories, and pica and rock eating are now generally considered to be behavioral disorders.

For the truly obsessed, anti-anxiety medications can help, but these dogs usually require careful management so they can't feed their obsession, literally or figuratively. Prevention is key, whether it means keeping the dog away from the inedible object, or the other way around. Basket muzzles, which allow dogs to pant and drink, may be required for the dog's own safety in severe cases where the object of obsession can't be removed from the environment, but should not be left on if the dog will be unsupervised. In some situations, particularly when the dog's obsession could result in his death, aversion training using a remote collar is warranted.

The Poop on Poop Eating

Bleccchhh! As far as people are concerned, there isn't much that dogs do that is more repulsive than poop eating. But to some dogs, there is no greater treasure on the planet than feces. Some dogs eat their own, or other dogs', while others prefer the delicacies the kitty-litter box has to offer. Still others prefer the dung of wild animals, with deer, geese, rabbits, and turkeys being common favorites. And for the lucky dogs that live on farms, it's a veritable smorgasbord!

It's a bit of a mystery why dogs engage in this disgusting behavior. Some may have a dietary deficiency, but the most likely cause is the way dogs smell. No, not how they smell to you—their sense of smell. You probably already know, by observation of your own dog if nothing else, that dogs' sense of smell if far more powerful than people's. But power isn't their only advantage. With people, the strongest scent tends to overpower everything else, so people only notice the strongest scent. Dogs' sense of smell allows them to smell kind of in layers, so they smell all the scents that are there, not just the strongest. This means they don't just smell the poop, but also they smell the undigested food that's in the poop.

E ALERT!

In rare cases, there is a physical reason for pica behavior. It is always a good idea to start any treatment of a severe behavior problem with a thorough veterinary examination. If nothing else, it will give you peace of mind.

Because this behavior is so self-reinforcing, management—supervising the dog and keeping the poop scooped—is necessary to control it. There are several products on the market for dogs that eat their own (or housemate's) poop that are supposed to make the poop taste bad (sheesh!), but they are only marginally effective. Without prevention through good management, aversion training is the most effective treatment.

The Zero-tolerance Policy for Teeth on People

Dogs' interactions with each other often involve their teeth. They use their teeth to play, to threaten or discipline, to control, and to some extent to communicate. Just because using their teeth is natural for them doesn't mean we have to accept them biting or nipping us. Whether their intent is play, communication, or discipline, teeth on people just isn't acceptable.

Take the Bite Out of Playing

Dogs' play with each other is mostly modified fighting and hunting behavior, with a lot of chasing, wrestling, and biting included. While this behavior is perfectly acceptable between dogs, it's certainly not acceptable for your dog to play with people as if they are his canine buddies or his littermates.

Puppies learn bite inhibition from the ages of three to twelve weeks. Puppies that were orphaned, the only puppy in the litter (a singleton), removed from their litters before seven weeks, or unsocialized with other dogs until twelve weeks may never learn to moderate the pressure of their bites. When they bite, they bite hard.

Play with your dog in ways that encourage cooperation, like teaching her to fetch a toy. Getting on the floor and wrestling or playing roughly will encourage her to treat you like a dog. Grabbing her muzzle, blowing in her face, or shaking your finger in her face also promote mouthiness. If she does have a momentary lapse of reason and puts her teeth on you in play, don't wait for her to get several test bites in to discover how much pressure is too much. Any sensation of teeth on skin is too much and grounds for ending the play session immediately, at least for a few minutes. Most dogs will become very careful with their teeth quickly, realizing that the fun stops whenever teeth come out.

Puppies learn bite inhibition, which means moderating the amount of pressure they apply with their teeth, from their mothers, littermates, and other dogs they play with. Dogs that apply too much pressure when they bite are disciplined by the victim with a sharp yelp, sometimes a snapping, yapping telling off, and usually the victim ends the fun by either turning away and refusing to play or actually driving the perpetrator away from the area.

Teeth Don't Work

If you've ever seen an episode of the old "Lassie" TV series, you've probably seen Lassie oh-so-gently take someone's hand in her mouth to lead them to safety, or to Timmy in whatever his crisis of the week was. While this looks really sweet on TV, in real life this kind of "communication" is all wrong between dogs and people. If you do allow your dog to communicate this way, he might think if you don't respond to his first request, that he's supposed to increase the pressure of his teeth. If your dog needs to tell you something, even that Timmy is stuck in the well, there are much safer and more reasonable ways for him to do it. Sitting and giving you eye contact is always a reasonable and polite way to ask permission. Even barking, within reason, is a more logical choice for what form of communication that you allow your dog to use for particular needs, like to go out.

ESSENTIAL

As far as puppy mouthing and play-biting are concerned, you should consider your shoes, clothes, and hair (or hair accessories) to be part of your body. If you're wearing it, or it's attached to you in some way, it is you, and the zero-tolerance policy applies.

Some puppies and dogs will use their teeth to get their own way, or to intimidate someone into stopping what they're doing. For most puppies, this starts as a threat only, with no application of teeth. If it works for the puppy, he'll try it again the next time something happens he doesn't like, and so on, until it becomes his first response to anything he's even slightly displeased about. If it's been working for him for a while, and then suddenly doesn't work, he might escalate the threat to an actual bite to get his point across.

Right from the moment you bring your puppy home, be very careful that you never let him "win" or get his way by threatening or biting. If he has a temper tantrum and flies into a piranha-like biting frenzy, grab him by as much of his scruff as you can hold, and hang on until he's over himself. If you can, keep his front feet elevated slightly off the ground while you're hanging on. Only release him when he's calm. If your dog already has a history of winning by biting, consult a professional trainer or behaviorist to help you get your relationship in order.

Dogs make very few mistakes with their teeth. They know exactly where their teeth are, and how much pressure they apply. For this reason, dogs almost never try to bite someone. They either threaten or they bite. Similarly, dogs, don't accidentally bite. Whether it's to protect themselves or some valued resource, or because they think they have the right to because of relationship issues, if they bite, they mean to.

Ouch! What to Do When Your Dog Mouths or Play-bites

Teeth on skin, especially those needle-like puppy teeth, are not only painful; they can also cause serious injuries and infections, even from apparently minor wounds that occur during play.

The First Line of Defense

With puppies particularly, you want to use the least amount of force or punishment that will accomplish your objective—in this case: to teach your puppy that humans are so delicate that they can't tolerate any teeth on them at all. The first thing to try when your puppy mouths you is to just yelp "Ouch!" loudly and walk away. Ignore your puppy for a few minutes and then let her make up with you. Repeat every time she touches your skin with her teeth for three days. If she's improving by decreasing the frequency of her mouthing or moderating the amount of pressure she applies, you're on the right track. If she's only a little better, you can try driving her away from you by scooching into her until she moves away. In other words, keep your feet close to the ground and scuff them on the floor as you move into her space and drive her away (into another room or her crate for a minute). Add emphasis by repeating "Ouch! Ouch! Ouch!" as you go.

Shark!

If the kinder, gentler way isn't deterring your little shark-mouth, then you'll have to add a correction. Since it's a mouth issue, you want to use a mouth correction by applying or squirting something that tastes bad into her mouth when she has her teeth on you. What you use will depend on your dog and what she doesn't like. The most convenient option is breath spray in a tube (made for people), but you can also try Bitter Apple, vinegar, lemon juice, or Tabasco. If you use one of the last three options, buy a small travel spray bottle (available at most drugstores) and dilute your deterrent in water. Whatever you use, make sure you say "Ouch!" at the same time you spray. It only takes most dogs a few repetitions for them to connect the "Ouch" with the bad taste. Don't threaten your dog with the spray—it tends to create a "fresh" back-talking puppy—either spray her or don't. Remember to arm everyone in the house and keep the deterrents handy so you can correct her promptly. As mentioned previously, if you have to go looking for a deterrent, it's too late.

Your puppy's mother would correct her for rudeness by grabbing her by the scruff and pinning her to the floor for a few seconds, until she submitted. This can be an effective technique for people to use if they have good timing and can execute it smoothly. It should only be used on pushy puppies, not soft or shy puppies who need confidence building.

If your puppy is in a frenzy of play-biting, try one of the scruff techniques described earlier, or give her a time-out in her crate until she can control herself again. If she's in a phase of biting frenzies, keep a leash on her so you can control her quickly without actually having to put your hands on her. Use the leash to hold her away from your body and keep a little tension straight up on the leash until she calms down.

Chapter 9
Jumping Up

Jumping up is one of the most common behavior problems that dogs have, or at least that dog owners complain about— it's not really a problem for dogs at all. Typically, nobody minds when a puppy or small dog jumps up on them, but when that puppy turns into a 50-pound adolescent or the little dog's nails are like an eagle's talons, suddenly it's not so much fun. What starts as only mildly annoying behavior can evolve into an obnoxious or even dangerous habit in just a few short months.

Why Dogs Jump

Like so many of the things that dogs do that people find unacceptable, jumping up is a normal part of canine communication and interaction. From the time they are identifying as dogs at three weeks old they use jumping up as a way to solicit things they want, and as a way to play and establish rank.

What Did You Bring Me?

If you've ever seen a nature show about any type of wild canines, like wolves, coyotes, or feral dogs, you've seen all the pack members who stayed behind swarm the returning hunters, jumping up and licking the corners of their mouths. It looks like a kiss hello, but what they're actually doing is soliciting a regurgitated meal. Sounds pretty icky to people, but it's another one of those this-is-what-separates-us-from-them things and is an innate part of being a dog. Since your dog never stops being a dog, this is part of his natural greeting behavior with his people, the returning hunters who provide his meals. Not that he's necessarily expecting you to give him a snack every time you walk through the door, but it never hurts to try, at least in his mind. However, just because it's part of his nature doesn't mean you have to go along with it. He will be happy to get your attention instead of a meal, so your job is to give him attention for what you like—four on the floor or sitting—rather than for jumping up.

QUESTION?

What's the best way to get my dog to stop jumping up on people?
It really depends on you and your dog. Any antijumping program begins with managing your dog so he can't jump on people. Also add training a replacement behavior for jumping. Some dogs may also require a correction or punishment if the behavior is a well-rehearsed habit.

It's Not Just Your Dog's Problem

It starts innocently enough. Your puppy is little, or she looks so cute, or you're not wearing work clothes, so you pet her and play with her sometimes when she has her feet on you. Or somebody else, a visitor, friend, or neighbor, does. It only becomes a problem when she gets too big, or she does it to the wrong person, or everybody, or when you are wearing nice clothes. For her, jumping up is always worth a try, because sometimes it results in good things, like petting and play. Even if something good doesn't happen, at least something happens, like some yelling or playful (to her, at least) pushing, adding a little excitement to an otherwise dull day. Pretty soon, she's jumping on everybody because she can always count on something interesting, and sometimes fun, happening.

Controlling Jumping While Training

You need to teach your little jumping bean what to do instead of jumping. During the process, you have to do something to keep him from being successful in getting his feet on people.

Controlling Jumping at Home

If your dog is like most pet dogs, he spends the majority of his time at home. Hopefully, for his socialization if not yours, you or family members have visitors on a regular basis. If he already has a habit of jumping up, you have to have a way to control him before visitors enter your home until he learns his new, more appropriate greeting behavior, Hoping for the best and yelling "Sit! Siddown! Get off! Sit! Sit! Sit!" while you make a mad grab for his collar probably hasn't been working too well so far, so it's time to do a little reconnaissance and make a plan.

Don't Wait For the Doorbell to Ring

You have to be ready with a way to control your dog before the doorbell rings. If you're not, it's going to be the usual hysteria, and one more deposit into your dog's jumping behavior bank. There are several easy things that you can do to control your dog when the doorbell rings:

- Install a short tether at least 6 feet from the door. Tethers can be attached to a strategically placed eyebolt in a baseboard or to a sturdy piece of furniture.

- Keep a dragline or leash on your dog, or at least near the door. You can step on the leash or use it to correct your dog if he jumps.
- Put your dog away, either crated or in another room, before answering the door.

If your dog gets hysterical when the bell rings, the visitor can stand out of his reach or you can physically restrain the dog. Have the visitor completely ignore him until he's calm; don't allow even eye contact! The visitor may have to spend some time with their arms folded, staring at the ceiling, until your dog can relax enough to respond to a sit command. Only then should the visitor pay him any attention. Start with just a little eye contact and some quiet praise and work up to petting. Quit if he starts to lose it, and quit on success, even if success means the visitor can only give him a quick glance for that session. It'll get better each time. Don't keep barking commands at the dog when he's wound up. Just stay calm and wait for him to calm down, too. If it's not a convenient time to work on it, tether or crate your dog.

Andrea steps on beagle Jack's leash so he can't jump on Kennedy.

Good boy!

Now Kennedy can give Jack some attention.

Outdoor Strategies

If your dog is going be around people, you must have a way to physically control him. This generally means a collar and leash because you can stand on the leash (with both feet), giving him just enough room to stand up or sit comfortably. He should only be able to get his front feet a few inches off the ground so if he tries to jump, he corrects himself. Every person who wants to greet him should use the same system you did with indoor greetings: by ignoring hysterical behavior and rewarding calm behavior.

Give Your Dog Something Else to Do

By now, you probably realize that it's not enough to just stop your dog from jumping up on people. You have to give her something to do instead of jumping, too. During the training process, avoid giving your dog the chance to make the mistake of jumping up, and insist that everyone who interacts with your dog follows the new rules.

Sit or Down for Greeting

Whenever you teach your dog a replacement behavior for a behavior you are trying to extinguish from your dog's repertoire, it's best to use a mutually exclusive behavior. *Mutually exclusive behavior* means that your dog can't practice the old behavior and the new one at the same time.

Sit and down both fulfill the exclusivity obligation, so pick the one that makes the most sense for you and your dog. If you're going to eventually want to have your dog become a certified Canine Good Citizen or therapy dog, then it makes sense to teach the sit for greeting, because it's part of both tests. If you have a dog that will be interacting with lots of small children, or has a tendency to paw, even when sitting, the down may be a better idea.

ESSENTIAL

Have a jumping-up training party. Invite five friends over, staggered out every 30 minutes. Work on not jumping up with each guest. If time allows, have each guest exit through another door and come ring the doorbell again for lots of repetition in a short time.

Get control of your dog in the position of your choice before the greeting. There can be no interaction until your dog is calm. As soon as he is, the person can approach, but don't have them pet yet. You or they can reward your dog for maintaining calm and the correct position. As long as all is well, continue until the visitor can pet and even kneel in front of your dog. If your dog gets hysterical and loses it at any time during the training process, the person should back off and ignore him until he's calm again. Be satisfied with a quick scratch on the chest to start, and keep the whole event calm.

The Easy Way Out

Sometimes it's easier just not to worry about having your dog greet people at all, and just give him something completely different to think about and do. Try throwing a handful of kibble on the floor the next time the doorbell rings. Your dog may be so preoccupied snarfing up all the kibbles that he doesn't even notice the pizza-delivery guy. A special or treat-dispensing toy that you keep near the door are other low-effort options for occupying your dog's attention.

If your dog's jumping habit is too ingrained, or you just can't seem to get your act together to provide consistent management and training, there are special body harnesses that are designed to reduce or eliminate jumping. They are somewhat effective for most dogs, and are worth a try, at least to avoid reinforcing the jumping habit.

The Determined Jumper

Determined jumpers are the dogs that jump on everybody, with no discretion. They are just as likely to jump on (or steamroll) a toddler as they are a teenager or a senior citizen. Most determined jumpers have been rewarded into the habit, but some personality aspects come into play as well. Some hysterical jumpers are just generally pushy and demanding, albeit affectionate; while others are submissive, and their jumping up is a classic gesture of submission.

Harsh corrections, yelling, or getting angry with submissive jumpers usually makes them worse. Like submissive wetters, when they're disciplined, they have to repeat the submissive gesture with more intensity to prove how really submissive they are. They are best dealt with in a calm, matter-of-fact manner. Give them specific tasks, manage them well, and reward correct choices.

When Jumping Turns Into Humping

How rude! Dogs humping people is never okay. It's not funny and it's not cute, even if it's a little dog doing the humping. Dogs that hump people are trying to establish dominance. Actually they're not even trying; if they're humping and getting away with it, they're already dominant. Even between dogs, humping isn't usually sexual in nature; it's about establishing rank.

If your dog consistently humps you or anyone else, the first thing to do is to put your dog on a leadership program. Make him earn absolutely everything, and don't allow him on any furniture or your bed. You also have to make sure that your dog is always dragging a leash or dragline so you can get control of him quickly. You may have to add some aversives to get your point across.

Effective Corrections

If you've been diligent about managing your dog and training a replacement behavior, and your dog is still jumping up, it's time to consider adding a punisher. When it comes to corrections for jumping, it seems like there are almost as many different corrections as there are dogs. And that's a good thing, because if what you're using as a correction isn't working to decrease the frequency or the intensity of the behavior within a few repetitions, you can switch to something else that might work better for your individual dog. Following are some common corrections for jumping up:

- **The knee-in-the-chest method**, mentioned first only because it's probably the most well known, not because it's the best. Use caution; it can injure you or the dog.
- **Walk into the dog.** With your feet close to the ground, scoot quickly straight forward into your dog's space, intercepting his jump before he has feet on you if possible.
- **Ignore him or turn your back on him.** The object is to wait until he stops jumping and reward that. Of course, this method is not really practical for determined jumpers.
- **Grab his feet or pinch his toes.** If you try this, you want to hold him up in the air for a little longer than he'd like to be there. Some dogs will get mouthy when you do this.
- **Step on his back feet.** This method requires you to be a bit of a contortionist. The idea is to lightly step on the dog's back toes so that he'll jump away.
- **Add an aversive.** Toss a shaker bottle at your dog's hind feet, or spray him in the mouth with breath spray or one of the other taste deter-

rents. This method is very effective, but you have to be armed and ready.

- **Bonk him on the head.** This method is not necessarily recommended, but it is effective for some dogs. It's not advisable for a soft or shy dog. If you try it, use something other than your hand that can't injure your dog, like an empty 2-liter soda bottle or a towel that is rolled into a log and taped. Show caution—some dogs will react with aggression, others with shyness.

Whatever correction you use, be prepared so you can correct your dog every time he jumps. Switch to something else if what you're doing isn't working reasonably quickly. Remember, just correcting him isn't enough; you have to teach him to do something else, too.

FACT

Some dogs find jumping up so self-reinforcing that they don't need any external reinforcement to continue the behavior. As mentioned previously, to them, jumping up is fun, or adds a little excitement to an otherwise dull day. They are more likely to need the addition of an aversive to reduce or eliminate the behavior.

How to Stop the World from Rewarding Your Dog's Jumping

Controlling and training your dog is relatively easy in comparison to trying to control and train the humans in the world. It's particularly difficult when they seem determined to undermine your efforts to make sure your dog is a polite and well-behaved member of society.

The "But I Don't Mind"-ers

You've seen them; they're the people with muddy paw prints all over their clothes. When you protest about your dog jumping up on them, the likely response is, "It's okay, I love dogs, I don't mind." That's just fine, but this is *your* dog. If *you* mind, it's *your* rules that have to be followed. You can either not let your dog interact with people who refuse to follow your rules, or you can try to convert them to your way of thinking. A little creative fibbing often helps. Try telling the "But I don't mind"-ers that your dog is in training to be a therapy dog or Canine Good Citizen, and that he's not allowed to jump uninvited to pass those tests—who knows, maybe it's even true (or will be someday).

You can also try getting these well-meaning but unhelpful individuals involved in the training process. Give them a couple of treats and let them lure your dog into a sit and reward your dog for maintaining the sit. You can unobtrusively step on the leash when your dog sits to prevent him from being successful if he has a lapse in judgment and tries to jump again.

Saboteurs

Saboteurs can be your biggest obstacles when it comes to teaching your dog not to jump on people. These are the people, often family members (teenage boys are most frequently the guilty parties), who deliberately encourage or reward jumping up. Their reasons vary, but it often comes down to "You're mean," because you won't let your dog express his joy at seeing people, or you're trying to "break his spirit," or you don't want him to have any fun. Of course, none of these are true, but try not to get involved in the argument.

As you learned in Chapter 5, a random schedule of reinforcement is the best way to keep a behavior strong, so if you have a saboteur that is rewarding your dog for jumping, even occasionally, it's going to be almost impossible to eliminate the behavior.

Make a bargain with family members or other people who, for whatever reason, want your dog to jump up on them. After your dog gives up trying to jump on people indiscriminately, you can teach your dog to "give hugs" or "paws up" on command.

Practice, Practice, Practice

Your dog has probably already had plenty of practice jumping up on people. Now it's your job to make sure he practices not jumping enough to override all the practice he's had, and all the reinforcement he's gotten, from jumping up.

FACT

Dogs that learn proper greeting habits from the beginning may never consider jumping up. From the moment you get your dog, make sure she is not reinforced for having her feet on people, and that the only way she'll get attention is by controlling herself, staying calm, and sitting (or whatever you want her to do instead of jumping).

Set Up Training Opportunities

Your dog's new mutually exclusive behavior to replace his default behavior of jumping up won't happen if you wait until you need it to work on it. You absolutely must set up training opportunities to get enough practice in for the new behavior to become the new habit. Have a jumping-up training party if you can, or at least invite (beg or bribe, do what you've gotta do!) a few people a week to come knock on the door for the specific purpose of training. Recruit anyone who happens to knock on the door to help. They don't necessarily have to pet or interact directly with your dog, but maybe they'd be willing to wait patiently while you get your dog into a sit. Maybe they'd even be willing to knock again in a few minutes so you have another chance to work on it.

Seek out real-world training opportunities, too. Take your dog to a pet store, or to your town green or park, and ask anyone that wants to pet your dog help you reinforce the sit or down for greeting. Most people who want to pet your dog will be glad to help you. If they are unwilling or unable to help you, either step on your leash so your dog can't jump, or don't let your dog greet that person.

Chapter 10

The Positions—Sit, Down, and Stand

Once you get a dog to understand the commands, the positions—sit, down, and stand—are finished behaviors in their own rights, but they're also much more than that. Separately and together, they provide the foundation for many other behaviors. From making your life with your dog easier during day-to-day activities to performing complex tricks, the possibilities for using the positions are practically endless.

10

Getting Started

Before you start teaching your dog the positions, set yourself and your dog up for success by preparing the environment with everything you need. In addition to preparing the environment, prepare yourself. Your dog should understand the meaning of his conditioned reinforcer (CR) before you start. If he doesn't, go back and play the eye-contact game until he does.

What You Need

You'll need to set up your training area with everything you need to control and reinforce your dog. To keep your dog with you and to help you achieve certain behaviors, keep a collar and leash handy. You can let your dog drag the leash if you want so you can step on it to keep him from wandering.

You'll also need treats, and lots of them. What you use will depend on your (and your dog's) preferences, but whatever you use needs to be something your dog likes and is willing to work for.

You may also want to have a few special toys in your training area. You can use them during play breaks, and to motivate your dog. As your training progresses, you'll also use them as distractions to challenge your dog.

Luring

As mentioned briefly in Chapter 5, with luring you'll use a treat to lead your dog into the positions. When luring, be sure to keep the treat pinched between your fingers, so you can control it until the right moment. Keep the treat close to your dog's nose and move it at the speed your dog can and will follow it. If the treat is too far away or you move it too fast, your dog will probably either lose interest in the treat, or leap or grab for it. Just bring the treat back to your dog's nose and start again. Use the corresponding command once as your dog moves into the correct position. In the first several sessions, you'll be CR/ treating every correct response. You can also use the command as part of your praise: "Yes! Good sit!"

Luring the Positions

You're going to teach dog to be able to move easily from any position to any position. So, in one set, you might do two repetitions of sit-down-sit-stand-down-stand. The order you work the positions isn't important, but you should try to avoid doing it the same way all the time, so your dog doesn't know what's coming next.

ALERT!

You can really distract your dog from the lesson if you're fumbling with and dropping treats all over the floor. If you don't have the dexterity to hold little pieces and dole them out one at a time, try using string cheese or hot dogs for training treats. Cut them into long strips that you can pinch off, or let your dog nibble a bit at a time.

Following are directions for luring the dog into a sit down sit stand down-stand:

- Hold a treat right in front of your dog's nose.
- Slowly lift the treat up and back, so your dog's nose is pointed straight up in the air. CR/treat when he sits.
- With your dog sitting, lower the treat from his nose straight down to the floor in front of his feet, then slowly away. CR/treat when he downs.
- Lure the dog back up into the sit, basically the same lure you used for the original sit, only you'll be raising your hand to lure him up into the sit after pointing his nose into the air. CR/treat when he sits.
- When he's sitting again, keep the treat at or a little lower than nose level and pull it straight away from him, parallel to the floor. CR/treat when he stands.
- As your dog is standing, bring the treat from his nose to the floor, pushing the treat toward him, between his feet. CR/treat when he downs.
- Bring the treat in a diagonal line up and away from your dog. CR/treat when he stands.

Amanda lures German shepherd Addie into a sitting position.

Luring from the sit to the down.

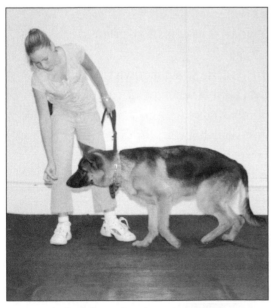

Luring from the sit to the stand.

Luring from the stand to the down.

Weaning Off the Treats

After just a few training sessions, your dog should be getting the idea of what you want, so it's time to start decreasing the dependence on treats to get him into position (you'll still be using treats as rewards). Do a little countdown:

- 5 repetitions with a treat in your hand, 1 without
- 4 with,1 without
- 3 with,1 without
- 2 with,1 without
- 1 with,1 without

Then count back up, the other way:

- 1 with a treat, 2 without
- 1 with, 3 without
- 1 with, 4 without
- 1 with, 5 without

When your dog can do the three positions in any order for 6 repetitions (for example, sit- down-sit-stand-down- stand) without a treat lure, don't use a treat to lure anymore; just use treats to reward. Within a few sessions of removing the treat from your lure hand, move to a variable schedule of reinforcement, then to a random schedule. Remember to reward the best efforts when you're on a random reinforcement schedule. They will be the examples of the behaviors that will stick as the final behavior.

Compulsion

Compulsion, or physically (not forcefully) positioning your dog, can be used to back up commands originally taught using luring, or to teach the behaviors if you don't want to use luring. As with luring, you'll use the command one time as your dog is getting into the position. Remember to CR/ treat if you're using this method to teach the command.

The Sit

To physically position your dog in a sit, hold her collar right behind her head with your right hand (or you can hold the leash so it's taut straight over her head), so there is light upward pressure. With your left hand, stroke down her back. You can try giving her a little pressure on her loin (where her waist is, if looking at her from above) or butt, but you may need to run your hand past her butt, into the dip in her hind leg. Use the side of your hand to tuck her into a sit. CR/treat if you're using this method to teach the sit, or praise her if you're using it to back up an ignored command.

Many dogs will sit in response to a little steady, upward pressure on the collar without any of the extra physical help. Try it after your dog has some understanding of the sit command. Release the pressure immediately when she sits.

QUESTION?

Should I give my dog a treat if I'm using compulsion to enforce a command my dog knows but ignored?
If you're sure your dog knows the command (you've taught it in lots of different places, and she usually responds on the first command), praise her when you get her into the position, but no treat. Save treats for rewarding correct responses that you don't have help with.

The Down

There are several ways to physically get your dog into the down position. For many dogs, the path of least resistance lies in a little "magic button." To find it, put your thumb through your dog's collar at the base of his neck. Keeping the collar low on your dog's neck, fan the rest of your fingers toward his tail. Find the valley between your dog's shoulder blades, and apply steady pressure with one finger. Do not try to smoosh your dog into the floor; just keep a little steady pressure on, and wait for him to fold into a down. You can try this method from the sit or stand.

Compulsion sit

Finding the "magic button" makes the compulsion down easy.

If your dog doesn't have a magic button, or you can't find it, you can try holding him by the collar with one hand, and with the other hand, in one sweeping motion, lift his front legs up and place him in a down. This method only works from the sit.

In a pinch, or if your dog is struggling with you physically, just stand on the leash so he can just barely stand comfortably and wait, for as long as it takes, until he lies down.

FACT

Like all mammals, dogs have an opposition reflex, which means they have a tendency to resist or push into pressure. For this reason, trying to use physical force to push your dog into a down usually results in your dog bracing himself against the pressure, resulting in confrontation instead of communication, and compromise between you and your dog.

Compulsion stand; notice Amanda's foot nudging German shepherd Addie's toes.

The Stand

If your dog is sitting, scoot your toes right in front of your dog's hind foot, just barely touching your dog's toes with yours. Most dogs will kick right up into a stand. You can add a little forward pressure on your dog's collar if necessary. If you need to use collar pressure, your hand (or the leash) should be under your dog's chin, with the pressure away from your dog, parallel to the floor.

Stimulus Control

Getting stimulus control of behaviors is a fancy way to say that your dog responds to your cues or commands with the correct behavior. There are two basic ways that you can communicate your commands to your dog: verbal or visual. Because people are verbal, we tend to teach verbal commands. Because dogs are visual, not verbal, they tend to have an easier time with commands they can see, like hand signals or other physical cues. It doesn't need to be an either-or situation though; you can easily teach your dog both visual and verbal cues.

Visual Cues

You can easily teach your dog hand signals for the sit, down, and stand while you are first luring the positions. Be conscious of your own body and how you're moving your hands. Exaggerate the beginning of the movement, then follow through with the rest of your hand lure. Do it the same way every time (practice without your dog in the mirror if necessary), and pretty soon, your dog will perform the behavior when he sees the exaggerated beginning instead of waiting for the rest of the lure motion. (Have a party the first time he does!) For example, for the down hand signal, start by pushing your open hand straight toward your dog, then follow through with the rest of the lure motion. Whatever your hand signals are, try to make them something that your dog will eventually be able to see from a distance.

For maximum signal impact, it's helpful to face your dog. If you have a small dog, work her on an elevated surface, like a grooming table, or on top of her crate.

Verbal Commands

When you first start teaching your dog the positions, you will be using the position's associated command just once, as your dog is assuming the correct position. After several days, depending on the frequency of your training sessions (about 75 repetitions), test your command by giving it before you follow through with whatever method you're using to get the behavior. If your dog responds correctly, have a party! If not, continue as you were for another few days and try again.

Jackpot! If your dog has a light-bulb moment and makes a breakthrough in training, have a mini party. Make a big deal about what your dog did right, with lots of praise and several treats given one at a time to prolong the impact. Quit the session on the big success.

Adding a Second Cue

If your dog already knows and responds reliably to one type of cue, it's easy to add a second cue. Give the new cue, followed within a few seconds by the known cue, and supported with help (luring, modeling) if necessary. So, you might say "Down," followed by your "Down" hand signal and lure (only if necessary). Do five repetitions per set. After several sessions, give just the new cue, and help if necessary.

Generalization

As mentioned previously, dogs are very context-specific animals, so just because your dog understands "down" in the kitchen before mealtime doesn't mean he'll understand it on the front stoop. He's really not trying to tick you off; he just doesn't understand the command or its relevance in a new situation, until you teach him.

Take Your Show on the Road

Over and over again, in new locations, reteach every command from the beginning. Each time you work a new location, test your cues to see what your dog really knows, and what you still need to work on. Pretty soon, no matter where you are, you can give a command and your dog will do it without hesitation.

Proofing for Reliability

Once your dog understands that he has to respond promptly and correctly no matter where he is, it's time to let him know that he also has to perform no matter what is going on around him. A little at a time, add variables to the environment and how you give the commands.

Keep distractions at a low intensity or far enough away so that he can be successful and rewarded early and often, and gradually increase intensity or move closer to the distractions as he overcomes each challenge.

Change how you give commands for another challenge. Whisper, or go around a corner, or turn your back to your dog when you give a command. For a real challenge, kneel on the floor a few feet away from your dog or lie flat on your back when you give command. If your dog can perform commands correctly in spite of all this stuff, give *yourself* a cookie; you've been working hard!

Discrimination Problems (What to Do if Your Dog Doesn't Know "Sit" from "Down")

Discrimination problems, or confusion about which command equals what behavior, are common in the early stages of training. They are easily solved, provided you don't let mistakes go uncorrected.

Help Your Dog

The most important thing to remember is to reward what you asked for. If your dog has moved on to something else, either ask for another behavior that you can reward, or gently place her back in the correct position. If she never went into the correct position in the first place, help her get into the correct position and praise but don't treat. If this happens frequently, you have some remedial work to do. Go back to her last level of success with the command and build stimulus control of the behavior back up again.

Build Duration

By building duration, or having your dog maintain a particular position for longer periods of time, you accomplish several things. You give your dog a deeper understanding of each command, you instill a bit of patience and self-control (he has to wait for the next command), and you lay the foundation for the stay.

When you are easily getting your dog through six position changes for one treat, pick one of the three positions (sit, down, or stand) to focus on in each set. When you get to that one, CR/treat your dog five times, about once per second to start, as long as he maintains the position. Instead of asking for the next position, release him with a pat on the side and a release command, like " free" or "release." Each set, work on a different position. Gradually extend the time between treats, so your dog can hold each position for five seconds. Finally, put it all back together again, so you're doing the set of six, with a five-second maintain of each position.

Chapter 11

The Recall—Teaching Your Dog to Come

The recall, or teaching your dog to come to you when you call, is arguably the most important thing you'll ever teach your dog. Undoubtedly, you want your dog to come to you when you call every time, not just when he wants to. It takes time and commitment to teach your dog a rock-solid, come-no-matter-what, reliable recall, but it's well worth the effort—it could even save your dog's life.

The Name Game—The Foundation for the Recall

The name game is a fun and easy way to not just teach your dog his name, but also to teach him that when he hears his name, good things are going to happen for him. This sets your recall training off to a great start, because he'll already be motivated to come to you before you even start teaching him to.

The First Week

The first week of recall training is all fun and games. Fifteen to twenty times per day, you're going to associate your dog's name with treats and fun. Every two days, you'll raise the criteria for reward.

First 3 days: Call his name, and no matter what he does, go give him several treats, repeating his name before each one. Repeat 15 to 20 times per day.

Next 2 days: Call his name, and only give him the treats if he (at least) looks at you. If he doesn't look at you, say "Too bad!" and make a big deal about going to and giving the treats to someone else, like another pet or family member—you can even pretend to eat them yourself! Repeat 15 to 20 times per day.

Next 2 days: Call his name, and only give him the treats if he comes to you. If he comes before the fifth day, have a big stinkin' party with lots of praise, smiles, treats, and some play. If not, do the "too bad" routine as above. Repeat 15 to 20 times per day.

By the end of the week, with very little effort, you have a dog whose name is just as good as his conditioned reinforcer.

Get the whole family involved in the training process by having each member call your dog five times a day. Your dog will get the benefit of lots of reinforced repetition, and one person won't get stuck with all the work.

Adding Commands

Now that your dog is happy to come to you when he hears his name, it's time to start adding some formal commands. As usual, the commands themselves aren't that important, but being consistent is. You'll probably want to teach your dog a verbal command, like "come," "here," or "front." Your dog's name should precede a verbal command, i.e., "Rover, come!" You might also want to teach your dog a "come" hand signal and a "come" whistle. To jumpstart the acceptance of each command, start each of them off with a week of the name game, with the new command filling the role of the name.

Set Your Dog Up for Success

It's always important to try to set your dog up for success in training, but it's of utmost importance in training a reliable recall. Don't put your dog in the position to make the wrong choice by calling him if you have no way to back it up. If your dog is allowed to fail to come to you when you call even a few times before he's reliably trained, he might always think that the recall is optional, rather than required. The dog needs to know that the first time you call, every time you call, he must come to you.

Failure Is Not an Option

There are a couple of ways that you can make sure your dog doesn't fail. The first is not to call him if he has the option not to come to you, especially if you already have the idea that he might make a choice other than coming to you. The second part of the equation is making sure that when you do call him, you have a way to enforce your command, like a leash or dragline. Until he's in the habit of coming to you, no matter how far away he is, or what distractions are going on around him, don't give him the freedom to fail. If he's in the position to "flip you the paw" when you call, don't waste your breath or dilute the power of your command by calling him repeatedly. Every time you call and your dog doesn't come, it reinforces his idea that the command is optional.

Slow Is the New Fast

Don't be in a hurry to get your dog unencumbered by his leash or dragline. Spend a few months getting him reliable before giving him too much freedom outdoors, even in your own yard. Freedom outside is no different than freedom in the house; it's a privilege to be earned., and he probably hasn't earned the privilege of that much freedom yet. He'll earn more freedom depending on his response to your commands. If he responds promptly and reliably on a long dragline 10 feet away, give him 20. If he's doing well at 20 feet, give him 50. If he's doing well at 50 feet, no matter what the distraction, drop the leash. If after two or three weeks he's still responding promptly and reliably with the leash dragging, it's time to gradually wean him off the leash by cutting a foot or two off the length every week until you're down to nothing attached to the snap. If at any time his training backslides, and he doesn't comply with a recall command, don't hesitate to put him back on a held line for a couple of weeks before weaning him off again.

If you're so addicted to leaving your dog free in your yard that you can't give it up for recall practice try this: every time your dog is out in the yard (or in the dog park, or anywhere else that you might have him off leash), call him for cookies at least five times for every time you call him to bring him in. If he's already in the habit of ignoring you when you call, spend a week or two approaching him and giving him treats, and also giving him treats every time he approaches you.

Teaching a Reliable Recall

Young puppies have a natural attraction and following instinct that keeps them with the pack and safe. But around five months, the flight-instinct period arrives, taking dog owners by complete surprise when the puppy who wouldn't stray two feet from their side yesterday is now in hot pursuit of every squirrel, person, dog, butterfly, and falling leaf in the vicinity. Teaching your dog to come to you when you call is a systematic process that takes repetition, time, and commitment to perfect.

Keep a Leash On

All early formal recall training should be done on leash—6, 20, or 50 feet—and retractable lines and leashes all have their place in the training process:

- Use 6- to 20-foot leashes for short, controlled recalls and group recalls.
- Use retractable leashes for recalls away from distraction and solo recalls.
- Use 50-foot draglines to gradually get reliable, off-leash recalls.

Leashes and draglines ensure success while your dog is building the habit of "rocket recalls."

Use retractable leashes with caution. They have been known to sever fingers if used improperly. Buying a good-quality retractable is a better bargain than buying a cheap but poorly made one. Read the directions and practice braking and releasing without your dog first, and resist the temptation to grab the cord if your timing is off with your brake and release.

Fido, Come!

When you call your dog, your tone of voice should indicate to him that you'll be happy to see him when he gets to you. Call him the same way every time, with his name first, followed by your recall command. Every time he comes to you, you should be able to touch him (or even better, grab his collar) before he gets his CR/treat. After he gets the idea that he's supposed to come to you every time you call, have him sit when he gets to you, before you grab his collar and CR/treat. There are several different ways you can practice recalls for lots of reinforced repetition in a short amount of time.

Always play recall games when your dog is motivated, and quit while he still wants to play.

Solo Recalls: With your dog on a retractable leash, let your dog watch you toss a visible treat, like a piece of breakfast cereal, several feet in one direction. Send your dog to go get it, and then call him back to you for another treat. Send him again in the other direction, gradually increasing the distance of the thrown treat.

Dual Recalls: On a retractable or long (at least 20 feet) leash, have a partner hold your dog by his collar. Take the leash by the handle and spend a few moments paying attention to your dog—really loving him up, petting him, praising him and then saying his name, followed by treats a couple of times—before running away to the end of the leash. As soon as you turn around, call his name three times, followed by your recall command, "Fido! Fido! Fido! Come!"—enthusiasm is critical! When he is straining to get to you, have your partner let him go. Praise him as he's coming (you have the leash to make sure he does), and CR/reward when he gets all the way to you.

Round Robin Recalls: Three or more people can play. Spread out in a circle 20 or more feet in diameter. Your dog should be dragging a line long enough to reach all the players. One at a time, call your dog and give him treats when he comes. If he decides the game is to run from person to person getting treats, only the person who calls him should pay any attention to him or reward him; everybody else should look at the sky. Use the dragline to enforce the recall if necessary.

Strolling Recalls: When you're out walking your dog, wait for him to lose attention on you. Back up several steps quickly and call him to you, reeling him in like a fish, if necessary. Praise like crazy and CR/treat when he gets to you.

Add a few extra recalls to your dog's day by calling him when he's already coming to you, or is likely to, like at mealtimes or when you're going to take him for a walk or out for some play time.

Body Language

Whether or not you use hand signals to call your dog, the physical picture you present to him when you call him, and when he gets to you, can have a major influence on the success of your recall training program.

Hand Signals

All of the hand signals that you teach your dog should be visible from a distance, but this is of particular importance with your recall signal, because your dog is more likely to be some distance from you. One to try, and that is instinctive for most people, is a big sweeping motion of your right hand, starting out at your right side and then sweeping in front of your body, with your hand landing on your chest. In the teaching phase, keep the leash in your hand as your hand is sweeping in front of your body to help draw your dog in.

Play the name game with your signal for a week to start (obviously, your dog has to be able to see you give the signal before you give him the treat). After that, or in slightly more distracting training venues, call your dog's name to get his attention, then give your signal, and follow immediately by a verbal command (if he knows it), and enforce the command with leash help, if needed.

Posture Counts

Your body posture during the recall is important, too. You want to present a welcoming rather than intimidating picture to your dog, but you don't necessarily want to have to squat to get your dog to come to you for the next fifteen years. If you have a shy dog, you may want to turn your side toward your dog when you call instead of facing him, but for most dogs, a relaxed, completely upright posture works just fine. When your dog comes to you, keep your hand(s), with your treats, close to your body, so he has to come all the way to you to get them. Keep your hands in the middle of your body and raise them slightly as he gets to you to lure him into an automatic sit. If you have a small dog, squat, rather than bending over, to give the treats. Big or small, most dogs will actually be pushed away, rather than drawn closer, if you bend over to meet them.

Adding Distraction

Once your dog knows what her recall command means and is responding reasonably reliably, it's time to start challenging her with distraction. By helping her overcome distractions and respond correctly in spite of them, you improve both your relationship with her and her reliability.

Using Distractions to Your Advantage

When you start adding distraction to your dog's recall-training program, take a gradual approach. You want to challenge your dog without completely overwhelming her. It's not a "gotcha" game; it's a process of building on small successes. Whenever you introduce a new distraction, it should be at a distance or intensity that she has a reasonable chance to make the right choice to come to you without your help to make her come. Of course, you will help her when she needs it, by way of a quick pop on the leash (or several) toward you, repeating until she gets all the way to you. Even when you have to help, praise her all the way. If using a retractable leash, the procedure is call, brake, pop toward you, release the brake to let the leash in, brake, pop, release. If using a regular leash, pop, then try to gather up the slack as quickly as she's coming so you can help her if she veers off course.

Kennedy distracts German shepherd Addie away from Jordan.

Jordan calls Addie, ready to give her a little pop on the retractable leash if she ignores the command.

Good girl, Addie!

Anything your dog is even remotely interested in can be used as a distraction, and you should make an effort to include a wide variety of still and moving distractions. You'll call her away from some distractions, and she'll have to pass others on her way to you. Food, toys, dogs, other animals, noises, and kids (especially running or playing kids) are all likely candidates to use as distractions, but be creative and use your imagination to come up with good distractions for your dog. Call her name to get her attention if she's focused on the distraction; then use your recall command and give her just a few seconds to respond before you help, if necessary.

Be the Better Deal

When you introduce distractions in your recall training program, there should always be something better than the distraction for your dog at the end of the recall. Why should he come away from interesting or exciting distractions for something boring or dull? Would you choose a saltine over a hot fudge sundae? Neither will your dog. There might be times you can use the distraction itself as the reward. He wants to go say hi to the kids at the park? Okay, but he has to come to you first; then you'll release him to see the kids. Over time, he'll get the idea that the fastest way to what he wants is to do what you want first.

What Not to Do (or How to Teach Your Dog Not to Come)

It's startlingly easy to teach your dog not to come when you call. Have you allowed your dog opportunities to ignore your recall command, or called her to do something she doesn't like? If so, it's not too surprising that she doesn't respond reliably.

Reality Check

Do an honest assessment of your dog's recall history so far. Have you made it your habit to call her from the yard to stick her in her crate and go to work? At the dog park, do you call her to put her in the car and take her home, ending her fun? Do you call her to punish her for something she did wrong, or to cut her nails, or do other things that aren't, in her opinion, going to be fun or rewarding for her? Is your tone of voice angry or harsh? Are you scowling at her when you call? Have you given her multiple chances to ignore you without consequence? If your recall habits are poor, your dog's will be, as well. It may be time to cut your losses and start over.

When to Change Commands

If your dog regularly ignores you when you call him, or is less than 75 percent reliable at responding to your first command, consider starting recall training over from the beginning with a new command. Be more careful about letting him get away with not coming when he's called, and making sure you're setting him up for success. Be prepared to give him plenty of repetition and opportunity to practice the new command.

FACT

There are some dogs who, by virtue of genetics, individual temperament, or long-standing habit, cannot be taught a reliable recall with the motivational techniques described here. These dogs require very careful management, and perhaps a recall taught with a remote collar for safety.

What to Do in an Emergency

There may come a time when your dog is on the loose. Maybe someone left the door open, or he slipped his collar, or he somehow got out of the yard. No matter what the reason, you have to get him—now.

Get Your Dog Back

If your dog is hightailing down the street, just about the worst thing you can do is chase her. Dogs are fast, way faster than people. Just when you think you've got her, she'll dart just out of reach again. Unless she stops to investigate something or potty, it's very unlikely that you'll catch her. What you need to do is use her own psychology against her and get her to come to you.

Get her attention and run in the other direction. If she likes to ride in the car, either get in yours or enlist the help of someone else to drive slowly up to her, open the door, and invite her in for a ride (hey, a ride around the block is still a ride). Try sitting, or even better, lying flat on your back on the ground. Most dogs just can't resist their natural curiosity, and have to see what their person is doing lying on the ground. If all else fails, grab a box of dog biscuits, and calmly walk her down enlisting the aide of any willing passerby to help.

Don't Get Mad

Although you are likely to be some combination of frustrated, angry, and scared when you do get your hands on your dog, you can't let him know that. If you take out your frustration on him, scolding him or even physically disciplining him, he won't understand that you're punishing him for taking off. In his mind, getting caught is the wrong thing to do, and he'll be harder to catch next time, guaranteed. When you do catch your dog, it should be the best thing that happens to him all day. Give him lots of praise, treats, and play, even if you have to fake it. If you don't have treats on you when you catch him, bring him home, praising him all the way, and take him right to the refrigerator and get something really special for him. This memory will make him easier to catch in the future, but you're not going to let him get away again, now, are you?

Chapter 12
Leash Walking

Taking your dog for a walk can be one of the most enjoyable parts of dog ownership. It's fun, relaxing, good exercise, and a great way to socialize your dog. However, if your dog pulls on the leash, dragging you down the street and practically pulling your arm out of the socket, it's not so much fun. With the right equipment and a little practice, you can teach your dog to go your way, and treat you and your leash with the respect you deserve.

Who's Walking Whom? (How Your Relationship Affects Leash Walking)

Like practically every other aspect of training your dog, the relationship you have with him affects how he walks on leash. Is he attentive to you, or more interested in everything else? Does he drag you toward things he wants to see or sniff, while you trail helplessly behind like a caboose on the end of a runaway train? If he does, it's time to get your relationship in order and teach him the rules of walking with you.

Leaders Lead

Sounds simple, huh? It is simple if you change your perception of why you're walking your dog. You probably have at least a few reasons for walking your dog now, like to let him potty, or for exercise. Instead of accompanying your dog on his walk, let him accompany you on yours. Go in the direction you want to go, and at the pace that you like. Stop when you feel like stopping, not because your dog wants to sniff or hike his leg on every blade of grass along your route.

QUESTION?

You mean I can't let my dog potty on walks?
You can let him potty on walks; you just can't let him potty at will. Give him a chance to go before you set out. Once you're walking, keep moving, and stop when you want to. Don't let him stop here and there, marking territory. If you want to give him a chance to go, have him sit and give you eye contact before you release him. Give him the length of the leash and a few minutes to go before you gather him back up and set out again.

Take the Reinforcement Out of Pulling

If you allow your dog to pull, you are teaching him that pulling is the right thing to do. If it's working for him, why should he give it up? Stop making forward progress if there is more tension on the leash than one or two fingers can easily hold. If nothing else, stop and wait for him to take tension off the leash before continuing. Even better is going in another direction; any direction is better than the one he wants to go in. You just have to make sure pulling isn't working for him, ever.

Equipment—Collars and Leashes and Harnesses, Oh My!

There is an extensive variety of tools available to make easier the job of teaching your dog to walk on leash politely. For training purposes, you'll need to outfit your dog with a well-fitting collar (for most dogs) and at least a couple of leashes. The type of collar you use for training will depend on your dog, or you may use an alternative to a collar, like a head collar or body harness.

Collars

The wide array of collars in your local pet store can be a little overwhelming, but with a little experimentation, and possibly an open mind, you'll find the perfect training collar for your dog. The following are several options:

Buckle Collars: These are leather, nylon, or fabric collars, sometimes adjustable, that fasten with a buckle or snap. You'll need this collar to hold your dog's tags, for the follow me game described later in this chapter, and maybe even for leash walking. This collar is not recommended for strong pullers because the pressure it can apply to the trachea can hurt such dogs.

Martingale Collars: These are also called no-slip or greyhound collars. They are especially good for dogs whose heads are smaller than their necks, since they are designed to keep dogs from backing out of them. Made of nylon, chain, or a combination of the two, they deliver a very mild correction by delivering pressure equally around the neck. Unless your dog is already a strong, habitual puller, this collar is an excellent choice for leash walking.

Choke Collars: Most often made of chain, but also available in nylon, this collar is the traditional choice for teaching leash walking. To be a safe and effective choice, the owner has to put the collar on correctly (it should form a "P" from the owner's perspective before being slipped over the dog's head), and have impeccable timing in its application. This collar has been losing favor in recent years due to the evolution of other training methods.

Prong Collars: Although these collars unfortunately look like medieval torture devices, they are actually much safer and (arguably) more humane than traditional choke collars. Like a martingale collar with rounded prongs for "power steering," they are the collar of choice for strong pullers or dogs with collapsing tracheas. Unless your dog has a very heavy coat, use the small size and add or subtract links to fit. Buy only the Herm Sprenger brand and let a trainer or knowledgeable person help you fit it properly.

Head Collars: Gentle Leader and Halti are the major brands of head collars. More like a horse's halter, these devices use the principle of controlling the dog's muzzle to control the rest of the dog. They can be very helpful in controlling strong or aggressive dogs, but are more of a management device than a training one when it comes to leash walking. Head collars require an adjustment period, and some dogs never stop fighting them.

Take your dog into the store to fit her collar. Buckle and prong collars should fit mid way on the neck, with just enough room for two fingers to fit between the collar and the neck. Choke and martingale collars should ride higher up, just under the ears to be effective, but must have enough slack for the "pop" action and to fit over your dog's head. Refer to the manufacturers' directions for fitting head collars.

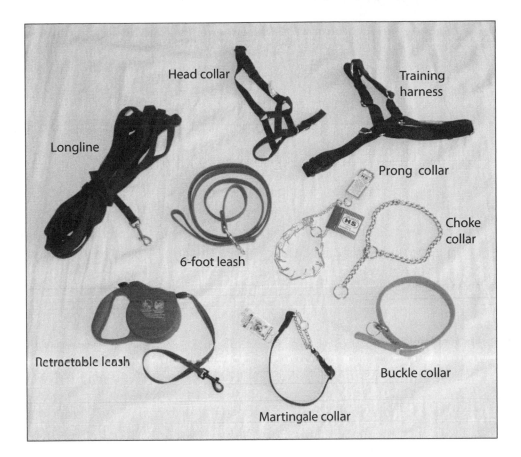

Longline

Head collar

Training harness

Prong collar

Choke collar

6-foot leash

Retractable leash

Martingale collar

Buckle collar

Leashes

You'll need at least two leashes for training purposes. For long-line walking, you'll need a 15-foot leash, and for regular walks and normal day-to-day control, you'll need a 6-foot leash. Your 15-foot leash should be made of cotton or mountain-climbing rope—whatever you prefer the feel of. For your 6-foot leash, you just can't beat a good leather leash, and a well-cared for one will last generations. If you're not good about making sure your dog keeps his mouth off your leash, use cheaper cotton until your dog matures. Thin nylon and decorative leashes may look cute, but they're anti-productive, not to mention often painful, for training purposes. If the leash doesn't feel good in your hand, it's useless.

For multiple reasons, retractable leashes should never be used for walking untrained dogs, not the least of which is the message they send to your dog about your relationship, which, if he's leading the way, is the wrong message. In addition, the constant tension that they produce on the collar actually teaches your dog to pull. While they are useful tools for recall and potty training (you can even snap one on your dog on potty breaks during walks), they shouldn't be used to walk dogs that don't yet have leash respect.

Harnesses

There are a few basic types of harnesses. Some are simply a way to keep hold of the dog while he drags his hapless owner down the street. These are cases where people felt sorry for their dog who was quite literally choking on a collar, but for some reason, couldn't or wouldn't train the dog not to pull.

There are also a couple of pulling-management harnesses available that use pressure points to discourage the dog from pulling. They vary in effectiveness depending on the dog. Like head collars, they are management, rather than training, devices, and the dog often has to use the device forever.

Follow Me—a Foundation Game for Leash Walking

The follow me game is a great foundation for both on- and off-leash heeling. By its very nature, it fosters your dog's attention on you and your leadership. You'll want to play this game when your dog is hungry and use high-value treats.

Location, Location, Location

To start, you'll want a fairly low-distraction venue. You can play the game anywhere, indoors or out, where you have some room to move in straight lines, preferably at least 15 to 20 feet in any direction, but smaller areas are okay to start with. Try basements, garages, basketball or tennis courts, your yard or another fenced area, or any open space that is safe and where the distraction level is reasonable or controllable. If you're working in a large or unfenced area, let your dog drag a long dragline so you can step on it if necessary to keep her from wandering.

Playing the Game

If you're in a fairly small, safe area, you can play this game with your dog off leash. Otherwise, let her drag a leash or dragline. Start out by facing your dog. CR/treat 3 times, then back away a couple of steps. If your dog follows you, CR/treat. Repeat 3 to 4 times, then turn so your dog is on your left. CR/treat your dog just for being on your left side. Take a few steps, CR/treating immediately if she follows. Start walking. Pay attention to your dog, but don't encourage her to follow you in any way. Just CR/treat, always by your left side, any time she attempts to follow you. At first, you'll be CR/treating every few steps. As soon as you've given her treats, take off walking again at a normal pace; don't wait for her. Don't worry about what she does; just keep walking, changing direction so you can pass her to give her a chance to follow you again if necessary. Once she has the idea and is trotting happily by your left side, getting CR/treated at varying intervals, try to lose her by turning to your right and walking away from her. Have a party when she catches up. Repeat a few times and quit while she still wants to play.

In subsequent sessions, try harder to lose her, and gradually add distraction to challenge her commitment level. As soon as she's showing some reliability under distraction, put her on a variable schedule of reinforcement to help the commitment stick, but praise often when she's getting it right. When she understands the game, insert your walking command, like "Heel" or "Let's go" before you start walking.

Long-line Walking—Teach Your Dog to Go Your Way

Long-line walking teaches your dog to respect your leash. You'll be walking your dog in a large square, stopping at the corners, nothing more. For this exercise, you'll need your dog, wearing his training collar, and a 15-foot leash. He should be pottied before you start. On this train, your dog is the caboose, and you're the engine.

A Place to Practice

Open space. That's what you need to find to practice long-line walking. You need to be able to move in a big square—at least 25 feet on a side. Finding level, unobstructed space to practice can be a challenge, but use your imagination. Church parking lots during the week, school lots or playgrounds on weekends, or office park and shopping center parking lots during off hours might work as well as more obvious choices like parks, where the distraction level may be too much for the early stages of training. Scout locations before you bring your dog for a training session, and make a mental or physical map of your training square.

Walking in Straight Lines

Walking in a straight line isn't as easy as it sounds, especially when you're trying to focus on several things at once. The easiest way to do it for this exercise is to walk your square once or twice without your dog. Start at your first corner and pick a focal point, like a telephone pole or an unusual tree—anything you'll recognize when you see it again—straight ahead, past where your next corner will be. Using your focal point as a reference, walk 25 paces (or more, if you have room for a larger square) toward it. Mark the corner if you want with a stake, flag, or even one of those little corncob holders. Turn 90 degrees, pick a new focal point, and count off an equal number of paces as you did for the first side of your square. Repeat two more times, turning in the same direction each time, until you get back to where you started.

FACT

Most people who do tracking with their dogs use the focal-point method to lay straight tracks, making note of the points on their physical maps. If you don't have a great memory, making a physical map of your training area with focal points may be helpful.

Walking the Square

Put the handle loop of the leash over your right thumb, and hold the leash in both hands, anchored right at your waist. Start at your first corner. Wait for your dog to pay any attention to you at all. As soon as he does, praise him, command, "Let's go," and take off to your next corner. Several things are possible. Either your dog will come right with you (more likely if you've played the follow me game a lot), or he'll go the other way, or he'll shoot ahead of you, or he'll fall to the ground like a rock, or he'll jump up on you, or he'll run around trying to wrap you up in the leash. Watch the leash so you don't trip, but other than that, plow ahead to your next corner and ignore everything that he does, except for enthusiastically and sincerely praising him for showing up at your left side. At each corner, pause for at least 30 seconds to give him a chance to stop paying attention to you. When he loses attention, say, "Let's go," and go to the next corner. By the second time around the square, he'll probably be paying closer attention, so end your session with a play break.

Holding the leash properly, with the loop over the right thumb, handle and slack anchored at Amanda's waist. Notice the slack in the leash between Amanda's left hand and Addie.

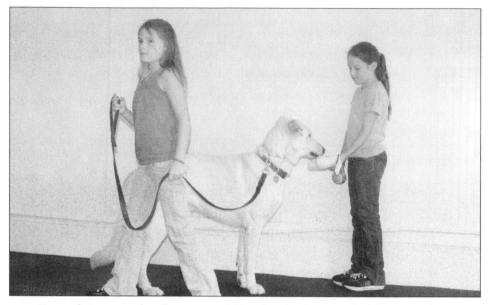

Kennedy turns and walks away quickly when Logan stops paying attention.

What a team!

Walking with a Regular Leash

Your basic 6-foot leash is what you'll be using in your everyday life with your dog. It's perfect for neighborhood walks, trips to the vet, and anywhere you need to control your dog's movement in close proximity to yourself. Now that you've spent some time playing the follow me game and teaching your dog leash respect on the long-line, the transition to your 6-foot leash should be a breeze.

The Walkaway

Before you take your dog out into the world for a training walk on your 6-foot leash, practice the walkaway without your dog, although a human stand-in is really helpful. Here's the move: Put the leash's handle loop over your right thumb, and grasp the rest of the handle in your right hand, anchored at your waist. Gather up the slack in one loop and hold it in your right hand with the handle. With your left hand, give your "dog " just enough slack to stand comfortably next to you, with a little dip in the leash between you and the "dog." Hold the leash lightly in your left hand, in a natural position at your side.

Start walking, and instruct your helper to go anywhere they want, except with you. The moment the slack in the leash disappears and you feel any tension, drop everything except the handle, turn abruptly to your right, and walk away as fast as you can. Your dog will get a "pop' on the leash and have no choice but to come with you. Praise and gather up the slack as quickly as you can and be prepared to do it again—quickly. Repeat until you can release, turn, plow on, and gather up the slack without thinking about it before trying it with your dog. Yes, your neighbors will think you've lost your mind, but it's all worth it for the cause. Now go practice with your real dog.

Be predictably unpredictable. Turn often, always opposite of the side your dog is on, at random times and angles. If your dog doesn't know which way you'll be going next, he'll pay much closer attention. Don't warn him that you're going to turn or wait for him at the turn, but do praise enthusiastically every time he catches up.

Hitting the Road

It's finally time to take your dog for a walk around the neighborhood. From the start, be ready to do the walkaway before the leash is tight. The only time there should ever be tension on the leash is the little pop your dog gets when he gets left behind on a walkaway. Do not guide or steer your dog on a tight leash, and do not beg him for his attention. Disappear if he's not paying attention, and make it rewarding for him when he does look to see where you're going. The first session, you may only travel half a block, and that's fine. The important thing is that your dog learns that he's coming with you, not the other way around. In general, the faster you walk, the more interesting you'll be to your dog, so put on some sturdy shoes and go! If you dawdle, he's much more likely to get bored and let his attention and discipline wander.

Heeling and Heel Position

So far, you've been teaching your dog to respect and pay attention to you and your leash. If you've done all the exercises, your dog should be walking pretty nicely by your left side with slack in the leash. Based on the theory that dogs will move away from discomfort and toward comfort, walking nicely by your side pays off. You give him attention or access to things he likes when he does, and you act like a lunatic when he doesn't, turning and walking away at the slightest tug on the leash. If you live in the city, or want to do competition obedience, you'll want to more precisely define where your dog should be in relation to you, and add an automatic sit when you halt.

Tracey takes shepherd mix Ralph on a leisurely stroll on a loose leash.

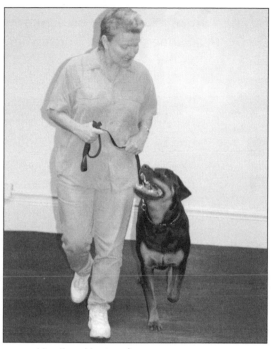

Heeling. Notice the precise position and attention that rottwieler Ebba maintains with Cathy.

Heeling or Loose-leash Walking?

Heeling, by competition standards, means that the dog maintains a position next to the handler's left side in which the area between the dog's nose and shoulders stays in line with the seam of the handler's left pants leg, as close as possible to without interfering with the handler's movement. The dog must maintain this position regardless of pace or turns, and must sit when his handler stops, neither forging ahead nor lagging behind. Heeling is necessary for competition dogs, but most pet dog owners are happy with dogs that don't pull, trip them, or cut them off, constantly weaving back and forth in front of them.

If you do want to teach your dog to heel precisely, great! It takes lots of practice, but done well, it has a ballet-like precision that is both beautiful to watch and a demonstration of amazing teamwork. It really helps to work with an instructor who has done competition obedience, but you can start by making sure you CR/treat your dog for being in the right place.

ESSENTIAL

If your dog has a tendency to swing in front of you to sit, it's probably because you've rewarded her in that position a lot. Teach her that sitting by your side in heel position is just as good as sitting in front of you by working with your dog between you and a wall, with just enough room for your dog to move freely. Move forward a step or two at a time, heeling and stopping, CR/treating for every sit by your side.

Competition-style heeling isn't really practical for real life, but there's no reason that you can't have the best of heeling and loose-leash walking. You can even do both; just teach and use separate commands, depending on the situation. If you want your dog to sit automatically when you stop walking, then practice it. When you stop walking, put a little tension straight up on the leash until your dog sits. Immediately release the tension and praise before moving out again. Repeat until it's habit for your dog.

Teach Your Dog to Take Up the Heel Position

The easiest way to teach your dog to take up the heel position is by luring. Start with your dog in a sit and face him. Hold the leash handle in your right hand, with the leash going from your dog's collar, past your left side and behind your legs. With a food lure in your left hand, start at your dog's nose and move your hand and your left foot back at the same time, moving at the speed he's following. Your hand should lead him in a little circle to his left and almost behind you. When he's turning toward you, step back up with your left foot. When his head is by your left side, lift the treat just high enough to lure him to sit, and immediately CR/treat. To start, reward every effort, and worry about perfect positioning later. As he gains confidence in his new trick, take the foot movement out, and put the behavior on verbal cue or hand signal. Once he knows what's getting rewarded, raise the criteria for reward until his positioning is perfect, and move it to a variable schedule of reinforcement.

Chapter 13

Now Wait Just a Second!

The wait command is one of the most versatile and useful commands you can teach your dog. Not only will you use it as a leadership tool and to instill your dog with self-control, but also, in virtually endless practical ways, it make life with your dog easier, safer, and more enjoyable for both of you. In addition to its real-world applications, the wait command is a necessity if you plan to do any kind of field or competition obedience work with your dog.

The Wait Command

The wait command tells your dog to pause, in whatever position he's in or you put him in, until you release him. Combined with the sit and eye contact you've already taught him, wait will be used more than any other command in the early stages of training your dog.

Introducing the Concept of Waiting

Your dog probably has no idea that waiting before he does something he wants is even possible, let alone desirable. To introduce the concept to him, start with him on leash, and toss a treat just out of his reach. Let him do anything he wants except get to the treat. Just hang in there and wait for him to stop trying to pull you toward the treat. As soon as he takes tension off the leash (even better if he looks at you), insert your wait command, "Wait," praise him, and give him a treat before releasing him, "Okay, take it" to get the treat on the ground. Repeat a few times, and you should notice the time he tries to get the tossed treat decreasing. At that point, say, "Wait" as you toss the treat. If your dog waits and watches you expectantly instead of lunging after the treat on he floor, have a little party and quit for that session. In future sessions, work toward having your dog wait before you toss the treat. Sometimes release him to it, and sometimes make him continue to wait while you pick it up and deliver it to him.

Wait in Motion

When he's doing well with the wait command, introduce it when he's in motion, first when he's just walking around the house, then when you're out for a stroll. You can use his name with the command, "Spot, wait! Yes! Good wait!" Step on the dragline, or give him a little pull on the leash if needed. Praise and pet him for waiting, then release him to go about his business. As he gets better at it, let him get further away before you call him to wait, or ask him to wait when he's trotting or even running.

Wait as a Leadership Tool

Wait helps you establish leadership by gently teaching your dog to give you control of the access to things he really wants, even when they're right in front of him. When he makes the choice to wait patiently, and willingly offers you power over his very existence, you get leadership without confrontation or violence. Yes, this does make you something of a dictator, but a benevolent one.

Have your dog wait while you throw his favorite toy. Hold him by the collar, and don't release him until he's not putting any pressure on it, then send him to get his toy with an enthusiastic, "Take it!" This game enhances leadership, teaches him a bit of self-control, and provides a foundation for competition retrieve work.

Sit, Wait, and Eye Contact for Food

Food is very important to most dogs—it's literally survival. By calmly and confidently making your dog's survival possible on a daily basis, your dog is much less likely to challenge your for leadership on other, bigger issues.

At mealtime, instead of dumping a scoop of kibble in your waiting (and maybe hysterical) dog's bowl, put the bowl on the counter. Prepare the food, and before putting it down, take your dog's leash (or dragline) in one hand, and hold the bowl in the other. The leash should not be tight, but shouldn't have any slack in it, either. Ask your dog to sit—once—then back it up with a little tension straight up on the leash, if he's not used to sitting in the midst of his excitement over mealtime. Tell him to "Wait" one time like you mean it and lower the bowl to the floor. If he gets up before you get the bowl all the way down, pick it right back up, and put tension on the leash until he sits again. Don't repeat your sit command, just keep the tension on his collar until he does. It doesn't matter at all how many times you have to repeat the process to get the bowl all the way to the floor with your dog holding his sit; it just matters that you calmly and matter- of-factly "win." As soon as he can sit there with the food bowl right in front of him, get eye contact by either waiting until he offers it, or making the tiniest noise to get his attention. Help as little as possible, and let him get CR/rewarded (the release to the bowl is his reward in this instance) for making the right choice.

ESSENTIAL

Anything given too freely loses value, and that includes food. You should not provide your dog with free access to food. It takes a vital leadership and training tool away from you. If you think your dog isn't motivated by food, try feeding him smaller portions twice a day. Whatever he doesn't eat in ten minutes, remove it and offer it again later, but only at the next scheduled mealtime.

If you repeat this exercise at every meal, your dog will probably offer the behavior unprompted within a week. Once he figures out that the sit, wait, eye contact routine is what is earning his access to the food, vary the amount of time you require him to maintain eye contact before releasing him.

Territory Boundaries

Territory boundaries are very important to dogs, or at least who crosses them first is. If your dog barrels past you through doors or on stairs, body-blocking you as she goes, not only is she being rude and disrespectful of you, but also she could injure you or herself in her haste to be first. On stairways and when going through doorways, insist that your dog wait for you to go first. Until she knows she has to wait for you to release her, try to cut her off before she gets out of position by giving her a verbal correction, like, "Aaaccchhh! Wait!" but be prepared to block her path several times, if necessary. There are detailed instructions for teaching your do to wait at doorways in the "Using Wait to Keep Your Dog Safe" section of this chapter.

Your Dog, With Self-control

Self-control is absolutely necessary for a calm, confident, and well-behaved dog. By nature, dogs are impulsive, often easily distracted, and driven to satisfy literally every whim that comes to mind. Until you teach him otherwise, your dog probably doesn't even know it's possible to control his impulses, but with your help, he'll learn both how to do it, and why he should.

Help Your Dog Control His Impulses

He's not going to do it just because you want him to. You have to have a way to make sure he doesn't get rewarded for the wrong, thing, like lunging at the food bowl before you release him. You can either set yourself up to help him control his natural impulse to dive on the food before he actually does it, or you can engage him in a conflict when you try to grab him by the collar and haul him off the meal he's scarfing down as fast as he can. Repeated conflicts like that could even make him defensive or protective of resources. Just avoid the confrontation altogether by keeping him on a leash or dragline until it's his habit to practice politeness and self-control. When you don't have to pick up the leash or dragline to help him make the right decision for six weeks, it's time to try him without it. Don't be shy about snapping it right back on for a few days here and there if his newfound freedom is a little too much for him to handle (it's kind of like taking the car keys away from a sixteen-year-old driver caught speeding).

Make Self-control Relevant to Your Dog's Life

If you're consistent about using and enforcing the wait command in your everyday activities with your dog, it'll become relevant to his life in a very short amount of time. When he can't get access to things he wants to see, smell, do, eat, or play with until he waits patiently for you to release him, it's in his own best interest to respond to your command promptly and without challenge. For now, the responsibility for making sure he does respond correctly, and doesn't get access to the good stuff until he's been released, is yours. Figure out all the ways that having your dog wait can make your life easier, and then teach him to follow your command in those situations.

Using Wait to Create a Habit of Politeness

For most dogs, consistent expectation and enforcement of polite behavior leads to that behavior becoming habit, or part of the normal routine, very quickly. However, if it's going to be your dog's habit to be polite, then you have to make it your habit to make sure you're giving her the direction she needs to make it happen.

ALERT!

It's not fair to your dog or your training program to sometimes let it slide if your dog doesn't wait or breaks position before being released. You don't want your dog wondering if you really mean it this time, or if your commands are really just suggestions. Mean it every time, or don't bother using the command at all.

How Your Self-control Helps

You don't have to fight or treat your dog harshly to teach him to wait. In fact, if you get frustrated and scream or lose control, chances are your dog is going to respond in kind. If nobody is in control, then, well, nobody is in control. A calm, assertive demeanor and an "It's just going to be my way" attitude are essential. Your dog is probably not purposely trying to defy you when he rushes to get to something he wants. By his rules of "normal," to the victor go the spoils. Be the victor by managing him to encourage cooperation. When he knows that you are simply going to wait for him to do the right thing, and make it impossible for him to be rewarded by doing the wrong thing, sit, wait, and eye contact will become his default (and polite!) way to ask permission for the things he wants rather than being pushy and demanding.

Recognizing and Testing Habits

You'll know polite behavior is becoming your dog's habit when you don't have to prompt her with a command or help to do it. For example, when you hold up her leash, does your dog sit and wait politely for you to snap it on her collar without being asked? If you pause before opening the door, does she automatically sit and wait, expecting that the command will come? When you see that she is automatically offering polite behavior before you have a chance to ask for it, it's time to start challenging her with distraction, higher-value temptations, or the need for longer duration. Always progress gradually, building on success.

FACT

The wait command is commonly used in performance events like obedience trials not just to keep the dog in position temporarily, but also to let her know that another command, like a recall or a retrieve, is coming soon. You can use the wait command in your training to add challenge to your commands by moving farther away from your dog before giving a command, or even disappearing around a corner before calling her to you.

Using Wait to Keep Your Dog Safe

There are so many ways that the wait command can help your dog stay safe. From dashing through doors or gates, to bolting from cars or crates, your dog can really put himself in harm's way if he doesn't know to wait and rely on your infinitely better judgment about whether it's okay for him to proceed.

Deterring Door Dashers

If your dog has a habit of dashing through open doorways or gates, only to lead you on a merry (at least for him) chase around the neighborhood, you must do whatever it takes to manage him to make sure he doesn't get to practice his technique anymore. Seeing your dog narrowly avoid being run over by a car—or worse—is an adrenaline rush you don't need, so in addition to managing him well, you also have to teach your dog that every time he wants to go through a door to the outside, he must sit, give eye contact, and wait to be released. Every single time until he does it without being asked.

To teach the wait, make sure you first have him sit in a position so that he's not blocking the door and you can open it all the way without hitting him. Tell him to wait, and then crack open the door. Gradually open the door enough for you to get through it, being ready to help your dog if he gets up by quickly closing the door and starting over, applying leash pressure as you did for putting the food bowl down, or both. When your dog can sit there on a loose leash with the door wide open, step through the doorway yourself, then call him through. Correct him as many

Shepherd mix Ralph waits for Tracey to release him before going through the door.

times as you need to so you can get all the way through the door with him waiting inside—no cheating by letting him go if you were "about to release him anyway." Either you release him, or he doesn't get to come through.

For safety during training sessions, and as a good correction, don't just have your dog on leash, but also let him drag a long (25 feet, with a knot tied every 5 feet in the line) dragline.

A Correction for Door Dashers
- Stand on the dragline with both feet fairly near the free end. Make sure there is at least one knot between your foot and the end, and that you're wearing sturdy shoes.
- Practice sit, eye contact, and wait for release at the door on leash a few times, making sure every time you come back in to the room after going through the door you step back on the line.
- After a few successes, make a show of quitting the training session. Say "all done" and remove the leash, but keep the dragline attached, and remain standing on the line.

- Without giving your dog a command, open the door wide, and if your dog bolts through it, shut the door on the dragline, so your dog is stuck out on the stoop all by himself (safely restrained from running by the line) and you're inside
- Wait about a minute, then open the door and make a big deal of welcoming your dog back into the house

There are some dogs that you won't be able to catch more than once with this little trick, but it is effective, and takes all the fun out of charging through the open door.

Bolters

If you learn nothing else from this book, learn this: never let your dog bolt out of a crate or out of a car—ever. Not even once, not even if he's happy to see you in your own home, not even if your car is in your own garage with the door closed. Maybe next time your dog will be in a crate at the airport, or you'll be parked on a busy street. Bad things happen in an instant, and when a tragedy is so easily preventable, there is just no excuse for letting him bolt. The beauty is that this behavior is easy to teach.

When you're going to let your dog out of his crate, open the door just an inch or so, closing it quickly and sharply with a firm "wait" command if he tries to shove his way through. Keep going until you can get the door all the way open and then call him out of the crate. Make sure you can touch his collar before he comes all the way out.

Your dog should be restrained in some way in the car, whether in a crate or with a seat belt, but the important thing is that he never gets the idea that he can come out of the car without having a leash on and being verbally released from it. Always attach the leash

Pug Boo waits to be released from her crate.

before detaching the seat-belt restraint, or using the crate method described earlier if he rides crated. Have him sit before snapping on the leash as an extra safety measure.

Practice your car-exit strategy in a safe environment regularly so the behavior will be there when you need it. If your dog only gets in the car a few times a year to go to the vet or groomer, he won't get enough practice to build the habit of waiting in the car.

How Wait Helps Dogs Learn Responsibility

You may have already noticed a recurring theme, which is to be proactive by giving your dog specific directions to follow, and by setting him and yourself up for successful practice by managing him in a way that it's always easy for you to enforce your commands. You're doing a lot of work to train your dog, but you can't do it all. Some of the responsibility is your dog's.

Controlling the Consequences

With consistent work (hopefully all of this is just a part of your lifestyle by now), your dog will learn that he can control the consequences of his behavior, both by offering appropriate behavior on his own and by responding correctly to your commands. The wait command gets the process going by giving your dog a balance between control and freedom. He can control himself by waiting patiently and get desirable consequences, or he can break his wait and get both repositioned and a delay before he gets what he wants. When he's offering polite behaviors more often that you have to ask him for them, you can start to relax the rules a bit. As long as he continues to treat people with respect physically, and to respond promptly and correctly, you don't have to make him wait every time for everything. This is what you've been doing all this work for, so you can finally give him more freedom, both physically (around the house and yard if he's earned it), and mentally (with more freedom to make choices). Of course, be prepared to help him be successful if he needs it, but give him a chance to offer the right behavior first. Unfortunately, where most dog owners mess up is doing it all backwards, giving freedom first and then trying to put the rules on when the dog is driving them crazy with obnoxious or dangerous behavior.

Let Your Dog Do His Share

So far in your training program, you've been giving your dog lots of guidance and direction, controlling practically every move he makes. It's time to let him take some of the responsibility for controlling his own behavior. With the wait, after you tell him to do it, don't keep constant tension on the leash, holding him in place. Make it his responsibility to maintain the position on a loose leash. Correct him promptly when you need to, but then give him enough room to make the choice between what you asked him to do and what he wants to do. When he realizes that he can control himself, and the consequences of his choices, he's on his way to becoming a teammate you can count on.

Chapter 14

The Fine Art of "Stay!"

14

Teaching your dog to reliably stay in a particular position is a lot of work, but the practical applications and usefulness are well worth the investment of time and energy. Whether you just want your dog to stay on the deck while the kids play in the yard, or you want to do competition obedience with your dog, the process is the same. Set your dog up to succeed early and often, and use that foundation of success to build a solid, reliable stay in any circumstances.

The Difference Between Wait and Stay

Wait and stay are quite similar in some ways, but vastly different in others. The stay is a bit more formal, requiring commitment and attention from your dog, sometimes for a long period of time, while the wait is a little looser and more temporary.

What Happens After the Command?

The wait command lets your dog know that he'll be verbally released fairly quickly, either to something he wants, like a meal, or to perform another job for you, like a recall or a retrieve. You might be right next to your dog when you release him, or you might be some distance away. The wait command tells your dog, "Hold on a second, something else is coming." The stay command, on the other hand, tells your dog in no uncertain terms, "No matter what happens around you, how far away I go, or how long I'm gone, do not move. I'm coming back to you."

Place, Position, or Both?

When you give him the wait command, you want your dog to stay where you left him, but the position he maintains is less important, as long as he waits for you to release him. With the stay command, you'll teach your dog to stay exactly where you left him, and in exactly the position you left him in, until you return to him and release him.

FACT

In obedience competition, breaking position in a wait is subject to a deduction, but the dog can still avoid being disqualified if he doesn't make forward progress until he's directed to. In the sit, down, and stand-stay exercises, however, the dog must maintain both his place and his position to receive a qualifying score towards an obedience title.

The Release Command

The release command is a combination of verbal and physical cues that let your dog know that he's done staying. To release your dog from a stay, you'll come all the way back to him (often to heel position), touch him, and verbally release him.

The Return

In the very early stages of stay training, you're not going to be moving much, basically just pivoting from heel position to being in front of your dog and then going back to heel position again. Later, you'll be walking around your dog and then to heel position. Move confidently, like you know your dog is going to stay there, not hesitantly, mincing along. Pay casual attention to your dog so you can interrupt him if he gets up to meet you, but you don't need to maintain steady eye contact; in fact, it's better if you don't. Don't reach for your treats, if you're using them to reinforce stays, until you're all the way back to heel position.

The Release

Like all of your commands, the cues you use for your release command are up to you. A collar touch or pat on the side combined with a verbal release, like "okay," "free," or "release" is fine, but use whatever makes sense for you. If you use a word like "okay" that is commonly used in everyday language, say it in a way that won't be confusing for your dog if he hears it in conversation. This is another reason for combining a physical release with the verbal one for stays. Praise is not and should not be your dog's release command. During stay training, praise tells your dog that he's doing the right thing and should keep doing it. Teach your dog the difference so he doesn't confuse praise with the release command. Challenge your dog by praising during the stay, first softly, then with more enthusiasm. Don't pet, just praise. If your dog breaks position, gently correct the broken stay and try again. If your dog resists the temptation of coming to get some love to go with the praise, give a big pat on the side with your release command and make sure your dog moves from the position.

Stay Basics

Although the position you leave your dog in will vary depending on the situation, there are some parts of the stay that will be the same every time. The release from the stay will be the same every time, as will the command.

QUESTION?

Should I use treats to reward stays?
It depends on your dog. Some dogs are too distracted by treats to focus on the stay, but if you can reward your dog and remind her to stay without her breaking, you can use them to reinforce maintaining the stay. If you use treats to reward stays, remember to always reward before the release, while your dog is still in the correct position. The treat is for holding the stay, not for breaking it.

The Stay Command

Like the release command, the stay command is a combination of a verbal and a hand signal, although you won't actually touch your dog with the stay signal. The command should always be clearly and decisively a command, not a question. The verbal command "stay" is given one time like you mean it, in combination with your right hand, open flat a few inches in front of your dog's face. In the early stage of teaching the command, you'll always be leaving from heel position, with your dog on your left side, so the leash will be in your left hand, leaving your right free to give the hand signal. Don't have treats in your hand when you give the stay signal!

During the Stay

After you've given your dog the stay command, the responsibility for staying is his. You'll correct if you need to, but don't do all his work for him by trying to hold him there with your hand extended, chanting "stay, sta-aaaaay, stay." If you pay attention to your dog, you'll quickly learn to read his signs and interrupt him while he's thinking about breaking the stay. In any case, you will correct him if he does break the stay, but he's responsible for staying. Let him do the work during practice. Think about it this way: how you teach it is how he's going to know it. A stay he won't hold unless you're constantly reminding him to isn't very useful for you, and you're doing this to make your life easier!

Clear and Reasonable Expectations

You should have a clear idea about what you expect from your dog when you give him a stay command so you can communicate it clearly to him. If you expect him to hold his place and position until you return to him, make sure he does during practice. Reliable stays take lots of repetition, and are dependent on building on success. Be realistic about the amount of practice you've done before giving your dog a stay command in a novel situation. Don't sabotage yourself, your dog, and your training program by using the stay command thoughtlessly, like to tell your dog to stay in the house when you're on your way to work.

If your dog doesn't lose it with praise, you can quietly praise occasionally, "Good stay," but don't pet your dog during the stay. If your dog has reasonable self-control in the presence of food, you can also slip your dog a treat occasionally with praise, and a gentle reminder, "Stay," to help build duration.

Teach Your Dog to Stay

Based on the work you've already done with the wait command, you'll start teaching your dog the meaning of stay as a self-control exercise. By building on small successes, you'll provide a good foundation for solid stays in practically any situation.

Self-control Sit-stay

Start with your dog sitting in heel position, on leash. Hold the leash a foot or so above your dog's head so that it has no tension or slack. Give your dog the stay command and signal. Drop a treat about a foot in front of your dog. If your dog stays, praise her, pick up the treat, give it to your dog, and release. If your dog gets up at any time before you get the treat to her, drop it back on the floor, quickly reposition your dog physically (don't tell her to sit), either with tension straight up on the leash, or tuck her into position, and remind her to "stay," firmly. Wait a few seconds, then reward/release as earlier. When your dog has had three to five successful repetitions, make it a little harder by throwing the treat a little farther away, so you have to take a big step out to get it. Repeat until you can get the treat about six feet away from your dog and have her hold the stay while you retrieve it. Every time you return, go all the way back to heel position before you reward, then release. Make sure your dog actually gets up and moves out of the position each time you release.

ESSENTIAL

If your dog isn't food motivated, don't despair; you can still do this exercise. Find a toy, a tennis ball, a stick, or anything that your dog adores, and use it as the temptation object instead of the treat.

Self-control Down and Stand-stays

Repeat the self-control sit-stay exercise with the down-stay and the stand-stay. Even if your dog is a superstar at the self-control sit-stay, start at the beginning, placing the treat right in front of your dog in the down and stand positions, gradually moving the treat out to six feet away, as you did with the sit-stay, getting three to five successes and coming back to heel position to reward and release each time before moving on. If your dog is having trouble holding the down, step on the leash so he can't get rewarded for breaking the stay. Depending on the size of your dog, you'll step on the leash from 2 to8 inches from where it attaches to the collar. You don't want your dog to feel tension on the leash, but you also don't want to give him enough room to break the position. When training the stand-stay, any leash pressure should be forward, and come from under your dog's chin, not upward, over his head.

Ring Around the Puppy

When your dog is holding the stay with the treat six feet away, instead of simply picking up the treat and taking it right back to your dog, take a step or two to the right or left, then walk away from the dog, pick up the treat, and bring it back to heel position to reward and release. Gradually continue adding a couple of steps per repetition to the right or left in an arc, until you can get all the way around your dog. When you can get all the way around in one direction, go the other way, again adding a step or two at a time before you go back to heel position to reward and release.

Again, Without the Treat

Repeat your whole stay training process without the visible treat on the ground. It should go very quickly the second time around. You only need one or two successful repetitions before moving on. If your dog gets stuck during the process and makes a mistake, don't panic. Repeat what he can do successfully several times before progressing. If you're doing multiple successful repetitions, reward variably, sometimes releasing with lots of praise and some play, sometimes with several treats before the release, sometimes with just a calm "good stay" and release.

ESSENTIAL

You don't have to use treats to train the stay, although it does usually make the process faster. Give the command the same way, and progress the same way, just don't drop the treat for your dog to focus on. During the ring-around-the-puppy exercise, do extra repetitions before crossing behind your dog so he doesn't pivot to follow you.

Help Your Dog Understand Stay Means Stay

Now that you've helped your dog learn what the stay command means, it's time to help him understand that even though it won't always be easy, stay always means stay. By turning the stay into an exercise that your dog thinks about and works to perform correctly, and challenging his commitment in various ways, you will help your dog become both confident and reliable.

Make Your Dog Think About Staying

Using your dog's natural opposition reflex, you can help the stay become an active exercise, rather than a static (and boring) one for your dog. Make sure the leash attachment is under your dog's chin before you start. Tell your dog to stay (in a sit to start), and pivot about 2 to 3 feet in front of your dog, so you're facing him. Very gently, pull toward your body on the leash, keeping the leash pressure as level with your dog's neck as possible, parallel to the floor. If your dog stays, praise him, and immediately go back to your dog, reward him, and release. Repeat 3 to 5 times, and then quit for a play break. In subsequent sessions, work all the positions, and gradually increase the pressure on the leash based on your dog's success until you can actually see your dog digging in and actively maintaining the stay.

FACT

It's easy for dogs to lose attention and forget what they're doing on extended duration stays if they haven't been taught to think about what they're doing and to actively resist physical pressure and temptation.

Slow Is the New Fast—Again

Stays, like recalls, are an area of training where people tend to fail their dogs, rather than the other way around. Inconsistency in training, unrealistic expectations for the level of training, and just plain lack of training are all ways that you can fail to teach your dog a reliable stay command. The stays are not a "gotcha" game, where you're trying to catch your dog breaking so you can correct him. Rock-solid reliable stays are built very gradually and systematically, while incorporating practically every possible variable into the training process.

Challenging Your Dog with the 3 D's

There are three basic variables to the challenges that your dog might face that will make holding the stay more challenging: duration, distraction, and distance. In fairness to your dog, and to increase the effectiveness and speed of your training program, get your dog reliable with each variable separately before putting them all together.

Duration

Duration is the first thing to build when proofing stays. If your dog can't hold a stay for at least one full minute with you right in front of him, there's no reason to think he can hold a stay in any other circumstance. Build duration gradually (of course!), making it harder two or three times, then easier, then harder again. So, you might do a session with repetitions of 5 seconds, 10 seconds, 20 seconds, 5 seconds, and then 15 seconds. At a bare minimum, your dog should be able to hold a stay for at least one full minute before you proceed with adding distraction. Use a watch; a minute seems like a really long time when you're just standing there looking at your dog.

Distraction

When your dog can hold at least a 1-minute stay, it's time to add distractions. Distractions should be challenging, not overwhelming, and gradually increase in intensity and in how close they are to your dog. Be creative when coming up with distractions—use squeaking toys, playing kids, running dogs, cats, chickens, or whatever else you have at your disposal. Praise your dog quietly for holding the stay in spite of distractions, and frequently reward and release. Pay close attention to your dog when you're introducing distractions so you can interrupt him if he's thinking about giving in to temptation, with a little leash pressure and an admonishment: "Annhh, anhhh, stay." Go back to heel position, and reward and release when your dog has recommitted to holding the stay, not when he's thinking about leaving.

Distance

The next thing to add to the stay equation is distance. Naturally, you'll increase distance gradually, proofing each jump in distance with duration and distraction before going farther away. You can move to 20 feet away in 3- to 5-foot jumps, making sure that your dog has been successful several times at that distance and distraction level before progressing. Past 20 feet add distance incrementally. Most dogs have a critical distance, which, when exceeded, causes the dog to lose either understanding or confidence in the exercise. To find your dog's critical distance, you'll have to experiment with distance a bit, spending the time to do a few extra reinforced repetitions at and past the difficult distance. For a good while, until you're certain that your dog truly understands the stay, start very close to your dog in every new location.

For competition obedience, and for your own convenience, there may be times when you leave your dog on a stay and go out of his sight. Obviously, training out-of-sight stays requires a safe location, and a way for you to know if your dog is breaking the stay. You can either recruit someone to be your spotter, or you can strategically place a mirror so you can observe your dog undetected. Keep your out of sight brief (just ducking around a corner and back again will do to start), and gradually build duration.

Just because your dog can hold a down-stay in the kitchen while you amble around the house doesn't mean he can hold a stay while you go into a store. Your best friend is too precious to take chances with, so use your stays, but use them wisely.

Practicing Stays in the Real World

The best way to practice stays after your dog has a foundation is to integrate them into your life. Out walking your dog, and stop to chat with a neighbor? Put your dog on a down stay. Writing a check at the pet store, vet, or kennel? Perfect time for a sit-stay. Your vet and groomer will love you if you teach your dog a solid stand-stay, not to mention how much easier it makes paw cleaning on wet or muddy days. The main thing is to put your work to use in your real life with your dog. You're not training him so he'll be trained from 5 to 5:30 in your kitchen; you're training him to be free to accompany you wherever life takes you.

Chapter 15
Settle (or, Go to Bed)

Ahh, the settle command. This command, once mastered, is your dog's ticket to freedom. It means that he can be contained in a designated area without actually being contained by a physical barrier. Instead of being locked away from the action when you have visitors, he can be part of it, or at least a spectator on the sidelines. He can accompany you anywhere because he can be trusted to calmly and quietly contain himself until you free him to do otherwise.

Settle or Down-stay?

Although the settle and down-stay commands are similar in that you expect your dog to lie down, that's pretty much where the similarity between the down-stay and the settle ends. The way you teach settle is completely different, as is what you expect from your dog when he performs it.

What Settle Means

Settle means that your dog should go either to a preassigned spot (more about assigning a spot in a minute), or a temporary place you designate, and make himself comfortable until you release him. He can flip from side to side, scratch real or imaginary fleas, or chew a bone. He can even get up, turn around, and lie back down again, as long as he doesn't leave the area. The duration of the settle can be very short, (say, just a few minutes), or up to 30 minutes or more. As long as your dog doesn't leave the designated area, and quietly contains himself, he can do pretty much what he wants. You're going to indicate to him early on in training that you prefer that he lie down, but after that it's all on him.

The Use of Settle

The more you use settle, the more uses you'll find for it. From letting the furnace repairman go about his work unassisted by your "helpful" dog, to waiting for your dog's appointment with the vet, to having lunch at sidewalk café, settle is useful in practically any situation. You can use settle to contain your dog when you have guests who don't necessarily adore being up close and personal with dogs, without actually having to put your dog in his crate or another room. Who knows, maybe they'll even change their minds about how they feel about dogs when they see a dog can be well behaved! Little League games, backyard barbecues, relaxing with a book in the park—anywhere that you want your dog with you but under control, is a great place to use settle.

The Settle Spot

Although you may have several of each type, there are two basic types of settle spots. The first type is a permanent spot that you use all the time in your day-to-day life with your dog. The second type of settle spot is portable, used for traveling with your dog (even a trip to the park is traveling). Both are easily identified by your dog no matter where he is.

Permanent Spots

Permanent settle spots are convenient areas around the house (or any-where you regularly take your dog) that you can send your dog to chill out for a while. You might have one spot in the kitchen or dining room where your dog can go when you're cooking or eating meals, another in the fam-ily room, one in the office, and still another in the bedroom. Anywhere that you hang out and want to allow your dog to hang out with you is a good place to designate a settle spot. Help your dog visually identify the areas (and be more comfortable) by providing something for him to lie on. You can use dog beds if you prefer, but a simple fleece mat will do just as well, especially for spots where he won't spend that much time.

QUESTION?

Where should the permanent settle spots be located?
Anywhere you want them. Some may be very close to where you sit, like right next to your chair or under your desk. Others might be used to keep your dog out of household traffic lanes, like in a corner of the din-ing room. Wherever you want your dog to be in relation to the activity is up to you.

Portable Spots

Portable spots should be, well, portable. There are lots of cute and por-table dog beds available, but anything that can easily be rolled or folded up, like a bath mat or towel, will do. It's not a bad idea to have at least one of your permanent spots do double duty as a portable. With training, your dog will instantly recognize it no matter where he is and know what's expected when he sees it and you tell him to settle. You can carry this portable spot literally anywhere for a visibly identifiable place your dog can call his own.

In time, your dog will understand that anything you put on the ground and tell him to settle on is his settle spot.

Teaching the Settle Command

There are two parts to teaching your dog what settle means. The first part is teaching her that finding and staying on her spot is what you want, and the second part is encouraging her to lie down and relax for the duration of the settle.

Teach Your Dog to Find the Settle Spot

Start by setting up one of your dog's settle spots (for this exercise, a mat works best) before you bring your dog into the room. Put the mat anywhere on the floor you want, and put a couple of treats in the middle of it. Bring your dog into the room (no leash is necessary) and stand near the mat. As soon as your dog investigates the mat (make sure he is actually stepping on it), CR/treat, then release your dog (your stay release is fine) and pick up the mat. Put it down somewhere else in the room and put another treat on it. Again, when your dog steps on the mat, CR/treat, release, and move the mat again. Repeat until your dog is rushing to get on the mat as soon as you put it down.

Over the next several training sessions, put going to the mat on command by pointing at the mat and saying "Settle" (or "Go to bed," or whatever you want to call it) before you let your dog step on it and CR/treat. Gradually raise your criteria so your dog has to have all four feet on the mat before CR/treating. If he steps off the mat before you release him, pick the mat up and put it down again somewhere else and work on gradually building duration in the next training sessions. When he immediately goes to the mat when you give your command and stays on it for at least 20 seconds in any position without any extra help from you, you're ready for the next step, getting comfortable.

It's Hard to Wait!

To start, make yourself comfortable in a chair or on the couch, with something to occupy your attention while you wait, like a book, the paper, or TV. Put the mat that you've been working with just to the side of where your feet will be when you're sitting. When your dog goes to check out her mat, praise her and drop a couple of treats on it. Step on the leash with both feet, giving your dog just enough room to barely stand on the mat comfortably. Have a seat yourself, and wait. Ignore anything your dog does, except when she lies down. When she does, say "Settle, good settle" and give her a couple of treats before you ignore her again. If she continues to lie down calmly, wait a few seconds, reward her again, and release her. Whether it takes twenty seconds of waiting or twenty minutes for her to lie down that first time, your dog will eventually lie down if you hang in there with her. The time that it takes for her to lie down will get shorter each time you practice, until she goes right to the mat and lies down. When that happens, have a party and quit for that session. Move to a variable reinforcement schedule as soon as she's regularly going immediately to her mat and lying down when you give her the settle command. Sometimes release her immediately; other times make her hold it for several seconds or more, gradually working her up to a minute before you reward and release.

Some dogs will not appreciate being restrained and will kick, buck, and generally throw a temper tantrum. The only thing that's important is that you keep your feet on the leash, ignore the rodeo, and wait for your dog to give up and lie down. The moment your bucking bronco hits the deck, reward and release. She'll figure out quickly that it's the calm behavior that's getting rewarded, not the wild behavior. You'll be using a couple of practical, around-the-house settle exercises to build duration and commitment even when you're not right next to her.

The Sitcom Settle Down

The sitcom settle exercise helps you build duration into the settle. Watching a 30-minute sitcom provides a perfect chunk of time to practice. There are several ways you can use the TV show as a guide for training, allowing you to enjoy the show and still get some training done.

And Now for a Commercial Break

Your first goal when building duration with the sitcom settle is to get your dog to maintain the settle through the opening credits to the first commercial break. To help your dog stay in a down position, step closer to the collar on the leash as soon as she lies down so she can't get all the way back up. Release her—only if she's quietly and calmly settled, not if she's struggling to get up—at the first commercial break, and use the break to work on something else, like position changes, or eye contact with distraction.

Over several evenings, gradually make your dog hold the settle for a longer period, a segment of the show at a time (the part between the commercial breaks), until your dog is maintaining it from the show's opening to the closing credits. When your dog can hold the settle for a whole show without trying to get up, try it without your foot on the leash. If he can hold the settle for the whole show without your foot anchoring him in place, challenge him with distraction.

Challenge Your Dog's Commitment

Get up and walk around the room, stepping on and squeaking one of his toys on your trip. "Accidentally" spill some of your snack on the floor near (but not too near—challenge, don't overwhelm) his settle spot and make sure he holds it while you clean up, maybe even treating him with one of your snacks. Alternate between settle and play, or settle and training. Work on settle during the show, and play or train during commercial breaks to help your dog learn to calm down from an excited state quickly and easily.

The Dinnertime Settle

Teaching your dog to settle during meal times has lots of positive side effects. It keeps your dog from begging at the table, or scavenging underneath it for dropped morsels—or away from your kids, who might sneak vegetables from their plates and into your dog. It has an added relationship benefit, as leaders eat first, then allow the lower-ranking members to eat. This is the main difference between the dinnertime settle and other settle exercises. In the other exercises, you occasionally reward your dog during the exercise.

For this exercise, only reward your dog when you are done eating. If you practice every time you sit down to eat a meal, your dog will probably automatically assume the correct position within a few weeks as soon as you take your seat. Some dogs will lie down whenever you eat.

Small Sacrifices

The sacrifices in this case are indeed small. At each meal during the training process, someone will have to commit to making sure your dog maintains the settle. At first, your dog will be right next to you, just like you've been doing in your training so far, so making corrections is relatively easy. As you move the mealtime settle spot to its permanent location, you may have to get up several times during the meal to make sure your dog is staying on the spot. When you don't give up, your dog eventually will acquire the habit of quietly accepting the restraint of settle, even in situations where he'd much rather follow his instincts, like getting as close as possible to the food on the table. So, meals may not be eaten in peace (or hot) for a couple of weeks, but it's a small sacrifice in the grand scheme of things.

Many people like to share food from their plates with their dogs. That's perfectly fine, as long the food is not harmful to dogs (some examples of foods to avoid are onions; chocolate; or anything too greasy, spicy, or salty). From a relationship standpoint, and to prevent annoying begging, don't share your food while you're eating it. Your dog and your relationship will benefit from waiting until you're finished eating to share.

Getting Distance

By the time you get to working on distance in the settle, your dog should have a solid grasp of the concept that when you give your settle command, his only option is to stay on the mat and lie down until you release him. Spend several days having your dog settle on his mat right next to you while you eat. If he can hold it for the entire duration of the meal with no help (no corrections, no feet on the leash), you're ready to start adding distance.

When you decide on the location of the permanent settle spot, do several short settles there before you do your first test run at a meal. Send your dog to his mat, then sit at the table for a few minutes before rewarding and releasing your dog. At mealtimes, send your dog to lie on his mat before you sit down. As long as he doesn't leave the mat, ignore him if he changes position. Praise him quietly occasionally as long as he's lying down: "Good settle." If he moves off the mat, don't say a word; just take him by his leash and bring him back to his mat and make him lie down again, either by stepping on the leash, or giving him collar pressure straight down, combined with the magic-button technique you learned when teaching your dog to do a down. If you have to correct him more often than three times during a meal, consider using a tether to keep him in place.

Using Tethers to Help Enforce the Settle

In the early stages of training, or when the lure of distractions may be overwhelming for your dog, you can make your own life a little easier by using tethers to back up your dog's place on his mat. You can also use tethers in outdoor situations to ensure the safety of your dog.

Using Tethers Wisely

While tethers can be extremely helpful in helping you enforce the settle, they can also be very frustrating for your dog if you just use them to restrain her without teaching her what she's supposed to do. Tethers are only to be used under direct supervision. You don't have to be close enough to touch your dog, but you should be able to see her. Provide something for your dog to chew on if she's going to be tethered for any length of time, and make sure the material your tether is made of is indestructible, like chain or vinyl-coated steel cable. Indoors or out, tethers must always be attached to something extremely sturdy. It doesn't do much good to hook your dog up to your lawn chair if she's going to drag it around the yard every time you get up for a beverage. The tether should be just long enough for your dog to stand up, turn around, sit, and lie down, slightly longer than the amount of leash you give her when you step on the leash to encourage your dog to lie down when you're working on settle close to you.

Weaning Off Tethers

While you can continue to use tethers to support the settle for your dog's whole life—and it's not a bad idea to do so outdoors, for safety reasons—you'll probably want to wean your dog off them as your dog gains confidence in the exercise (and you gain confidence in your dog). Before you do start weaning off tethers, make sure your dog has been thoroughly proofed and will maintain the settle under a variety of distractions, in multiple environments, both indoors and out.

To start decreasing the dependence on tethers, you're going to do the exact opposite of what you did with the recall: you're going to gradually give your dog more length on the tether, so he has room to make the choice to leave his mat, but not to completely leave the area. Try to ignore him for a few minutes if he leaves his mat and see if he'll return to it on his own. If you have to help your dog stay on his mat a lot, he's not ready for more freedom yet, so continue as you were for a few weeks and then try again. Each time you give him more freedom, double the length of his tether, until it's 6 to 8 feet long. When he can hold the settle in any situation with 8 feet of room to make a mistake, detach the tether from its attachment point and let your dog drag it for another few weeks, then start shortening it a foot or so at a time, like you did when training the recall.

Using Settle in the Real World

You haven't spent all this time working on the settle so your dog will do it when you're watching TV; you've been doing it to make your life easier in the long run. For your dog to really know the settle command in all situations, you need to work on it in all situations.

A Day at the Beach

Plan short outdoor field trips in your local area to work on settle. The beach, the park, your town's downtown area—anywhere that you can find a place to sit and be comfortable yourself is a good place to practice the settle. Start in somewhat low-distraction venues, then move to busier areas. Coffee shops or cafés with outdoor seating are great places to practice—you get to enjoy yourself while you work the settle. Step on the leash or tether your dog if necessary when you first start working on the settle in new or distracting locations, but give him the least amount of help that gets the task accomplished. The settle is his responsibility to maintain, not your responsibility to "glue" him into position. By the time you get to this point, he will have had enough practice to understand what's expected.

The Great Indoors

There are tons of indoor places to practice and use the settle command. Any place that allows dogs is fine, but also try places that might be similar to places your dog may accompany you to. Implore friends to let your dog come practice settle at their house (with your supervision, of course). Local shopkeepers often welcome dogs, and it never hurts to ask if there is no posted policy. Your vet's reception area will work as a practice venue (and is a good place to use the settle command anyway), but the important thing is that you get your dog out and do it!

Chapter 16

He Can't Always Have What He Wants

There are going to be lots of things in your dog's life that he wants (or wants to chase), but isn't allowed, either for his own safety or for the safety of the objects in question. Maybe he has a tendency to shred your kid's stuffed animals; or he picks up cigarette butts on walks; or he chases cars, cats, or deer. For these and other reasons, it's incredibly useful to teach your dog a "Leave it" command.

The Leave It Command

You'll teach your dog the leave it command with treats, and then transfer the meaning to other things he would otherwise pursue with abandon if unimpeded by your command. During the process of teaching your dog to "leave it" on command, you'll also teach your dog to "take it" on command, so this is really a two-for-one lesson deal.

In the Beginning

To start, you're going to teach leave it as a food refusal exercise. You're going to need lots of soft, pea-sized treats, so make sure you have them ready before you start your training session.

The following shows the procedure to follow:

- Hold 1 treat pinched between your thumb and index finger, say, "Take it," and give your dog the treat. Repeat 3 times.
- On the next repetition, present the treat as before, but don't tell your dog to take it. Hold the treat securely, so your dog can smell it but can't get it. Keep your hand as still as possible and let your dog do whatever he wants, short of chomping on you. If he does, boink him lightly right under his nose with the fingers that have the treat in them.
- Wait for your dog to give up trying to get the treat, even if the only reason he does is to check the floor to see if you dropped the treat.
- The moment he stops trying to get the treat, insert the command and CR, "Leave it! Yes! Good leave it." Say "take it" and give him the treat. Repeat 5 times
- On the next repetition, say, "Leave it" as you present the treat.
- CR/treat if he immediately backs away from the treat. If not, don't repeat the leave it command; just wait until he gives up trying to get the treat again and insert your command as you've been doing, then try again.
- As soon as your dog is readily leaving the treat, raise your criteria so he also has to give you eye contact before you CR/treat. Make a tiny noise to get him started if you need to.

When your dog is leaving the treat immediately upon command and giving and maintaining eye contact with you, it's time to move to the next step.

Now You See It

For the next step in the "leave it" teaching process, you're going to move the treat from between your pinched fingers to the palm of your hand, so your dog can see, not just smell, what he's leaving. The first few sessions, you can start with a couple of repetitions of "leave it," as he already knows it, with the treat pinched between your fingers. On the third repetition, instead of pinching the treat, place it on your open palm, and bring it down to, or a little lower than, your dog's nose level. Say, "Leave it" as he sees the treat. If he backs away and gives you eye contact, immediately CR/treat. If he can't resist the sight of the treat and tries to get it, quickly close your hand around it . Do not tell him "no" or jerk your hand away. Just close your hand around the treat, and if you catch a whisker or lip in your fist with it, poor puppy, he should have listened! As soon as your dog stops trying to get the treat from your closed hand, open it so he can see the treat again. CR/treat or close your hand again, depending on what he does. Make sure you only CR/treat when he is making the choice to leave the treat and look at you when your hand is open. If your hand is closed around the treat, he's not leaving it; you're just preventing him from getting it. Repeat 5 times per session. When your dog doesn't even think about looking at the treat in your open hand after you've said, "Leave it," you're ready to move on to the next step.

Good timing is essential for this exercise, both to insert the command at the exact right time, and to CR/treat your dog for getting it right. Practice some of the timing exercises in Chapter 5 to help you help your dog be successful quickly.

Paying Attention Pays Off

Now that your dog has some understanding of the leave it command in very controlled circumstances, it's time to kick things up to the next level, incorporating more realistic scenarios into your training program. During this time, you'll teach your dog that paying attention to your command is more rewarding than paying attention to what you're getting her to leave.

FACT

There is a very practical reason for requiring eye contact as part of the leave it. Opportunist that he is, if your dog is still staring at the treat after you've given the "Leave it" command, he hasn't really left it. He may not be actively trying to get it, but he's either plotting his next attempt or waiting for an opportunity.

Horizontal Surfaces

Just about every horizontal surface in your home is a potential source of temptation for your dog. Kitchen counters, the dining-room table, the coffee table, kids' tables, and even the floor are all likely candidates for places to practice (and later use) your leave it command. During training sessions (and of course, for management until your dog is trained), keep your dog on her leash or dragline so you can make sure she isn't rewarded for the wrong thing, like grabbing the treat off the floor or table.

Start your horizontal leave it training by placing the treats on the surface you're practicing on, and later dropping or tossing the treats (moving things are much more interesting to your dog, so this subtly challenges her commitment). You can also set up the environment before you bring your dog into it for a more randomized practice session. Use your command as she notices the planted treats. Until she's really reliable, don't release her to dive on treats on the floor; pick them up and give them to her. In other words, you're the source of the good stuff, not the floor.

Dory gives Lab mix Bailey the "leave it" command for the cookies on the floor.

Good boy, Bailey! Dory rewards him from her pocket first, and then might give him one of the cookies.

Takin' It to the Street

If you've been progressing according to your dog's success, he should have a good understanding that when you say "Leave it," you want him to not only not go after whatever you're telling him to leave, but also that he should turn his attention away from it and onto you. This is especially important when you're taking your leave it show out of the house, and into the great big world full of distractions and temptations. When you do venture out for leave-it training sessions, bring two types of treats. The first type is something visible and relatively low value to your dog, like plain breakfast cereal, while the second should be something really exciting to your dog, like last night's leftover roast beef. Try to be sneaky about tossing the visible treats out in front of your intended path, so your dog doesn't see you do it. When you come upon one of your decoys, command your dog to leave it. Make sure he doesn't get the treat on the ground, and CR/treat when he gives you his undivided attention. First give your dog one of the better treats that you have on you, and then pick up the lower-value treat and give that to him, too.

Sometimes You Can Get What You Want

In real life, when your dog is well trained, there will be times that you'll tell your dog to leave something that she can, in fact, have access to, just not right this second. Leave it in this case might be temporary, until you can make sure that the situation is safe, or you might not allow her access at all at the time, rewarding her with something equal or better than what she left.

FACT

Teaching your dog a reliable leave it could quite literally save her life. Puddles of antifreeze, poisonous snakes, toxic plants, and garbage are just a few of the possible attractive (to her, anyway) hazards that could seriously injure or kill your dog if she comes into contact with them. Running into the street in pursuit of a cat or other animal is another very real danger that a solid leave it can prevent.

Using Life's Rewards

You want your dog to be friendly to your neighbors, but you don't want her mindlessly zooming across the street to greet them every time she sees them. You might tell her to "leave it" when she sees the neighbors, and then escort her to go say hi when she gives you her full attention instead of coveting the neighbor's. Even squirrel chasing is relatively harmless if you can easily call your dog off. Your dog decides what she finds rewarding, and no reward is more powerful than what she actually wants, provided she does what you want first. So there's no harm in giving her the occasional tissue to shred, if that's what floats her boat, as long as she isn't stealing them, and leaves them and all the other stuff alone when you tell her to.

Advanced Leave It Practice

As your dog gets better at leaving the things she wants on your single "leave it" command in real-life situations, challenge her by asking her to leave things she's fully engaged with, like her food bowl, or a bone that she's gnawing, or something that she's not allowed to have or pursue. Make sure there is something awesome in it for her when she does leave it, and let her return to whatever she left for you, if it's something that's legal. If not, redirect her to something even better.

Using Leave It to Stop Car Chasing

Predators that they are, moving objects are always of special interest to dogs, and cars are no exception. Herding breeds, terriers, and the bull breeds especially have reputations for car chasing, trying to grab moving tires, or both, but any dog can be vulnerable to this potentially fatal obsession. Leave it, sometimes combined with an aversive, is the solution to this hazardous habit. If you're walking with your dog on leash, it's relatively easy to use and enforce the "Leave it" command and then reward and/or redirect your dog to a more appropriate activity than chasing cars. If for some reason your dog has freedom around moving cars (not a good idea in any case), or is obsessed to the point of physically overpowering you to get to them, you'll have to teach the dog that coming near moving cars means something bad is going to happen. The next sections will help you get a handle on car chasing.

Timing Is Everything

You already know how important timing is to many aspects of training your dog. To be effective, particularly in the teaching stage, the leave it command has to come when your dog first notices the car, or when he's thinking about chasing it, not when he's already running down the road after it or having an hysterical fit at the end of the leash trying to get to it. When your dog can perform the command easily before he's in full chase mode, then you can try it when he's a little more stimulated or has more freedom, gradually working up to calling him off something he's chasing.

Deterring Determined Car Chasers

As mentioned previously, really determined dogs who either have very high prey drive, or who have had so much practice that the behavior itself is reinforcing may need an aversive associated with moving cars to deter them from chasing and keep them safe.

You'll need at least two helpers to assist you in teaching your dog that cars sometimes strike back. One person can drive the car, while the other can toss the aversive, in this case, big water balloons, out the window at your dog if he approaches the moving car. For safety, the car should be moving very slowly at first and your dog, of course, should be on leash. Repeat the exercise with several different types of cars, and even beg for the mailman or regular deliverymen to get in on the act with you. Yeah, you're going to get a little wet, along with your dog, but it's worth it. If your dog is not deterred from car chasing in several sessions, consider a bigger correction. For life-and-death issues like this, a remote collar is a reasonable choice to deter dogs obsessed with chasing cars.

Using Leave It to Reduce Dog Aggression

Dog aggression, particularly on leash, is an unfortunately common problem in today's world, where dogs often suffer from lack of socialization with their own species. Some dogs who have forgotten how to speak dog well, decide on a "the best defense is a good offense" strategy when dealing with other dogs, just because they don't know what else to do. They need to learn leave it as a coping strategy. Others truly are dog aggressive, so for them, leave it is both a safety measure and a mutually exclusive behavior to challenging other dogs.

Teach Your Dog What to Do Instead

In order for leave it to be an effective measure for reducing dog aggression, it is absolutely imperative that you time your "Leave it" so you're giving the command when your dog indicates that he has seen another dog, not when he's lunging at the end of his leash, barking, snapping, and snarling his head off. As your dog gets really good at leaving other dogs at a distance, turning his attention away from them and onto you, you can gradually work on your training closer to them. When you first start working on aggression issues, reward your dog the moment he gives you his attention, but don't stop there. Keep his attention on you by giving him specific tasks to do. Turn around and move away if necessary to give your dog the space he needs to be in his body and functional, rather than "over there" with the other dog mentally.

ALERT!

Interdog aggression can be an extremely serious and dangerous issue. If your dog makes ugly faces and noises at other dogs, but hasn't actually been involved in a serious fight or attacked another dog to the point of injury, proceed with the leave it training described below, along with getting your relationship with your dog in order. If your dog has ever seriously fought with or injured another dog, or you don't feel physically capable of controlling your dog, consult a professional trainer or behaviorist to help.

Building a Habit

Dog aggression is an issue that isn't going to go away overnight. The more practice your dog has had at his habit of unsociable behavior with other dogs, the more he'll need to practice his new behavior of looking at you instead of at other canines. While he's building his new habit, it's very important to avoid setting your training back by allowing him to get in altercations with other dogs.

You'll know you're doing well when your dog automatically looks at you when he sees another dog, even before you've seen it yourself, or had the chance to tell him to "leave it." Along with being a coping strategy for dealing with other dogs, this method can actually teach your dog to welcome the presence of other dogs, because he knows good things happen for him when they're around.

Most dogs aren't truly dog aggressive; they're just poorly socialized, and so they lack the proper canine communication skills. Well-meaning but overprotective owners who mistake normal communication between dogs for aggression can cause their dogs to behave aggressively with their own behavior, by either isolating their dogs from others or by reacting nervously around other dogs. An obedience class can help resolve both owner and dog socialization and confidence issues.

Leave It for Life

Leave it is such a practical command, with so many possible everyday applications, and is so easy to teach that there really is no excuse not to take a little time to do it right. It will take some time, and lots of repetition, for your dog to fully understand the command in all situations. If you want the command to be there when you need it, you have to work on it a lot so your dog doesn't even consider not turning his attention to you, even when what he has to leave is intensely interesting to him.

Meaning It

The command is not "Leave it, leave it, leave it, LEAVE IT!" or "Leave it?" The command is, simply, "Leave it." Say it once, just loudly enough for your dog to hear you, but avoid shrieking, even if it's an emergency. When you need to use the command, it should sound the same way your dog has heard it hundreds of times before in training, albeit perhaps with more volume depending on the circumstances. For your dog to believe you mean it when you say "Leave it," or that he has to, you must have a position of leadership with your dog, both so he will leave things that he wants, and so he trusts you not to let anything bad happen when you make him turn his attention away from something he thinks he's defending himself or you from.

Backing It Up

If you've done your part by giving your dog sufficient repetition in a wide variety of situations to really know the command, you may never need to correct your dog for ignoring a command (does the phrase "building on success" ring a bell?). If you haven't done enough training, or your dog was already obsessed with something before you started, particularly something dangerous, you may need to back up your command with an aversive. Depending on your dog and the danger level, you might use a shaker bottle, a squirt gun, water balloons, a remote collar, or whatever else works to stop your dog in his tracks.

FACT

Remote collars come in several varieties. Some deliver a warning tone, with or without a squirt of citronella or lemon oil, or a static shock. They are commonly used to "snake break" dogs who live in areas populated by poisonous snakes. Consult a trainer or behaviorist to figure out which type of collar is best for your dog's temperament and behavior.

Can I See That?

If you didn't see your dog grab something he shouldn't, then it's too late to tell him to leave it, so you should also teach him to "drop it" on command.

Starting Out Right

You want your dog to willingly give you anything she has in her mouth when you ask for it, whether the item is hers, yours, or a stick from the yard. The way to get her to be happy giving you anything, even high-value items, is to do literally hundreds of object exchanges, or trades, with anything and everything she puts in her mouth from the moment your bring your dog home. Any time you notice her chewing or carrying something, approach her with a really good treat. Ask, "Can I see that?" (or "Drop it," "Give," or whatever you want your command to be) as you bring the treat right to her nose with one hand, and either lightly grasp or hold your hand out to catch what she has in her mouth. The instant she drops it, CR/treat. Inspect whatever she gave you, and if it's something legal, give it back to her. If not, redirect her attention and interest with something else.

Keeping the Drama Out of Drop It

How you approach your dog when he has something you're going to take from him (even temporarily, as a training exercise, or to make sure what he has is safe), makes all the difference in whether he's more likely to willingly give it to you, or feel the need to defend it. Approach him calmly, even if the item he has is something valuable to you. If you go storming after him, chances are he'll run from you, destroying or eating the object in his haste to keep it, or even become aggressive in his attempt to keep his treasure.

Don't neglect "drop it" training! You never know what you might need your dog to drop. Whether it's his own toys during fetch or tug-of-war games, or chicken bones from the trash, you need your dog to drop it the moment you say it, no matter what it is—it could save his life!

From the time you bring your dog home, never scold him or punish him for bringing something to you, even if it's something he wasn't supposed to have. He won't understand that you're punishing him for taking the item. To him, the punishment is for presenting it to you. Be happy to receive anything your dog brings. If your dog habitually picks up forbidden objects, good management of him and your stuff is crucial, unless you want object exchanges to be your full-time job until your dog matures.

From Object Exchange to Drop It

After several days of random object exchanges, your dog should be happy to see you approaching him when he has something in his mouth, knowing it means a good deal for him. At the very least, he'll get something good in exchange for what he has, and he might even get what he has back again. Now that you have the behavior you want, the next step is to put it on command.

Drop It on Command

After you've done at least 25–30 successful object exchanges with a treat at your dog's nose when you give the command, try doing it without the treat. Do everything else the same way you have been: ask your dog, and hold your hand out for, whatever he has, just without the treat in your hand. If he gives the object to you, have a little party with several treats in a row. If he doesn't give it up on your command, say, "Too bad" and eat (or pretend to eat) the treats yourself. The next time you try, go back to using the treat with the command for another 25 repetitions, then try again without the treat.

When your dog is readily giving up what he has without the treat in your hand, start giving your command before you reach for what he has. Not that that's how you're going to do it all the time, but you do want him to respond just on the verbal command, without the additional hand cue. That way, you can tell him to drop something from across the room or yard, and have confidence that he will.

Speed-training Drop It

For extra oomph in your training program, and to teach your dog to drop it on command quickly, don't just wait for him to have something in his mouth to work on training; set up training opportunities. Use a variety of low-, medium-, and high-value items so the behavior is there when you need it, no matter what it is you need your dog to drop. Start with items of lower value, the stuff your dog has access to all the time, like his normal toys and chewies. Encourage him to "take it" before asking him to give it back to you. You can reward him with a separate treat, or by giving the original item back to him. Move up to higher-value items like marrowbones. Give him the higher-value item, but keep your hand on it. Ask him to give it to you several times before you let him keep it. For extra practice on really high-value items, try cooking a piece of bacon on a paper plate in the microwave. Eat the bacon yourself (or crumble it up to use as extra special training treats), and crumple up the paper plate. Leave the paper plate on the floor so you can practice the drop it command when your dog picks up the plate to get to what he thinks is inside. For an extra kick, use the bacon as his reward for dropping the bacon-scented plate.

If your dog won't drop something, don't panic. Approach him calmly, stepping on his leash or dragline to prevent him from taking off. Grasp the top of your dog's muzzle with your left hand, inserting your thumb and middle finger just behind his canine teeth (the "fangs"). Use your right hand to hold the lower jaw, approximately the same way, and use your left pointer finger to put slight pressure on his gums or incisors (front teeth) until he opens his mouth. When he does, use your right middle or ring finger to hold the lower jaw down while you quickly retrieve the item. It takes practice to get it right, and like all training, you should practice opening his mouth (and perhaps popping a treat in) when you don't need it, so you know it'll be there when you do. If your dog behaves aggressively when you try to get something from him, consult a trainer to help.

Chapter 17
Kids and Dogs

Kids and dogs are, as Forrest Gump said, like peas and carrots, they just go together. However, the relationship between kids and dogs isn't always rosy. This is no time to let them figure it out for themselves. Mutual respect, appropriate behavior, and great relationships don't usually spontaneously occur. Supervision, management, and training— of both parties, not just the dog—are required to ensure the safety and emotional health of everybody involved.

Supervision Equals Safety

Supervision of kids and dogs is the single most important step you can take to ensure the safety of both. Along with allowing you to see any inappropriate behavior by either, supervision affords you an opportunity to referee and teach both how to play together productively.

FACT

According to *www.dogbitelaw.com*, about 70 percent of serious dog bites are inflicted on children, usually younger than 10 years old. Most of the bites are to the face, and are inflicted by a family dog or another dog well known to the child. Lack of supervision and clear direction for both kids and dogs is at the root of most bites.

The Under-six Rule

Children under six years old should never be left unsupervised with any dog, even your beloved family pet. Young children are so impulsive, and they can and will do all kinds of things to dogs that even if well intentioned, may cause the dog to feel that he needs to defend himself. Toddlers need particularly close supervision, as their jerky movements, high-pitched screams, and tendency to tightly grasp things (in this case, maybe your dog's ears, feet, or tail) are unsettling or downright frightening for many dogs.

The relative size and strength of kids compared to your dog is another factor to consider. Even small dogs can quite easily overpower a child that is three or four times their size. Dogs, especially young ones, often treat small children like littermates, thinking nothing of mouthing; body-blocking; knocking them down; and snatching snacks, toys, or other items out of children's hands. In addition, the small stature of young children often puts them at face level with dogs, encouraging some dogs to believe that a child staring at them is challenging them for dominance, an invitation for disaster.

Playing Nice

Of course, if you have both kids and dogs, chances are they are going to play together. How they play is important both for safety and because of how it affects the overall relationship between them. Any physical play between dogs and kids should be closely supervised, and children should never play physically competitive games with dogs, like tug of war or wrestling. Any time the dog wins a competitive game with a child, it encourages the dog to believe that he is above the kid on the relationship totem pole. Instead of competitive games, teach kids and dogs to play cooperative games, like fetch or find it. Both kids and dogs usually love playing find me, in which a parent or someone else who can physically control the dog restrains him (or, if his level of training allows, leave him on a wait) while the child hides, then calls the dog to find her, rewarding the dog with lots of praise and treats when he gets there.

Teaching Kids How to Behave with Dogs

Some dogs are extremely tolerant of even rough handling by children, and will happily accept being used as pillows, or being dressed up in baby clothes and wheeled around the neighborhood in a stroller. However, dogs, even those that are considered to be members of their human families, are animals first, and will defend themselves as such if necessary. It is important to teach kids to handle dogs gently and with respect.

Teaching Kids to Control Themselves

How children conduct themselves around dogs has a big impact on how dogs react and respond to them. Kids must be taught early on that dogs aren't toys provided for their amusement. Instead, help kids understand that dogs are not just living and breathing, they're also thinking and feeling creatures that deserve kindness and compassion. Like young dogs, young people often have very little self-control, and may have to be restricted from interacting closely with dogs until they're able to behave calmly in the presence of them.

Do's and Don'ts:

- Don't allow kids to run up to or by your dog.
- Do teach kids to let sleeping dogs lie undisturbed.
- Don't allow kids to tease your dog through a fence or with food.
- Do teach kids to talk to dogs calmly, not scream or shriek at them.
- Don't let kids harass your dog if he's chewing on something.
- Do involve kids in your dog's socialization and training program, even if they're not your own children.
- Don't allow kids to handle your dog roughly.

A little common sense goes a long way. If kids don't behave appropriately around dogs, or vice versa, then they don't get to interact until more training has been done.

Respect for the Dog's Space

Like people, dogs have an invisible circle around them, defining their personal space. The size of the circle depends on the temperament and personality of the individual dog, as does the dog's likely response when the boundary is crossed. Some dogs are quite accepting of their boundaries being crossed, depending on the circumstances, while others will flee, and still others will defend their space with threats or outright aggression. Much of what kids want to do to dogs, like hugging them tightly around the neck, is quite naturally perceived by dogs to be acts of dominance or aggression. In fact, unprovoked dog bites inflicted on children are relatively rare, although the provocation that preceded the bite might not be obvious to the casual observer.

ESSENTIAL

Dogs should be provided with their own kid- free zone, whether it's their bed, a crate, or an unused, out-of-the-way or little-used room in the house. Kids must be taught to leave the dog completely alone when the dog retreats to his safe zone—no poking fingers in the crate, reaching for him, or whining allowed.

Leadership and Kids

You already know how important leadership is for dogs to be happy and well behaved. Leadership is just as important for kids, both to model for them how to treat your dog, and to ease your dog's mind that someone is in charge of the miniature (and often loud, erratic, and quick-moving) humans in their lives.

Rules of the Game

If kids behave in an out-of-control fashion around your dog, there is a good chance that one of three things will happen:

1. Your dog will try to flee the scene.
2. Your dog will behave in an out-of-control manner along with the kids,
3. Your dog will discipline the kids herself—and probably not in a way you'd like.

If it's your dog, then it's your game, so you make the rules and enforce them for both dogs and kids, even if the kids aren't yours. You have no apologies to make to anyone for insisting that your dog is both respected by and respectful of people, no matter what their age. If either your dog or the kids who want to interact with her get out of control, it's up to you to give the offender some time out to get a grip on themselves before resuming activity.

Helping Kids Get Leadership

Kids over the age of six can start to establish leadership with dogs with some parental assistance. Using the same control-the-valuable-resources method that you have been implementing all along, put your child in charge of some of the good stuff in your dog's life. For example, with sit, eye contact, and wait until release well established in your dog's behavior repertoire, transfer some of the responsibility for feeding the dog to your child.

Anything your dog wants from your child, like petting or play, should be met with a request for a simple task, like sit, for the dog to perform first. When the feeding ritual is well established, do the same thing you've worked on before at doorways and stairways—the kid always goes first, then the dog. For the best results, regularly involve your child in the training process for all the commands, including stays, recalls, and walking nicely on leash.

Back It Up

The easiest way to teach your dog that your child is in charge is to back your child up, provided, of course, that what your child is asking of the dog is reasonable. Backing your child up could be as simple as following up your child's command with your own, much like when you add a second cue for a behavior your dog already knows. You may also have to back your child up physically, either by making sure the dog does what your child asked, or by helping the child control or restrain your dog.

ESSENTIAL

Help your child practice giving commands with a commanding tone of voice, not a shrill or plaintive tone. Practice without the dog first, and make sure your child isn't repeating commands. Kids need all the power their voices can command, and repeating commands dilutes the power of the first one.

Walking the Dog

Walking is a great way to establish leadership, but you want to make sure that it's the child doing the leading, not the dog. As a general rule, unless the dog is very well trained, kids under twelve shouldn't walk dogs by themselves if the dog weighs more than 50 percent of the child's weight. An adult should back the child up with either their physical presence or even a second leash, if necessary. Training tools like prong collars or head collars may also be used to give the child a no-strength-required advantage.

Fun Stuff Kids Can Do with Dogs

There are an abundance of activities that kids and dogs can enjoy together. From organized and competitive events to backyard fun, you're sure to be able to find something that both your child and your dog will enjoy.

Just for Fun

Give your kid a clicker (or teach her how to use a verbal CR, like "Yes!") and a bag of treats, and start working on shaping tricks, like shake, roll over, speak, spin, back up, and crawl. Backyard obstacle courses can be purchased or made from household items to provide an opportunity for exercise and teamwork, not to mention fun. Nothing beats a good game of fetch for cooperative fun, but make sure your child isn't snatching the ball from your dog, or prying it out of her mouth to get it, along with making sure your dog isn't snatching the ball back from your child. For extra impact, your child should have your dog sit and wait some of the time before the ball is thrown. Any rude behavior by your dog toward your child calls for an immediate end of the game for at least 20 minutes. In other words, your child should simply walk away if your dog displays any rude or pushy behavior like jumping, mouthing, or pawing. It doesn't take most dogs long to figure out they'd better play nice if they want to play at all.

FACT

There are several online resources for kids with dogs that are both fun and educational. The Web sites ✎www.loveyourdog.com, ✎www. pbrc.net/poppysplace, and ✎www.dogplay.com are designed to be kid friendly and are loaded with info about dogs, dog safety, training, and fun things for kids and dogs to do.

For the Real Dog Lover

Some kids have a natural affinity and ability with animals in general, and dogs in particular. They want to do and learn everything they can with their canine companions to have a great friendship and partnership. For

Jordain and Cairn terrier Duncan train for agility.

the special kid that is really committed to the care and training of her own dog, look into organized activities in your area. Kids are welcome, and in fact, encouraged to train and compete in several performance events, including agility, rally, obedience, and conformation, in addition to junior handling in the American Kennel Club and other national and international kennel clubs.

4-H Clubs are active in many communities, and many of them have dog-related activities, including obedience competitions and volunteer work with dogs. With their parents' assistance, some kids even raise puppies for assistance-dog organizations or take their own trained therapy dogs on visits to hospitals, nursing homes, and other therapeutic venues. Along with the responsibility of caring for a dog, a child learns a lot about grace under pressure, good sportsmanship, and civic responsibility from participating in organized activities with their dogs. It's a win-win situation: a well-behaved dog and a responsible kid. What more could you ask for?

Stranger Danger

Sometimes kids' natural affection for dogs can get them into trouble. Your child needs to understand that not every dog is friendly or safe, and that even the cute ones can be dangerous. There are several simple precautions for your child to take when approaching or being approached by strange dogs.

Unattended Dogs

Unattended dogs are never to be approached, followed, or touched by your child. If your child does run across an unattended dog, he should turn quietly and calmly walk away, even if the dog appears friendly. He should not, under any circumstances, run, scream, stare at, or call the dog, or try to get the dog to fetch a stick. The first thing your child should do if he is pursued by a dog is to become a tree—in other words, be perfectly still, with his "branches" (arms) wrapped tightly around his body. Your child should look up, not at the dog. If a dog knocks him down aggressively, or is growling or snapping, your child should curl up into a tight ball with his fingers laced on the back of his neck.

ALERT!

The no-touching-unattended-dogs rule doesn't stop at strange dogs. It extends to dogs your child knows belonging to friends, neighbors, and family members. He also should not reach through or over a fence to pet a dog, even if the dog knows him and is wagging his tail.

Making New Friends

Children should be instructed to always ask before petting a strange dog, both out of safety and as a matter of politeness. New dogs, even those described by their owners as friendly, should be handled initially with caution. Along with adult supervision, the child should allow the dog to smell her closed fist first before attempting any petting. Petting, if it happens at all, should be limited to a few quick scratches under the chin or on the chest to start, not over the dog's head. Children should never attempt to hug or kiss a dog they don't know very well, and even then it's often a risky proposition, as many dogs do not perceive such a display as affection but as aggression. Adults present should monitor the interaction closely, watching the dog for freezing, showing the whites of the eyes, hard staring at the child, or soundless lip curling—all can be indications that a bite is about to occur. If the dog seems wary, nervous, or uncomfortable, don't allow your child to go near it, and particularly should not pursue it if it attempts to get away.

Jordain introduces herself and asks permission before petting Goldendoodle Linus.

Petting under the chin, not over the head.

Bringing Home Baby—Infants and Dogs

Bringing home a new baby is of course a time of joy, but it can also be very stressful for new parents as well as their dogs. From the time a new baby comes home, everything is different—the schedule, sights, sounds, and smells. Last but not least, the lion's share of what was the dog's attention and affection get bestowed on the newcomer instead. With a little planning, good management, and a conscious effort to meet the dog's needs as well as the baby's, the transition to the new pack order is made much easier.

Preparing for the New Arrival

Don't wait until the baby comes to practice how you're going to manage your dog. Where will he be when you're nursing or providing for the baby's needs? Is he even allowed in the nursery? Make those decisions and practice with a doll long before your real baby comes home. Go ahead and set up the nursery, bouncers, and other baby equipment as soon as you can so your dog is already familiar with them before the additional impact of a baby. Take a walk with your dog and your empty stroller to work out any leash-walking kinks before you actually need to walk your dog while pushing a stroller with your baby in it. Make sure your dog is responding reliably to the commands "sit," "wait," and "settle," no matter what position you're in when you give the command—sitting or lying on the couch or in the rocking chair, or with a baby carrier strapped to your chest.

ESSENTIAL

There are quite a few baby-noise CDs available to help you accustom your dog to the new and unusual sounds that he'll hear when your new baby arrives. Start playing the recordings at a low volume to start, gradually increasing the volume as your dog gets better at following commands and remaining calm in spite of the racket.

When the baby is born, sacrifice an old T-shirt or sweatshirt to the cause. Let dad wear or sit on it for a little while, then mom, and then wrap the baby in it (or roll it up with the one of the baby's hospital swaddling blankets). Give it to your dog to use as a bed or crate mat before you bring the baby home. The mixture of scents will familiarize your dog with the scent of the new baby, along with reassuring him that mom and dad have already accepted the baby into the pack.

After Baby Comes Home

Some dogs will quite happily accept anyone their people do, but others will need some assistance and reassurance during the adjustment period. To hasten the acceptance process, include your dog in the baby-care process just by allowing him to be present. Don't isolate your dog, but instead make sure good things happen for him when the baby is around. The dog should get some special treats whenever he responds calmly in the baby's presence. Your infant should never be left unattended with your dog, even if your dog is normally very good and gentle with your baby. Even the nicest dog can unintentionally hurt an infant, along with the possibility of the sounds and movements of an infant inciting the dog's natural prey drive. It only takes a moment for tragedy to occur—it's just not worth the risk.

Your time will be precious, especially the first few weeks, while you all adjust to the changes in the household. Be creative and find ways to productively occupy your dog to replace some of the attention and exercise that he'd normally receive. Feed him from a treat-dispensing toy like a Buster Cube, Leo puzzle, or stuffed Kong toys, instead of from a bowl for a few weeks to occupy his attention and energy without making him feel left out. If you have a high-energy dog, arrange for someone (a family member, friend, neighbor, or paid dog walker) to come and exercise your dog once or twice a day for at least the first few weeks until you're adjusted to your new routine. It's not unusual for dogs to revert to grabbing inappropriate objects like they did in puppyhood just to get some attention.

Chapter 18

Games Dogs Play

Most dogs love to play, and playing properly with your dog strengthens your relationship, as well as providing your dog with some fun mental and physical activity. The games you play with your dog are just as important as how you play them. Along with having fun with your dog, incorporating play into training (and training into play) creates a dog that not only has great attitude about working for you, but also is much easier to control, even when he's excited.

Control the Games, Control the Dog

There are lots of ways to play with your dog: physical games, games with toys, and mental games. When you play with your dog, it's important to play in a way that doesn't undermine your dog's training or your relationship with him. The way to do that is to control the games, both what games you play and how you play them.

Playing with Toys

Toys are necessary for some of the games you play with your dog, like fetch and tug of war, and provide your dog with legal outlets for some of his natural hunting behaviors. But whose toys are they, and what toys should you use for which games?

Some toys you use to play with your dog will be your toys, available to your dog only when you bring them out for a game. The toys you use to engage your dog in games of tug-of-war and fetch are examples of toys that belong to you, not your dog. Other toys are your dog's, and available to him to play with all the time, with or without you. Plush toys, interactive-puzzle toys, and chew toys are your dog's to play with as he pleases.

ALERT!

Many dogs and people love to play Frisbee, but veterinarians see a lot of injuries from playing with the wrong type or in the wrong way. Only play with soft, flexible flying discs, and keep throws low enough for your dog to catch without jumping or twisting.

The types of toys you choose for your dog and yourself really depend on your dog, his playing and chewing style and strength, and what he likes. Don't let your dog take and make toys out of your stuff, even if the items are old or unwanted. If you didn't give it to him, it's not his! Using old shoes and socks or discarded kid's toys as dog toys is almost never a good idea, as it will be difficult for your dog to figure out which shoe is legal to chew on and which isn't. Every dog is different, so you may have to do a little experimentation to see what kind of toys work best for you and your dog. Suggestions for tug and fetch toys are in the sections later in this chapter for those games.

Don't keep all of your dog's toys available to him all the time. Like kids, many dogs will pull out everything they own and still not be able to figure out what to play with. To keep your dog interested in his toys, keep a few—three or four—available all the time, and rotate them once or twice a week. New stuff is so much more fun than the stuff you see every day!

Starting and Ending the Game

All of the games you play with your dog should start when you want them to, not when she shows up and shoves a toy at you. If you do want to play when your dog wants to, great, but have her do a few simple tasks for you first—a few position changes or a brief stay is fine—then engage her in the game of your choice. Better than waiting for your dog to ask you to play is surprising her with a game at a random time, or even in the middle of a training session. Whipping out a toy for a quick game of tug during heeling or recall training is a great way to keep your dog motivated and focused. Interrupting games with a brief training session, even if it's just one repetition of one behavior, is another way to very subtly but powerfully teach your dog to reliably respond to your commands.

How and when you end games is important, too. You always want to end games when your dog still wants to play—in other words, leave her wanting more every time. Decide on some way to let your dog know you're done playing. Simply putting the toy away (if you're using one for the type of game you're playing) and holding up your empty hands with a verbal "All done" or "That's it" works nicely. Ignore any attempts by your dog to goad you into continuing the game once you've decided it's over. If your dog is already in the habit of controlling the games, you may have to be patient while you wait for her to give up pestering you to play, but she will figure it out if you don't give in to her demands, providing her with yet more evidence that you're the leader.

Playing by the Rules

Rules are an important part of every game, including the ones you'll play with your dog. If your dog doesn't play by your rules, whatever they are, then he doesn't get to play. That being said, disciplining yourself not to continue playing when your dog breaks a rule is probably the hardest part.

Making the Rules

Each game you play will have some basic rules. When excited, some dogs have a tendency to lose self-control and get completely hysterical. Rules aren't there to keep you or your dog from having fun; they're there to keep the fun safe. The rules can be as simple, like, "if a tooth touches human skin, game over" (in fact, that's a good rule to apply to every game you play with your dog). Or, your rules can be more formal, like "fetch toys have to be delivered to the hand, and not dropped until they're asked for." How simple or elaborate you want the rules of your games to be is up to you, but they should all ultimately include rules that promote safety and deference to people.

Sticking to the Rules

Whatever your rules are, one thing is for sure: if you don't stick to them, neither will your dog. Inconsistency is always the enemy of dog training, so be clear with your dog about whether the behavior he exhibits during play should be rewarded by continuing the game or punished by ending it. Particularly if you choose to play physical or wrestling-type games with your dog, you need to draw clear, consistent boundaries about just how physical your dog is allowed to get, and that level of physicality has to be acceptable to everybody who plays with him. If your dog plays with small kids or elderly people, but also with teenagers, what the kids and elderly can tolerate has to be the limit all the time, even with the teenagers. People that can't play by your rules can't play with your dog, period.

Fetch

The ultimate game of cooperation, fetch (or retrieving) is a terrific way to both build cooperation and wear your dog out. Some dogs are natural retrievers, but most dogs with even a slight interest in toys can be taught to enjoy retrieving.

For dogs that are obsessed with retrieving, there are several toys on the market, the Chuck-it, for example, designed to greatly increase the distance of the throw. These involve low effort for you, and great exercise for your dog!

The Two-toys Game

The two-toys game is a great way to get your dog started retrieving. As you've no doubt already guessed, you'll need two toys to play. These toys are yours, so they are not available to your dog to play with all the time. The toys you use should be identical, like tennis balls, or short lengths of rubber hose (you can get pieces of rubber hose cut at most auto-supply or home-improvement stores), but it really doesn't matter what you use as long as you have two of them and your dog can be enticed to pick them up. The beauty of this game is that by its very nature, it encourages your dog to come back and give up the toy right from the beginning, with no begging, pleading, or chasing required.

To start, take your dog to a fairly open area, at least 20 feet across. Stand in the middle of the area, and get your dog interested in one of the toys by teasing her with it, throwing it in the air and catching it a few times, or squeaking it if it has a squeaker. When she's excited about the toy, throw it a short distance—5 feet or so—to one side. As soon as she picks up the toy, start playing with the second one. Keep playing with it until your dog drops the first one, then toss the second toy in the opposite direction, again, just a short distance for now. As she's on her way to pick up the second toy, pick up the first one. Repeat the process a few times, gradually increasing the distance of the throw.

It is very important during the early stages of playing this game that you quit each retrieve session while your dog is still very enthusiastically retrieving the toy, even if that means quitting after just a few repetitions. You can increase the number of retrieves as she builds desire for the game, along with introducing the fetch command as soon as she's regularly picking up and returning with the toy. As her retrieving skills improve and become reliable, challenge her by having her sit and wait while you throw the toy, and then release her to fetch it. You might also raise your criteria for reward (in this case, throwing the toy again) by teaching your dog to bring the toy to you by sitting in front of you with it and waiting until you ask for it, or by delivering it to your hand, rather than dropping it at your feet.

If you're planning on doing obedience competition with your dog, it's a good idea to work with an experienced instructor to help you teach your dog a correct competition-style retrieve. It's always wise to teach your dog how to do it correctly from the beginning, rather than trying to undo old habits.

Working with the Non-retriever

Even dogs that don't retrieve naturally can usually be taught to enjoy the game. There are several of ways to go about teaching the non-retriever to fetch. If your dog has any interest in toys at all, figure out what kind of toys are his favorites, remove them from his environment, and put them somewhere where he can't get them. This is just a temporary measure to build motivation; he'll get his toys back. You are going to play the two-toys game, so make sure you have two of his favorite toy, even if you have to buy two new ones. Bring one of the toys you'll use for retrieving out and play with it by yourself, squeaking it, and then tossing it in the air or between family members. Show it to your dog, entice him to follow it, and whip it away before he has a chance to grab it. Put the toy away. Repeat a couple of times a day for several days, never letting your dog actually take the toy. When you can predict that he'll be excited to see the toy, get him all worked up, then toss one of the toys a couple of feet away, and do just one repetition with the second toy the first time (get the second toy back with an exchange for a treat if necessary). Each day, add distance and repetition until he's reliably fetching.

If your dog doesn't care about toys, you can shape a retrieve using your CR, treats, or both to mark and reward tiny steps toward the finished retrieve. Make sure each step is solid and on a variable reinforcement schedule (your dog will perform each step several times for one CR/treat) before raising your criteria for reward. You might break down the shaped retrieve into the following steps:

- Looking at the retrieve object.
- Nosing it.
- Mouthing or licking it.
- Gripping it.
- Holding it (you can teach your dog to hold until you ask for the object at this point if you want).
- Picking it up from floor.
- Chasing and picking it up from a short toss.
- Returning with it.
- Adding distance.

Depending on your dog, you might add or delete steps. Be patient; it may take several weeks of consistent work to teach your dog to retrieve.

Tug of War

There is quite a bit of controversy over whether or not playing tug games with your dog is a good idea. For the average dog, teaching her to play tug by the rules is a great way to let her have fun, in addition to giving you exquisite control of her mouth. For many dogs, tug is so reinforcing that it can be used to reward other behaviors. In addition, tug games can help build confidence in shy dogs if you let your dog "win" (end up with the toy) often.

Who Should Play Tug Games

Most dogs are good candidates for playing tug games, provided, of course, that the games are started, played, and ended appropriately. Dogs that have ever threatened or bitten people should not play tug games unless they are under the instruction and supervision of a qualified professional trainer as part of a training or behavior-modification program. For safety, dogs should not play tug games with small children or other people who are easily overpowered.

FACT

Many dogs growl when they play tug games. Don't panic! As long as your dog doesn't growl at you or threaten you in other situations, he's probably not threatening you during play. In fact, growling is a normal part of playing for many dogs.

Playing Tug Games Properly

A person should always instigate tug games, not a dog. When you invite your dog to play a game of tug, it's a good idea to use a specific toy designed for that purpose. The best tug toys are made of cotton rope or rubber, and have handles built into them. Do not let your dog talk you into playing tug with old socks or towels, although if you're willing to sacrifice his plush toys to play tug, that's perfectly acceptable. As long as it's you (or another person) who invites your dog to pull, not your dog who presents a toy and then starts pulling when you put your hand on it, you're doing fine. If your dog does try to get you to play tug by pulling when you put your hand on a toy, simply release the toy as soon as you feel any tension on it.

To start a game, bring out one of your tug toys. Like fetch toys, tug toys are yours; bring them out when you want to play, and put them away when you're done. Tease your dog with the toy until he grabs it and starts pulling. Hold on and pull back, shaking the toy slightly up and down or side to side. Insert your tug command (whatever you want to call it—try "pull it" or "tug"), several times, along with praise for a tug well done. When your dog is really into the pull, slip a treat right under his nose, and give your "drop it"

Kennedy and German shepherd Addie play tug by the rules.

Addie drops the toy, sits, and gives eye contact immediately when asked…

So she can play some more!

command. When your dog opens his mouth for the treat, put the toy under your arm or behind your back for a moment, then present it again to continue the game. Before long, you won't need a treat to get your dog to drop it, and you can use the continuation of the game as his reward for giving you the toy when you ask for it. Like every other command, your dog should instantly release the toy on the first command. If he doesn't, let go of the toy and walk away. During the game, if your dog moves up the toy and his mouth touches your hand, stop the game immediately with a loud "ouch" and walk away. When you're ready to quit the game, ask for the toy, and reward your dog with something: a treat, another toy, or whatever your dog likes. If your dog likes to retrieve, you can play with a combination of fetches and tug sessions for variety.

Physical Games, Mental Games

The more time you spend with your dog, the more ways you'll find to play with her. Some games will be discovered, and some invented. Some of the games will be physical, while others will be mental. Some of the best games combine physical and mental play to keep your dog engaged and productively occupied.

Physical Games

Physical games occupy your dog's body and include the standards, like fetch and tug-of-war, but the fun doesn't stop there. Depending on the temperament, size, and energy level of your dog, you might play modified wrestling, keep-away, or tag games with your dog. Remember, you make the rules of the games, so be sure to stop the fun before things get out of hand if and when your dog tests the boundaries of acceptable play.

Mental Games

Mental games, like find it require your dog to exercise his brain, which is often more tiring than physical exercise. Don't just play find it games with treats; use toys and people (who doesn't love a good round of hide and seek?) for extra fun. Hide the object of the game in successively harder or more unusual locations. Teach your dog to find specific toys by name. Briefly interrupt games with a random obedience command, releasing him the moment he complies with a continuation of the game. Not only does it make training part of the fun, it increases the speed at which your dog responds, so he can continue his game.

Playing with Other Dogs

Playing with other dogs is great exercise, along with being important for your dog socially. But not every dog is a potential playmate for yours, even if it's a nice dog that plays well with other dogs.

Finding Suitable Playmates

Finding suitable playmates for your dog isn't always as easy as it sounds. It's not so much a size issue as it is a playing-style issue. Dogs, like people, have different playing styles. Some are very physical, wrestling, play-biting, mounting, etc., while others prefer tag-type games in which the dogs alternate chasing each other, with or without any physical contact. Some dogs play well with other dogs by using toys, playing tug of war or keep away. But for others, toys are something to be protected from other dogs, not shared with them. Sometimes you can find good playmates at dog parks, but you are often just as likely to run across dogs that shouldn't be at the dog park at all, let alone off leash and interacting with your precious companion. Many training centers and some pet boutiques offer supervised play sessions that allow your dog to socialize and play in a relatively safe and controlled setting.

Your Job

Your job during doggie play dates is pretty simple. For the most part, all you have to do is to stay out of the way so you don't get knocked down in the foolishness. Don't be surprised if the dogs' play involves a lot of growling and barking. In fact, usually the more noise you hear, the less there is to worry about.

Dogs are great for at least one thing: observing how dogs behave with each other. Go to the park without your dog, and watch until you can recognize specific postures, facial expressions, and vocalizations and predict how other dogs are likely to respond to them. Watching dogs play is both entertaining and educational!

Reading dogs' communication is easy with practice. You'll see dogs communicate with each other (and with you, if you pay attention) constantly, with a variety of body postures, facial expressions, and vocalizations. See if you can figure out what the dogs are "saying" to each other. Is it "Will you play?" or "Get away from me!"?

Speaking Dog

If you watch dogs interact, you'll notice an almost ritualistic array of physical communication. Some behaviors are displayed to calm or defer to whomever the communication is aimed toward. Other displays indicate an alert, assertive frame of mind, or even an invitation to play.

Facial Expressions

Dogs have an array of facial expressions. A relaxed and happy dog will look that way; his eyes will be soft, his ears will be relaxed, and he'll often be panting and almost seem to be smiling. A frightened dog, on the other hand, may not make direct eye contact with you. His head will often be lowered or turned away or he will keep glancing away, showing you the white of his eye. An assertive, alert dog will have an expression of alertness, and everything on his face will be forward: his ears, his attention, even his whiskers.

ESSENTIAL

Dogs' eyes really are windows into what their emotional states are. A fearful or assertive dog ready to bite will usually have dilated pupils, show you a "whale eye" (the white rim around the eye), and may look at the exact spot they intend to bite before doing so. A happy dog has a soft eye expression, while a dog seeking to appease someone will often squint.

Watch dogs' faces. Like us, they use every part—eyes, ears, and mouth— to nonverbally express their state of mind. Even their lips speak volumes without a word: Are the teeth covered or exposed? Are the lips relaxed or tight with anxiety or determination? Are the ears pricked forward alertly, relaxed, or pinned tightly to the head in a display of fear or submission?

Shape Shifting

Dogs use their bodies to communicate, too. From their shoulders, to their toes, to their tails, every part tells a story. Piloerection, or raising the hackles, doesn't necessarily indicate aggression. It often signals alertness, and sometimes even uncertainty or fear (especially if the hackles are raised from withers to tail). A dog that stands squarely on his feet with his head and tail in relaxed positions is calm, while a dog that stands high on his toes with everything—ears, head, and tail—raised and rigid is on alert. A frightened or submissive dog will literally shrink away, with a lowered head and tail, in an attempt to appear as small and unthreatening as possible.

FACT

Because of selective breeding for specific physical traits, like prick ears or tails that curl over the back, some dogs may have a little trouble giving or recognizing normal dog communications.

Greeting Rituals

How dogs initially greet each other often indicates whether or not they will get along, play, or ignore each other. Dogs that want to get along don't face each other straight on; they approach from an angle or from the side. Eye contact will be brief. They'll probably spend some time sniffing each other pretty thoroughly. Depending on the dogs involved, there may be some attempts at pawing or humping by one or both dogs. An elbows-on-the-ground, butt-in-the-air posture is a classic "Let's play!" pose, while a dog that stands tall, freezes, and gives direct and sustained eye contact is often saying "Don't mess with me." This last signal, combined with a very low growl and perhaps a lip curl, can indicate an imminent attack. Dogs that know each other well, or who are confident and well socialized, will often mimic some of the more assertive gestures in an attempt to get their counterparts to play, but the difference in expression is obvious to careful observers.

Calming Gestures

Dogs have quite a few ways of trying to diffuse aggression or hostility. They will often yawn, lick their nose, sniff the ground, or turn their heads as a way of saying "I mean you no harm, and I want no conflict." They may move in an arc, in slow motion, or turn away completely as they attempt to both exude and instill calm and peace. Some dogs may even freeze in a sit or down to avoid inciting the aggressive advances of another. Watch your dog to see what calming gestures she offers when interacting with other dogs and with you.

Chapter 19

Fun Stuff to Do with Your Dog

You got a dog to be a companion, friend, and playmate, right? Well, now that you have a well-behaved dog (or at least you're well on your way), it's time to get out there and have a good time with him. There are tons of things you can do to both have fun and enhance your relationship. From hiking and swimming to formal, competitive dog sports, you're sure to find something that suits both of your fancies!

Training Classes

Practically every dog and owner team can benefit from taking a few obedience classes together. They allow you to work your dog under distraction, and some schools offer a variety of activities that can help you keep your dog's energy and intelligence directed in a positive way—and you get to socialize with other people who love dogs, too.

What Classes to Take

Depending on your dog's skill level and the school's policies, you might want to start with the school's basic class. Be honest about your dog's level of training if the instructor asks so she can help you get into the right class. Plus, it never hurts to reinforce the basics in a new environment. If your dog's skill level is obviously already beyond the basics, most instructors will be happy to move you into a more advanced class.

Depending on your interests and the school's offerings, you might take advanced classes, therapy-dog classes, agility (competition style or just for fun), rally, or competitive obedience classes. Some schools even offer field trips for a real-world training experience. You may have a choice of private lessons, group classes offered from independent dog trainers with their own schools, community-education classes, and offerings by local kennel clubs, so you may need to do a bit of research to find which offers the best match for your goals and learning style.

Choosing a Training Center

There are several ways to find a trainer or school. Of course, you can always start with an Internet or Yellow Pages search, but don't stop there. Ask friends, neighbors, vets, groomers, dog walkers, and even the local shelter whom they recommend. Once you have a few names, make some calls. Is the trainer respectful of you, or dismissive? Do they seem to care about you and your dog, or do they just want to give you a sales pitch?

One of the best ways to make your final decision is to ask if you can observe a training session or class. If the trainer won't discuss their methods and doesn't want you to see how they train, keep looking. When you do watch a class, are you comfortable with the student/ teacher ratio? Does the trainer seem to be in control of the class? Does she seem to like dogs and their owners? Are her explanations of exercises understandable? Do the people and dogs seem to be getting the individual help they need? The dogs may not be well behaved (that's why they're there), but does the instructor handle them well? Most importantly, are you comfortable with the methods used? When you find a place you like, sign up and enjoy the quality time with your dog.

Traveling with Your Dog

If you're one of millions of people who travel with your dog, you'll not only want to travel safely, but you'll also want to make your trips as pleasurable for yourself and your canine companion as possible. Along with being fun and exciting, being away from home can also be stressful, but there are some simple steps you can take to make your trips enjoyable and relaxing.

If possible, bring several days' supply of water from home, along with your dog's food to minimize the possibility of digestive upset. If your dog does have a bit of loose stool from dietary change or stress, a spoonful of canned solid pumpkin (not pie filling) added to a couple of meals will usually firm the stool up quickly, with no negative side effects.

Traveling Safely

Your first consideration when traveling with your dog is safety. If you are going to travel by car, your dog will need to be safely restrained for the ride. Think it looks cute to see a little dog riding on the driver's lap, with the dog's front feet on the door, ears blowing in the breeze? Every year, hundreds of dogs are injured or killed when they are thrown out of the open windows they're half hanging out of, sometimes with their owners still holding the leash. Your dog should not ride sitting on someone's lap, and especially not in the front seat, where he's not just a potential distraction or hazard for the driver; he's also a potential projectile in an accident or during sudden braking or turning. The safest way for your dog to ride in the car is in a crate, but a seat belt is the next best thing.

If you are flying with your dog, or you are crossing state or international borders, your dog will need a health certificate from your vet before your trip. You will also want to make sure you bring a copy of your dog's rabies vaccination and license certificates, and prescriptions for any medications your pet is on, just in case. No matter how you travel, you'll want to make sure your dog is always wearing a well-fitting collar

Shepherd mix Ralph is strapped in and ready to go for a ride!

(that he can't slip out of) and is always leashed in unfenced areas. You can use a longline or retractable leash to give him some room to stretch his legs, but even trained dogs shouldn't be off leash in unfamiliar or unsafe (highway rest stops come to mind) areas.

ALERT!

A dog lost in unfamiliar surroundings might never be recovered. A properly fitting collar, with your current phone number (cell is often best), along with permanent identification like a microchip, can help your lost dog find his way home. If your dog is chipped, add the phrase "ID by microchip" to the tag instead of your address.

Flying with your dog can be nerve-racking, particularly if your dog is too big to fly in the cabin with you. You can breathe a little easier if your dog is small enough to fit in one of the widely available under-seat carriers. Whether your dog is able to fly in the cabin or not, it is not recommended to tranquilize your dog prior to flying. It depresses the respiratory system, and your dog needs to be able to pant to help regulate his body temperature. Most airlines will not fly animals in extreme weather conditions, so make your travel plans accordingly. If your dog does end up flying down below, there's nothing wrong with waiting until you're absolutely sure your dog is on the plane before you board. You should also always try to get nonstop flights when traveling with your dog, but if you must change planes, make sure that your dog makes it on the next leg of the flight with you before the plane takes off. The large majority of dogs make it to their destinations just fine, but it never hurts to make sure your precious cargo is okay.

There are several Web sites that specialize in travel with pets. Check out ✍www.petswelcome.com, ✍www.petfriendlytravel.com, ✍www.dogfriendly.com, ✍www.tripswithpets.com, and ✍www.travelpets.com for all kinds of info on traveling with your dog, including destinations, lodging, and travel tips.

Pet-friendly Destinations

Maybe you're lucky and have access to pet-friendly destinations already, but if you're creative, you can find a variety of travel and vacation options to meet practically any interest and budget. For outdoorsy types, camping is fun, and leashed dogs are welcome at many privately owned campgrounds, as well as at some state and national parks. If you're not into the idea of roughing it, pet-friendly lodging is available in every variety, from the most basic motor lodges, to intimate bed-and-breakfasts, to the most cosmopolitan hotels in large cities. If you're determined to bring your dog with you on vacation, do you have a plan for what your dog will do when you're visiting local attractions? Some of the larger hotels offer dog-walking services, but you may want to arrange for day care in the area if you're going someplace your dog isn't allowed.

Outdoor Activities

Outdoor activities that you can enjoy with your dog abound. Depending on the energy and fitness level of your dog, and his individual proclivities, outdoor fun might include simple backyard games like Frisbee, swimming, or hiking, but could also include more exotic activities, like skijoring (see the info on skijoring later in this chapter).

The Casual Sportsman

Hiking, camping, and backpacking are wonderful ways to spend time with your dog, get exercise, and enjoy nature. Leave the cell phone and laptop at home, and take your dog on a hike or even an overnight backpacking/ camping trip. Even the most pampered couch potato enjoys getting out and acting like a dog now and then. Swimming or a run on the beach, maybe combined with some water retrieves or a good game of Frisbee, can help keep your dog happy, not to mention well-exercised, and therefore calm and well behaved at home.

Summer Camp

In the past several years, the idea of vacationing/camping/dog training has really caught on, leading to the development of several camps that are geared to dogs and their owners. From basic activities to competition camps, you can find one to suit your fancy at *www.dogplay.com*.

Basically, if your dog is allowed to be there, why not include him in the fun? Sure, you'll probably have to do a little extra management and training in new situations at first. But any of the training you do reinforces all of the other training you've done, and before you know it, you have a dog that is trained everywhere.

Something Extra

Some dogs have all the luck! They get to accompany their owners, and in some cases, work for them (most dogs' dream) on a regular basis. Skijoring, or snow skiing while your dog, in harness, pulls you, is gaining popularity, as are road trials, particularly for Dalmatian fanciers, in which horse-rider-dog teams compete in endurance events. Mushing or sled-dog racing isn't just for huskies anymore—there has been at least one team made up entirely of standard poodles.

Be creative. What are your interests? How can you involve your dog in them? If you own a purebred dog, what was he bred to do? Maybe you'll even find a new hobby. Most people who compete in dog sports started out as just dog owners who wanted a well-behaved pet, but got bitten by the competition bug when they were exposed to the variety of venues and types of competition available.

Pet-assisted Therapy

Pet-assisted therapy has become more popular in recent years. There are a variety of types of pet-assisted therapy and venues in which to pursue it. In some facilities, therapy work is primarily an entertainment source and stress reliever for the patients, but in others patients are put to work in some fash ion with the dogs. It is a commitment of time and emotional and physical energy to pursue therapy work with your dog, but the reward of helping others is its own payback.

FACT

There are several organizations that test and certify therapy dogs. The Delta Society is probably the largest and most well known, followed by Therapy Dogs, Inc., and Therapy Dogs International, among others. Do your research, and decide which group's policies, tests, and guidelines are the best fit for you and your dog's capabilities.

The Right Dog for the Right Job

If you want to do therapy work with your dog, you're going to need to do a little more than basic training. Depending on your dog's energy level and personality, you may choose to engage in some therapy activities and avoid others. Some common forms of therapy include companion entertainment, motor-skill development, and reading assistance. In the first type, dogs are used primarily to help people feel better by virtue of their presence as something to pet, hug, and kiss. They may also provide entertainment by performing tricks or obedience skills, or by arriving at the facility dressed up in costumes. Some types of therapy involve the patient brushing or walking the dog, or throwing a toy for the dog to retrieve. One of the newest variations has kids with learning disabilities reading aloud to their nonjudgmental canine therapists.

The Down Side

As rewarding as therapy work is, it does have some potential drawbacks to consider before getting involved. The first is to remember that it is a commitment of at least several hours at least once a month. People are counting on you to show up; you can't just do it when you feel like it. It's not just showing up, letting some infirm people pet your dog, and going home. You have to keep up with your dog's training, and ideally continue teaching her new things so she's both comfortable and comforting. You'll have to bathe your dog and clip and file her nails before each visit.

The biggest toll to doing therapy work is often an emotional one. Therapy work can be extremely stressful and sad for both you and your dog. Being realistic with yourself about what you can handle and what your dog will both be good at and enjoy is an important step in guiding you to the right type of therapy work to pursue. While you're being realistic, be realistic about your dog. Some dogs just aren't cut out to be therapy dogs. Of course, safety—of the patients, your dog, and yourself—always has to be the first priority. And don't forget that you're doing this as an activity to enjoy. A dog that is shy or afraid of strangers isn't going to enjoy the experience, no matter how well trained she is, so you may have to consider other outlets for your philanthropic efforts if therapy work isn't right for your dog.

Competitive Performance Sports

For every type of person and dog, there is a type of competition to suit their interests. Some are popular, like the conformation show the Westminster Kennel Club puts on every year that is nationally televised. Others are more obscure, although just as well loved by their devotees. There are two basic types of competitive events for dogs; the first showcases the dog's beauty, grace and precision teamwork, and the second, while still often requiring teamwork, is often a stunning display of skill, training, athletic prowess or some combination.

The Showman

Conformation events are often considered to be nothing more than beauty pageants, but their real purpose is to identify the dogs that most closely represent their breed standard. In fact, ideally, the dogs aren't really so much competing with each other as they are with the judge's mental picture of perfection for the breed. Other events, like obedience, rally, and freestyle, showcase an owner's commitment to an exceptional relationship and teamwork with their dog. A well-trained and synchronized team is a thing of beauty to watch. The "Showman" events include:

Conformation: As mentioned previously, dogs compete against the breed standard for points toward a breed championship. How the dog is presented (groomed) and handled has a huge impact on the success of a show career.

Obedience: Also as mentioned earlier, obedience titles are earned by successfully completing the required parts of all of the exercises in the Novice, Open, or Utility classes multiple times with a minimum score of 170 out of 200. Scores are based on precision and accuracy. Titles include the Companion Dog, Companion Dog Excellent, Utility Dog, Utility Dog Excellent, and Obedience Trial Champion.

Rally Obedience: The newest competitive dog sport, rally is less formal and a nice bridge between pet dog training and traditional competition obedience. Rally has owner-dog teams follow a preset course of signs with both stationary and moving exercises.

Freestyle: Quite literally, freestyle is dancing with dogs. Owners choreograph elaborate routines to music, in which dogs move in synch with, and in contrast to, their owners.

While the "showman" events do require training, and a great deal of it at the advanced levels, they don't require dogs to be particularly athletic to participate in them at a winning level.

The Athlete

The second type of canine performance activities utilize or showcase a dog's natural abilities, which have been directed and honed to perfection by their owners. Although all dogs can compete in these events, they do favor the more naturally athletic breeds or individuals. They include:

Agility: High speed balanced with precision, agility is fun and exciting to watch and compete in. With too many available titles to list, agility competition is offered by several organizations. Dogs qualify by completing an obstacle course within the allowed amount of time, and depending on the class, few or no mistakes, like dropped bars on jumps.

Flyball: Fun and usually loud, flyball is a relay race of sorts, with teams of four dogs negotiating four jumps, jumping on a box that launches a ball for them to catch and return over the jumps so the next dog can go.

JoAnn and Havanese Mickey enjoy agility training.

Tracking: Tracking dogs must follow a human scent trail that is often several hours old and indicate articles left by the person who laid the track. The age, distance and terrain depend on the title being pursued—Tracking Dog, Tracking Dog Excellent, Variable Surface Tracker, and Tracking Champion.

Schutzhund and French Ring Sport: These sports are designed as tests of the working dog. Schutzhund has three phases: tracking, obedience, and protection. French Ring forgoes tracking for agility. They are both great, if misunderstood, activities for the high-drive dog and committed owner.

ALERT!

Because of the bitework involved, Schutzhund and French Ring Sport are suitable pastimes only for responsible people with very stable dogs. This is not the sport for the out-of-control biter that terrorizes the neighborhood. It is absolutely imperative that you get qualified instruction before undertaking any bite or protection training with your dog.

No matter what type of activity you want to pursue with your dog, plan on spending a good bit of time practicing to meet your goals. Your goals may be "just" to get that title, or you may want to strive for perfection and national rankings. Like any game, learn the rules before you play. It is a good idea to find a local group—either a club or private trainer—with similar interests to guide you. In addition to the activities mentioned earlier that are open to essentially all breeds, there are others that are breed or group specific.

Breed-specific Activities

In the AKC, the largest registry in the USA, breeds are split into groups based on their purposes. Many of the groups and some individual breeds have competitions or titling events. Unlike the types of competition listed earlier, open to essentially all breeds (including mixed breeds, depending on the registry the club offering the event is affiliated with), these events are open specifically to the breeds that would historically do the jobs the events mimic.

FACT

Every dog is eligible, and in fact, encouraged, to do the training necessary to earn the AKC's Canine Good Citizen certificate. The CGC program stresses responsible dog ownership and basic manners. The ten-part CGC test is also used as the partial model for many therapy-dog tests. Testing is available at locations around the country throughout the year. Visit *www.akc.org/events/cgc/* for more info.

Find Out What Your Dog Was Bred to Do

Nothing is more satisfying for most dogs than doing what they were bred to do, whether it's hunting, herding, or ridding the farm of vermin.

Breed-Specific Activities:
- **Herding:** In addition to the traditional herding breeds like Border collies, German shepherds, and Shetland sheepdogs, flock drivers, like rottweilers, Samoyeds, and Greater Swiss Mountain Dogs may also participate.
- **Field trials:** There are several different types of field trials, separated by type. There are pointing breed trials, retrieving breed trials, and spaniel or "flushing" breed trials, as well as individual trials for the various scent hounds, like coonhounds, basset hounds, and beagles. Hunt tests are another type of field trial open to multiple hunting breeds.
- **Earth Dog Trials:** Go to ground! These tests are open to terriers and dachshunds and are designed to test and preserve the instincts of the original critter getters. Dogs must crawl underground through a tunnel and go after vermin with enthusiasm.
- **Lure Coursing:** Open to the sight hounds, like Afghan hounds, borzois, and salukis, these events test the dogs' ability to hunt by sight by following a fast-moving lure around a 600- to –800-yard course.

- **Working Dog Titles:** Offered by many breed clubs, working tests demonstrate that a dog can perform (or at least has the instinct to perform) the job for which he was bred. Ranging from water rescue work titles for Newfoundlands and Portuguese water dogs, to carting and weight pulling for the draft breeds like Bernese mountain dogs, many breed clubs offer opportunities to earn working certificates.

What to Do If Your Dog Didn't Read the Book

Sometimes, two great musicians can produce a tone-deaf child. And so it is with dogs. Maybe your golden retriever isn't a natural swimmer or retriever, but he loves lure coursing. And maybe your pug seems to be a typical Labrador reincarnated, swimming and retrieving with the best of them. Or perhaps you have a mixed breed or a breed that isn't recognized for competition by the major show-licensing registries. Just because your dog can't compete in the activity, doesn't mean you can't train for it and pursue it for fun and that your dog won't enjoy it, even she isn't eligible for a title. A Shih Tzu going to ground like a terrier? Why not?

With the variety of activities to suit literally every interest and commitment level, there's really no excuse not to get out and do something with your dog.

Canine Good Citizen test #8: reaction to another dog. Cairn terrier Duncan and shepherd mix Ralph pass with flying colors!

Trick Training

Trick training is more than teaching your dog cute behaviors. Like all training, trick training helps your relationship with your dog, improves your timing, and reinforces your dog's other training. And if you do therapy work with your dog, your audience is likely to be very appreciative of even the simplest tricks.

Capture It

Shaping is the primary method you'll use to teach your dog most tricks, although you'll combine it with some luring and modeling as well. But there are some behaviors that your dog already offers; you just have to get them on cue. Behaviors that you can "capture" and then name include barking, sneezing, yawning, and pawing. Anything that your dog does that you want him to do again is something that you can mark with your CR (say "Yes!," click, and so on) and reward. Your CR will have to be well established for your dog to realize that you're marking something he's done. Remember, the CR bridges the gap between what your dog did and the treat, so make sure you follow your CR with a treat to build behaviors quickly. Don't name a captured behavior until your dog is predictably offering it, expecting it to be marked and rewarded. Once you have stimulus control of the behavior (your dog will do it when you say it), don't mark or reward it if your dog offers it without being asked.

ALERT!

When you ignore your dog for offering behaviors you didn't ask for, be prepared for him to go through what is known as an extinction burst, which means he'll try harder before he gives up. Think about the last time you were waiting for an elevator and it didn't come as quickly as you expected, or at all. Did you press the button again, maybe several times, rapidly? After a while, you either waited, or took the stairs. That button –pressing frenzy is an extinction burst.

Make It Happen

For some tricks, you'll need to aid your dog in some way to get the trick to happen. You can use food lures to easily teach your dog to crawl, roll over, sit pretty, dance, and spin to the left and right. Remember to keep lures close to your dog's nose and only move them at the speed she's following. If you need to, break up the finished behavior into small segments for CR/reward, then raise the criteria for reward until the behavior is complete.

For example, to teach your dog to roll over using a food lure, you would start with your dog in a down position. Lure from your dog's nose, to the floor, and then to her side next to the last rib. Move the lure up the rib, toward the spine. Some dogs will lie flat on their sides without help at his point; others need a little pressure on the shoulder to help. If you want you can stop and name (side, bang, play dead) this part of the behavior before proceeding. Continue luring around to the other side until your dog is belly up. Again, you can name this separately. Continue the lure until your dog is all the way over. This is not a trick to force; it's not easy for some dogs, and can even be painful for dogs with back problems. Make sure your dog is completely relaxed and comfortable at each stage of the behavior before proceeding to the next step. If you're going to name each part of the behavior, only work on one named part per training session.

You can also use physical aids to help behaviors happen. Physical aids can include barriers for your dog to crawl under, or to help him learn to back up in a straight line. You might also use targets to teach your dog to go to, touch, mouth, paw, sit, or lie on very specific places or objects. You might even use a physical aid to get your dog to bark, by knocking on a wall or ringing the doorbell. And there's nothing wrong with giving your dog a little help by physically positioning him so you have something to reward. This could be as simple as picking up his foot and placing it in your other hand to teach him to "shake" if you can't get him to offer it on his own.

Chapter 20

Dogs Will Be Dogs: A Troubleshooting Guide

Even the best dogs can sometimes have behavior issues that need to be addressed. Some behavior problems are problems only in the owner's mind, because their dog is exhibiting a behavior like scavenging for food that, while normal for dogs, is unacceptable in human households. Other problems, like separation anxiety, are more psychological than behavioral, but the damage resulting from them is just as troublesome, if not more so. Treating behavior problems requires consistency, good management, and patience.

When Good Dogs Act Bad

Even the best dogs make occasional mistakes, or have momentary lapses in judgment. Sometimes their mistakes stem from following their natural instincts, but just as often, misbehavior has been reinforced in some way.

Nature or Nurture?

Dogs are naturally curious and thoroughly explore their surroundings, usually with their noses first, but also by sight. When something interesting appears on their sensory radar, their natural impulse is to investigate. Depending on the immediate result of the investigation, they learn to either repeat or avoid similar situations in the future. Certain behaviors, especially those that might result in the dog getting something tasty to eat, like trash raiding and counter surfing, are especially problematic, because it only takes one success for the dog to try again and again. Since random reinforcement is the most effective way to keep a behavior strong, your dog doesn't have to find something good very often to encourage him to keep trying.

Some dogs find certain behaviors, barking, for instance, self-reinforcing, meaning they don't need an external reward to continue. The behavior itself becomes the reward. Or, your dog may be getting a reward from his behavior, but you just aren't aware of it, or understand what it is, or why your dog is rewarded by it. The reward might just be in your dog's mind because he's associated his action with something else that happened at the same time. Whether or not his behavior had any effect on the outcome in reality is irrelevant, because in his mind he caused it. Barking at the mailman, for example, is a classic case of incorrect association of behavior to consequence. The mailman comes and goes every day, but in your dog's mind, he drives the mailman away every day, and is quite pleased with himself for a job well done.

He Knows He Did Something Wrong!

Dogs have a few basic ways to relieve stress, with biting, chewing, and vocalizing high on the list. It's not surprising that those are often the first activities they turn to in times of frustration, anxiety, or boredom. What is often surprising, especially to new dog owners, is the extent to which some dogs will express themselves in these ways. After-the-fact punishments don't help because they make the dog more anxious, leading to more stress relief, followed by more anxiety... Well, you can see where this is going.

A lot of people truly believe that their dogs know they did something wrong when they chewed up the sofa cushion or raided the trash because the dog looked or acted guilty when they came home, sometimes even before the damage was discovered. The truth is, the dog knows the visible results of his binge will make you angry, but he doesn't connect the displeasure with his action unless you do. His guilty look is a way of appeasing you before you get mad. Some dogs will even do their damage to relieve their own stress over the anticipation of their owner's anger. If you insist on setting your dog up to repeat his mistakes, it's an interesting experiment to set up a video camera to see when the destruction occurs and the attitude of your dog when he does it.

Trash Raiding

Garbage digging, trash raiding, or dumpster diving—whatever you call it, it's both annoying and dangerous. If you're lucky, you'll clean up the mess and your dog will just have a mild case of diarrhea from his dietary indiscretions, but the consequences of this behavior are potentially much more serious, even fatal, if your dog is poisoned or gets an obstruction or perforation of his digestive system.

The best time to teach your dog to stay out of the trash is when he's a puppy and before he's successful the first time. Set up the booby traps described later on all the trashcans in the house before your dog manages to gobble up some goody he stole from the rubbish bin, and be the sympathetic savior when he causes his first correction.

Manage the Trash, Manage the Dog

Trash raiding really goes right to the very root of what a dog is, an opportunistic scavenger. Your dog doesn't know scavenging is wrong. In fact, to him, he's doing exactly what a smart dog should do when he stumbles across some food-—eat it—even if he's not particularly hungry. Even if there's not much to eat in the trash, there's usually something of interest, at least to a dog, to be thoroughly investigated, if not chewed, shredded, or eaten, even if it's not technically edible. If you come home one night and think there's been a snowstorm in the house, think again; it's probably just some shredded tissues from the trash.

To prevent an occasional indiscretion from turning into an obnoxious if not deadly habit, you need to be proactive about managing both the trash and the dog until you're sure he won't get into it, or you're sure that the trash is securely out of his reach. Either the trash has to be secured in a dogproof trashcan, or the trash has to be inside a cabinet (possibly with childproof latches), or maybe even locked in another room or outside if you have an especially astute problem solver.

Of course, if you're there, you can use your leave it command if you notice your dog eyeing the trash, as well as keep him crated or out of rooms containing trash cans when you're not around. Having some of your management enforcement tools, like shaker bottles or squirt guns handy is really helpful, so you can provide an unwanted consequence if he just can't keep himself from helping himself to the garbage when you're with him.

The Sky Is Falling!

Along with managing your dog and your environment, you need to take the reinforcement out of garbage-can raiding. To deter your dog from trying again in the future, you'll have to connect some big negative consequences with the act. The negative consequence has to outweigh the possibility of reward if you want it to have an impact on the frequency of the behavior. You don't want your dog's behavior to be dependent on your presence (i.e., you want him to stay out of the trash whether you're there to correct him or not), so your best bet is to devise a booby trap for your trash can. Depending on your dog's personality and his individual sensitivities, you have several options.

One booby-trap option is to make something light but noisy fall on and around your dog if she tries to take something out of the trash. Start by preparing your bait. Cook a piece of bacon on a paper towel, or a small chunk of hot dog in waxed paper in the microwave. Eat the bacon, or use the hot dog for training treats. The paper is the bait, and the dog can smell it. The next step is to prepare your trap, out of view of your dog, please. Gather 6–12 shaker bottles or aluminum cans, and tie them about 12–18 inches apart. Put them on a counter, preferably out of view, over the trashcan. Trail the string to the trashcan, and tie the bait, the paper used to cook the goodies, to the end. There should be just enough slack so the string is lying unnoticed on top of the trash. Now all you have to do is wait to hear the racket so you can "save" your poor dog and redirect her to something else. Set up similar traps around any trash can she's even thought about visiting, using different kinds of bait, so she doesn't start to think bacon and hot dogs are the source of evil!

If such measures aren't having a significant effect on her behavior in a short time, like three or four repetitions, it's time to try something else. You can set up a booby trap that will dump water on your dog for grabbing bait out of trash as an alternative to the Chicken-Little treatment. In addition, Scat Mats, which deliver a mild, static-type shock when the pet steps on them, or indoor electric fences work for many dogs, although these are more management devices than training—which is perfectly acceptable. There are some dogs who are so obsessed with food that no correction is strong enough to overcome it. In this case, management is your best option.

The Counter Surfer

Counter surfing, like trash raiding, is tough to stop once it starts because of the random reinforcement received by the surfer. Hey, some dogs just enjoy looking, and don't even need to get anything to have a good time browsing. The ones that are successful, even rarely, tend to be pretty devoted to the pastime if some serious intervention doesn't happen quickly.

Keep It Clear!

Your lunch, a tray of chocolate chip cookies, or your Thanksgiving turkey; even your sunglasses or important papers. Anything left unattended is a potential target of consumption or destruction for the determined counter or table surfer. The easiest way to curb counter surfing is obvious–don't leave attractive stuff up there unattended. Of course, you also have the option of not allowing your dog to have freedom in the rooms where he's likely to make poor choices.

You can also try making the surface unattractive for him to put his paws on. Try putting some of the clear vinyl carpet protector that is sold by the foot on a roll in home-improvement stores. Get the type that has the longer nubs on the bottom (intended so the vinyl will grip the carpet). Tape it to the countertop upside down, so the points are up. Scat Mats and sticky-side-up shelf paper or tape are other unattractive surfaces to try.

Booby Traps

In addition to booby traps similar to those described earlier in this chapter, you can also try putting shallow trays (lipped cookie sheets work great; get a bunch at the dollar store) of water on the counters. Let them hang over the edge as much as possible, so they come down easily when your dog puts a paw on them, water and all. Snappy Trainers are a safe mousetrap-type device that startles some dogs enough to deter them from counter surfing (and trash raiding).

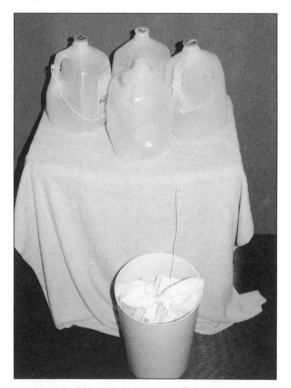

A typical booby trap set up for a trashcan

Excessive Barking

Barking is a normal part of being a dog, and some barking is to be expected. Dogs that bark excessively, however, aren't just a nuisance to their owners, but also to their neighbors.

What's All the Racket About?

There are as many reasons for excessive barking as there are barkers. Some dogs bark to warn away intruders, real or imagined. Others bark because they're bored, anxious, scared, frustrated, or excited. Some dogs, like many of the herding breeds and hounds, seem to bark just because it feels good, while terriers bark to alert you to the presence of every dog, person, squirrel, and falling leaf in the neighborhood. Many dogs have been rewarded into excessive barking by their owners, who jump at their dog's every command, whether it's "Let me in," "Let me out," "Play with me," or "Pay attention to me now!."

Lack of clear leadership contributes to many cases of excessive or uncontrollable barking. If your dog thinks that he is the ultimate protector and decision maker, he'll not only bark, he'll also ignore your requests for him to be quiet. Separation anxiety, also often owner induced, can also be a cause of troublesome barking.

Nip It in the Bud

Getting your dog to "zip it" means you need to nip barking in the bud before it gets out of control. How you control your dog's barking depends on your dog, the reason she's barking, and how persistent her barking is.

If she's alarm barking, is it reasonable? For example, is someone in your yard or at the door? If your relationship is in order, a simple "Good, girl, that's enough" may be enough to let her know that you recognize and appreciate her effort, but that you can control the situation. If your dog barks out of boredom, more exercise can help–sleeping dogs don't bark–as does controlling your dog's exposure to her barking triggers, like not leaving her alone in the yard, or closing the blinds if she barks at every jogger she sees outside.

Don't add to your dog's barking problem by rewarding barking. Unfortunately, many people teach their dogs to be persistent barkers by allowing their dogs to "win" or get their way by barking to get some reaction or attention, or to be let out of their crates, or to get you to hang up the phone, or whatever else it is they want. Even yelling at your dog to "shut up" is better than nothing, from her point of view. It can be tough to wait out a barking dog, but you either have to wait it out and reward quiet, or add a meaningful punishment.

Some people have had success controlling their dog's barking by using shaping to teach their dogs to bark (and then quiet) on command. It doesn't work for every dog, but it's worth a try, and you'll have taught your dog another cute trick, if nothing else.

Meaningful Corrections

For something to be meaningful to your dog, it has to have an almost immediate effect on the behavior. Within 3 or 4 repetitions, either the frequency or intensity has to decrease, or it's not meaningful, it's nagging.

You guessed it, you have to figure out what's meaningful for your dog, but you can try a squirt bottle (maybe with a little bit of vinegar or Bitter Apple in it for an unattractive flavor), a shaker bottle, a spritz of breath spray right in your dog's mouth, along with the word "Quiet," said firmly, not loudly. After you've connected your new quiet command with the correction that works for your dog about ten times, try the command by itself. If it works, have a party; if not, follow through with your correction. It's very important not to give your dog empty threats. He needs to know that if he didn't listen to the first command, he's going to get the correction.

If you don't have good timing, or your dog barks persistently when you're not home, you may have to consider a bark collar. There are two basic types of bark collars. The first sprays a mist of (usually) citrus-scented oil in the dog's face when he barks, and the second delivers a static shock. Some of the shock collars are self-adjusting, increasing the level of the correction if the dog continues barking. Neither of these collars works on every dog. Some dogs aren't deterred by them; some get worse (sometimes before getting better), and some are smart enough to turn their heads away from the mist as they gleefully bark away. If you choose to try a bark collar, make sure you get one that is activated by your dog's vocal cords, not by noise, so he doesn't get corrected for noise he didn't make.

QUESTION?

What about surgical debarking?
Surgical debarking should only be considered if all other options have been exhausted and the dog is in imminent danger of losing his home or his life because of excessive barking. Dogs do still make noise after debarking, which is sometimes even more annoying than the barking was.

Treating Separation Anxiety

True separation anxiety is fortunately relatively rare, but when it is diagnosed, it can be extremely difficult, and in some cases, impossible, to treat successfully. Separation anxiety often has a genetic component, but can also be caused or encouraged by poor handling, usually by babying the dog and having constant contact with him.

Preventing Separation Anxiety

Preventing separation anxiety is easy if you can discipline yourself. From the moment you bring your dog home, insist that you spend some time apart, whether you're home with her or not. If you're home, she should be in her crate or behind a baby gate for several short periods throughout the day. Only let her out if she's calm and quiet. When you're hanging out with her, don't let her have constant physical contact with you. Make her settle in her bed sometimes, and pet her when she's earned it, but dole it out in small doses. Don't let her get literally addicted to your hands on her every moment of every day.

When you leave, don't make a fuss, kissing and apologizing to her for five minutes before you go. Put her in her crate, give her a treat or stuffed Kong, say "See ya later," and be on your way with no emotion or emotional response to her protest. When you come home, completely ignore her until she's calm. This is really hard for people, because it just plain feels good that somebody is that happy to see you. When she's calm, let her out of her crate (make her wait until you release her, please), have her sit, and then pay attention to her for no more than 20 seconds, then go about your business.

Separation Anxiety or Bored and Underexercised?

Just because a dog is destructive when no one is home doesn't mean he has separation anxiety. Most destructive dogs just have too much energy and are bored, or seize the opportunity to scavenge or chew something they don't normally get the chance to when the people are home. These dogs don't have a psychological problem to solve; they just need better management.

True separation anxiety is a panic disorder, and it almost always involves barrier destruction (of door or window frames) and destruction of personal items like clothes and shoes (rather than household items like sofa cushions). Separation anxiety–afflicted dogs also often vocalize excessively and often eliminate, sometimes on the owner's property or bed. These poor dogs suffer to the point that they will mutilate and injure themselves in their panic, sometimes to escape confinement.

One of the best ways to diagnose separation anxiety is to set up a video recorder. Most of the damage in separation anxiety usually occurs in the first hour after departure, and the dog will usually be visibly panicked or frantic, often shaking, pacing, and panting. Frustrated and bored dogs appear relaxed and to be having a good old time, shaking the sofa cushions, and parading around the house with the remnants of the trash.

Treating Separation Anxiety

Treating separation anxiety often involves the use of antianxiety medications in addition to behavior modification. Medications range from prescription drugs to herbal remedies, and it may take some experimentation to discover what is most helpful to your dog.

The behavior-modification process includes desensitizing the dog to the triggers that precede departure (putting on your coat, getting your keys), getting physical distance from the dog when you're home, limiting physical contact, increasing exercise and training, and giving the dog a coping mechanism.

Many dog owners have reported success in treating separation anxiety and other panic or phobic disorders, like thunderstorm phobia, with natural remedies, including flower essence remedies and melatonin, without the negative side effects sometimes present with traditional medications.

For some dogs, it's helpful to feed them all their meals from a stuffed Kong or other food-dispensing toy. This is started with the owner present, then in another room, and finally out of the house for gradually longer periods of time. In the meantime, it's important not to allow the dog to rehearse the panicky behavior, so the services of a pet sitter or day care may be necessary.

Easing the Pain of Thunderstorm/ Fireworks Phobia

Thunderstorm and fireworks or noise phobia are similar, but slightly different disorders. The treatments, however, are virtually the same.

Can Your Dog Predict the Weather?

If your dog starts worrying and displaying nervousness–panting, shaking, pacing, trying to escape or hide–long before you hear the first rumble of thunder or see a drop of rain, your dog is probably suffering from thunderstorm phobia. If, however, the storm comes and he gets nervous only when the lightning really starts cracking, there's a good chance that he has a fear of loud noises. Some dogs are only afraid of specific noises, while others worry about every noise louder than their comfort level.

Dogs that are noise phobic for only one or two sounds are usually easier to treat than dogs that are thunderstorm phobic or that have generalized noise phobias. It is impossible to control the weather, and it's pretty tough to control everything that makes your dog nervous, if she's afraid of everything, too. True thunderstorm phobia is very dangerous, as dogs can and will injure themselves to horrifying extremes in their frantic attempts to escape. Some dogs are so sensitive to storms that they start to panic when the barometric pressure starts to drop.

What Works

Desensitization combined with counterconditioning certainly works to improve noise sensitivity. If noise is the only part of storms that bothers your dog, you can buy noise tapes made specifically for desensitization purposes. It is important to eliminate your dog's exposure to his panic triggers during the behavior-modification process.

FACT

Many thunderstorm-phobic dogs attempt to hide behind the toilet, or in the bathtub. One theory is that the tile surfaces are insulation from electrical shock. Whatever the reason, if it makes him feel better and he's not doing damage to himself or the bathroom, let him ride out the storm wherever he feels safe. You can't make him feel better, so let him be.

If your dog is really thunderstorm phobic, you will probably have to use one of the pharmacological or alternative antianxiety treatments available. Melatonin, at a 3 mg dose, is commonly used, as are custom-blended flower essence remedies. You will need to work with your vet to determine the best treatment to try, but if something doesn't work, don't give up; try something else. There is a good deal of anecdotal evidence that body wraps made from athletic bandages, or vests made for this specific purpose, are very beneficial in reducing panic disorders in many dogs. The concept is borrowed from T-Touch, a type of therapeutic touch originally developed for horses, then modified for dogs.

Chapter 21

Special Dogs, Special Issues

It is always something of a challenge to integrate a completely foreign species into a human household successfully. Because dogs have been living with us in our homes for so long—at least tens of thousands of years—it's almost as though we expect them to become human, forgetting that they are a complicated and complete species on their own, with a markedly different perception of what is normal or acceptable behavior. Living with dogs successfully includes understanding, accepting, and relating to them for what they are, and not just for what we want them to be.

Single Dogs, Multiple Dogs

Whether you only have one dog, two, or a whole pack, each scenario has its own unique set of benefits, drawbacks, challenges, and realities.

Living with a Single Dog

Living with only one dog is, for the most part, a little easier, or at least less labor-intensive than living with multiple dogs. However, only dogs can sometimes have a skewed sense of reality, and become antisocial and spoiled if their needs for regular socialization with their own species are neglected. Oftentimes, owners of single dogs are overprotective of their "furbabies," and cater to their every whim to the point of obsession, unfortunately often resulting in a dog that is a neurotic mess.

To be really happy, your single dog needs leadership, boundaries, exercise, affection, training, and socialization more than he needs to be showered with loads of undeserved adoration.

Living with Multiple Dogs

Living with multiple dogs has its own challenges. In general, or at least without really good leadership, the more dogs you have, the more they tend to act like dogs. You have to make an effort to make sure each dog bonds to you and respects you as the leader. To some extent, you have to let the dogs sort out their own pack order, but you always have to be the pack leader, without an iota of doubt in any of your dogs' minds.

ESSENTIAL

Don't get a dog as a pet or playmate for another dog. You never know how they're going to get along, and if you don't have the time or energy to exercise and play with one dog, you definitely don't have time for two! Littermates are exceptionally difficult. They usually overbond to each other, and basic temperament traits like dominance or shyness tend to become exaggerated.

It's a lot of work each time you add a dog to your household, who will naturally bond easily to other dogs, but probably not as easily to you. Crate the new dog separately, and do lots of individual work with her (and with your other dogs). She should have some freedom within the pack, but much of her early time in her new home will be spent tethered to you. When you can easily call her away from playing with the other dogs, she can have more freedom with the rest of the pack.

Living with a Disabled Dog

There are some special challenges to living with a disabled dog–emotional, physical, and sometimes financial. But dogs play the cards they're dealt, without self-pity, so if you do share your life with a disabled dog, you can give him a full and fulfilling life.

Just a Dog

Here's a little secret: disabled dogs don't know or care that they're disabled. They don't feel sorry for themselves, and neither should you. Give them the respect a proud dog deserves, and treat them just like any other dog, with consideration for their abilities and limitations.

You do have to make some adjustments in how you live with them and train them for safety reasons, but that doesn't mean that they should be put in a bubble. For example, a reasonable accommodation for a deaf dog would be to not let him off leash, at least in unfenced areas. Don't move the furniture around if you have a blind dog, or get steps, a ramp, or even wheels if you have a physically disabled dog.

Push it to the Limit

Disabled dogs don't need pity, but they do need leadership, management, socialization, and training just as much as any other dog; in some cases, more. You may have to make some adjustments to the cues you use, or in how your dog performs the exercises, but do engage their minds and bodies to the limits of their abilities. The Web site *www.petswithdisabilities.org* has a wealth of information, not to mention inspiring stories, about living with a disabled dog.

Living with a Shy or Fearful Dog

Living with a shy or fearful dog requires patience, commitment, and realistic expectations. If your dog is genetically shy, you're not going to change who she is, no matter how much training you do. You can, however, help her become more comfortable in her own skin, more reliable in her behavior, and more confident in you—all at the same time.

Causes of Shyness

Dogs exhibit fearful or shy behavior for several reasons. The prognosis for successful treatment often depends on the cause. Is the fear new or ongoing? How old was your dog when you first noticed she was fearful? Is she afraid of one or two identifiable things, or is she always skittish and nervous? Early onset of generalized fear and anxiety often indicates a genetic component, while fearful responses to specific things are usually learned.

ALERT!

Genetically shy dogs and dogs that weren't socialized early in their lives have a relatively poor prognosis in comparison to dogs who have learned to be fearful in response to specific triggers or events.

As mentioned in the sidebar, some dogs learn to be fearful, either in response to a specific, traumatic event, or because fearful behavior has been rewarded, usually by a well-meaning but misguided person trying to make the dog feel better.

What You Can Do to Help Your Dog

As the owner of a shy or fearful dog, your first priority is to get your dog a thorough physical, including blood work with a thyroid function test, to rule out the possibility of a medical basis for fear or anxiety. Then, provide her with calm, confident leadership–all the time, not just in times of stress or crisis—and she'll know you're in control, and won't let anything bad happen to her. By putting yourself between her and whatever or whomever she's afraid of, and giving her specific directions to follow (sit, stay, look), you take the pressure of decision making off her, so she doesn't have to make the awful choice between fight or flight. Fighting (biting) would probably be her last choice, but she would if, in her mind, she had to defend herself; flying (running away) does nothing to solve the problem, and she could possibly injure herself in her panic.

Don't Make It Worse

Never punish or reinforce your dog for exhibiting fearful behavior. It will only make her worse and possibly add aggression to an already unstable temperament. You may feel pity for her, but keep it to yourself, and put on an assertive and cheerful front—pity does her no good. You can live with her the way she is and manage her by limiting her triggers and making sure she is supervised in a way so that she doesn't harm herself or others. Or you can do everything in your power to work her through her fears and gratefully embrace each bit of progress as a milestone. There are some prescription medications that, as an adjunct to behavior modification, can help, as well as alternative treatments like flower essences and therapeutic touch.

Desensitization and Counterconditioning

You have a good chance of modifying your dog's fearful behavior with desensitization, a systematic process of reducing fear; and counterconditioning, which teaches the dog a new reaction in response to his fear triggers. Before you start, make sure you have you have sit and look on command. You're already presenting yourself as a good leader, right?

Desensitization
- Identify the trigger you want to work on, skateboards, for example.
- Present your dog with his trigger at a low level of intensity. In this instance, distance is one way to lower the intensity, and making sure the skateboard doesn't move is another. You will have to experiment

to find your dog's critical distance, or the closest he can be to the trigger without fear.

- Teach your dog to sit and "look" at his critical distance. CR/treat for success. Repeat until he's not even thinking about the trigger at that distance
- Move a little closer to the trigger (or it can move closer to you), 1–5 percent of the distance to start. Work on sit and "look" until the dog is comfortable again.
- Very gradually, always based on your dog's success, move closer, until you are right next to the trigger and he can still function.
- Repeat the process with each trigger or each variable (a moving skateboard, for example).
- If your dog shows fear at any time during the process, back up to where he can be successful.
- Be patient! It can take days, weeks, or months to make progress.
- End each session with success.

Control the Triggers

It is important to reduce (or eliminate, if possible) your dog's contact with fear triggers during the desensitization/counterconditioning process. Some fears, like thunderstorm phobia, are more difficult to treat, both because you can't control them, and because your dog may be reacting to more than just the obvious triggers (like barometric pressure, not just thunder). Thunderstorm phobia treatment is covered in Chapter 20.

Dangerous Dogs? Breed-specific Considerations

Some breeds of dogs have reputations, although not necessarily deservedly so, as being dangerous. It's not that they necessarily bite more often than other breeds, but due to their physical nature—their size, strength, and bite force—when they do bite, the resulting injury tends to be much more serious (and newsworthy) than that of a less powerful dog.

The Realities

The owners of breeds that are usually on dangerous-dog lists—German shepherd dogs, rottweilers, bull breeds, and some of the mastiff-type dogs among them—have more work to do than do the owners of other breeds. They must make an extra effort to make sure their dogs are well socialized and behaved to help their dog become a canine ambassador for his breed. They also have to manage their dogs responsibly, and not allow them to roam. Unfortunately, some areas have already enacted breed-specific legislation making it illegal to own banned breeds. Of course, criminals aren't law abiding to start with, and aren't known to be the most responsible of dog owners, so when they're the only ones who own the "dangerous breeds," it doesn't help the reputation of the breed in question.

Many of the so-called dangerous breeds, pit bulls among them, were originally selectively bred to be specifically not aggressive to people, but some irresponsible breeding and handling of individual dogs led to preventable tragedies that have permanently tarnished the breeds' image. The sad statistic is that about two-thirds of serious dog bites are inflicted by pit bulls and rottweilers combined. Unfortunately, nice examples of the breeds in question and their owners often pay the price for the few infamous examples.

FACT Many insurance companies refuse to insure owners of certain breeds, deemed by them, sometimes arbitrarily, to be dangerous. Check with your homeowner's insurance company to see what their policy on your breed is. Some companies may accept otherwise-banned breeds if they have passed the Canine Good Citizen or therapy-dog test.

What You Can Do

If you own and love a breed of dog that has an unsavory reputation, it's in your best interest, as well as the interest of your individual dog and that of his entire breed, to make sure that he behaves impeccably. If you haven't done the work, or he has some behavior issues, manage him well and train him often to improve both his behavior and image.

Get involved in your dog's breed club to get the advantage of power in numbers to battle issues like breed-specific legislation. It is a big responsibility owning a breed labeled dangerous, but you can make a difference in the future of your chosen breed if you have the energy and commitment to make the effort.

Breed Tendencies and Individual Personalities

Dogs are who they are. Some tendencies are normal for all dogs, but are enhanced in certain breeds, or certain traits were selected for when those breeds were being developed. In modern society, dogs are often purchased on impulse for their looks or size, with no regard for what the breed's intended purpose is (or was). But just because dogs are chosen based on their looks doesn't mean they lose the instincts that have been bred in for generations.

Understand the Dog You Have

If you have a terrier or herding dog, he probably barks a lot and loudly. That's the dog you chose. Ideally, you researched the breed thoroughly before you chose it and can accept a certain amount of your dog's natural doggieness. If you didn't research the breed before you chose it, do it now, for a better understanding of your dog's natural tendencies, if nothing else. You are not ever going to train the instincts out of your dog, but you can learn how to manage your dog and modify or channel some of the behavior.

Dog Aggression

Some breeds have been selectively bred for fighting, often with other dogs. Although some individual dogs in the fighting breeds get along fine with other dogs, many don't, and serious injury or death can result from negligent handling of seriously dog-aggressive dogs. Training can help get control of the dog and teach him an alternate behavior to instigating fights, at least with his owner present, but good management is a big part of living with any dog that has a hard-wired or genetic tendency to fight with other dogs. Owners of dogs that are aggressive to other dogs are smart to work with an experienced trainer to help them modify their dog's behavior.

ALERT! Do not get in the middle of a dogfight! You could be seriously injured for your trouble, and there's a good chance that you won't stop the fight by getting in the middle of it anyway. You can try throwing water on the dogs, or wedging a broomstick in between them.

Shaping Positive Behavior Patterns

Although you are going to have to live with a certain amount of your dog's normal, if annoying, behavior, you can modify the behavior somewhat and reduce its frequency with good management and training, and by actively pursuing legal outlets for your dog to bark, or dig, or chase, or whatever, with the exception of fighting. Teach your dog to bark on command, and let him bark his head off once or twice a day. Make a digging pit for your terrier. Play fetch or Frisbee or set up a lure course for your high-prey-drive dog.

It's difficult, if not impossible, for most dogs to understand not to do something, particularly when that something is as natural to them as breathing. Managing the triggers that cause your dog to engage in the behaviors you want to limit is an important part of modifying behavior. If your dog goes ballistic at the front window every time he sees a jogger go by, close the drapes, or don't let him have access to that window. You may have to do a little investigation to discover what your dog reacts to so you can limit his access to it while you're training.

Dog Bites and Liability Issues

Dog bites are a serious issue, not just for the person who is bitten, but also for the health and safety of the dog and the dog owner's property.

Preventing Dog Bites

The large majority of pet dogs will never bite anyone, but it's always important to remember that dogs are animals first and pets second, and any dog can and will bite in the right circumstance. Preventing dog bites is relatively easy for most dogs. Early and continued socialization, good management, and consistent handling and training all go a long way to preventing dog bites. As already mentioned, children must know how to behave around dogs, both those they know and strange dogs.

FACT

Although the number of dogs has stayed relatively steady, around 65 million, the number of reported bites has increased dramatically, from about 585,000 in 1986 to about 800,000 in 1994 according to ✍www .dogbitelaw.com.

Dogs that have already bitten someone are much more likely to bite again than dogs who have never bitten. It is a serious liability issue to have a biting dog, not to mention the physical and emotional damage a serious bite causes. Liability can take several forms. For example, a person who is bitten can sue the dog's owner for personal injury. In addition, pets are considered personal property by law. A person whose dog, cat, or other pet is injured or killed by a dog can sue the attacking dog's owner for property damage. In some states, the owner may not be liable for the first bite of a dog without a violent history if the dog's owner takes reasonable measures to control their dog. In other states, however, the owner will be liable for a bite regardless of the dog's favorable history or the careful steps undertaken to prevent the situation from repeating itself. Dogs that have already bitten have to be managed very carefully so they're not in the position to do it again. Don't make excuses for a biting dog—"But he's so sweet most of the time"—it doesn't really matter why he bites, it just matters that he doesn't have the chance to do it again.

What to Do if Your Dog Bites Someone

If the unthinkable happens and your dog does bite someone, the first thing you have to do is to remove your dog from the situation and securely contain him. Next, check on the victim to see if the bite requires medical attention. Any bite that breaks the skin is a potentially dangerous bite, due to the risk of infection, and should be checked by a doctor. If the bite is serious enough to require medical attention, you should immediately contact your insurance carrier, your lawyer, and a dog behaviorist.

Laws regarding dog bites vary widely from state to state, but you can always be held civilly liable for any damages caused by your dog. You absolutely must not allow your dog the freedom to bite another person. Serial biters don't survive very long. If you feel that you can't deal with your dog's problem, you can't just give someone else your nightmare without being honest about his history. In fact, you could be sued if you knowingly place a biting dog with someone else without disclosing the information. The sad truth is that people are not knocking down shelters' doors hoping to adopt a biting dog, so there is a good chance you or someone else will have to euthanize your dog if he has a history of serious bites.

Chapter 22

Your Healthy, Happy Dog

Keeping your dog healthy and happy is a lot more involved than making sure he has food, water, and exercise. Training and socialization are important, as you already know, but your dog will also need regular veterinary care, as well as grooming and possibly boarding, or in-home pet care. If your dog is lucky, he'll get to travel with you, at least occasionally, and there are several simple things you can do to ensure a safe and happy trip.

Veterinary Care

One of the most important people in your dog's life is her veterinarian. If you start out with a puppy, you'll get to know your vet pretty well in the first year. And of course, accidents and illnesses—minor and major—can occur despite even the best intentions and efforts. The time to develop a relationship with your vet is before such an event occurs.

Routine Care

Your dog will need to see the vet at least once every year for her annual checkup, heartworm, and intestinal parasite tests. In many areas, dogs are routinely tested for Lyme disease in combination with the heartworm test. Depending on your dog, your vet, and your personal preferences, you may also want to have blood work, vaccinations, or titer tests.

Your dog will also need to be spayed or neutered, usually around the age of six months. Leave breeding to the professionals who are committed to improving the breed, and let your kids learn about the miracle of life from a DVD. It's not worth losing your dog in whelp (giving birth). Also, it's expensive and a full-time job raising puppies. Heat cycles are messy and last for three weeks, usually twice a year, and leave your dog vulnerable to mammary cancer. If you have a male dog, he'll be much easier to live with, and will have a much lower tendency to run away or develop aggression problems if he's neutered. You'll also eliminate the possibility of testicular cancer and prostate cancer as he ages.

Your dog's vet should check out unusual or foul smells coming from any part of your dog's body. Maybe your dog just needs his teeth cleaned, but better safe than sorry.

Minor problems are bound to crop up in your dog's health. Skin and ear infections are common, as are urinary-tract infections and minor accidents. You are your dog's best friend in more ways than one. It is your careful observation of your dog, his body, and his behavior that will help you catch any health issues before they become serious. At least once a week, thoroughly examine your dog's eyes, ears, mouth, body, and limbs, noting any unusual appearance, including lesions, pustules, growths, or the presence of parasites like fleas or ticks.

Emergency!

Before you need it, know what your veterinarian's policy is for after-hours emergencies. For some reason, serious veterinary emergencies usually occur outside of normal business hours. Many areas have veterinary emergency clinics that are open after normal hours. Write down the number near the phone and take a drive there one day so you won't have to try to find it when you're already distracted by an ill or injured dog and your emotions. If you do need to visit the emergency clinic for real, always call before you leave the house so the staff can prepare to take care of your dog immediately when you get there.

When to Seek Emergency Care
- An obviously broken or seriously injured limb (your dog will not bear any weight on it, or it hangs at an odd angle).
- Being hit by a car—even if it doesn't immediately appear serious, your dog could have internal injuries or head trauma that aren't obvious.
- Unexplained or profuse bleeding.
- A bite or scratch from another animal that breaks the skin, especially punctures or bites that swell or bruise severely.
- Sudden swelling, especially of the face, which often indicates a serious allergic or anaphylactic reaction to a vaccine or insect bite)
- Eye injuries, even apparently minor ones, can turn major in a short time. Get them checked ASAP.
- Ingestion of toxic substances.
- Heatstroke or hypothermia/ frostbite.

- Burns.
- Any sudden dramatic behavior change including respiratory distress, aggression, or neurological signs like seizures or circling blindly.

ALERT!

Use extreme caution when approaching or touching a sick or injured dog. Even the nicest dog can bite if he's sick, scared, or in pain. Fashion a muzzle out of a piece of rope or a leash, and get help if possible before moving the hurt dog.

The best thing you can do for your dog in an emergency is to breathe and stay calm. Panicking won't help, and could even get you injured if you use adrenaline to guide your actions instead of your good sense.

Bloat

Bloat is always a veterinary emergency. This condition, which strikes terror into the hearts of many owners of deep-chested breeds, like Doberman Pinschers and Great Danes (although any breed can be affected), is a simple term for gastric dilatation and volvulus, which causes the stomach to fill up with air, and if left untreated, twist. There is some evidence that feeding dogs a grain-free diet from elevated feeders, in addition to resting the dog for an hour before and after meals, can help reduce the chances of bloat, but it is a very real threat for susceptible dogs. This is a life-threatening condition requiring immediate treatment.

Alternative Medicine and Therapies

There are a variety of alternatives to traditional or Western medicine, including homeopathy, acupuncture, chiropractic, and herbal- and flower-essence remedies, in addition to several types of physical therapy, healing, and therapeutic touch. Veterinarians who practice alternative, complementary, and integrative medicine, sometimes in addition to traditional treatments, are often referred to as holistic practitioners. What this really means is that they approach treatment from the view of the whole dog, not just the acute symptoms of the current problem. If you're interested in finding out more about alternative or complementary medicine, visit *www.altvetmed .org* for information and links to organizations for each specialty, so you can find a vet in your area.

Vaccinations

There are a variety of diseases that dogs are commonly vaccinated against, including distemper, parvovius, adenovirus, hepatitis, parainfluenza, leptospirosis, Lyme disease, kennel cough (Bordatella), coronavirus, and rabies.

Puppy Shots

Most puppies will be vaccinated for most or all of the above diseases as a matter of course during their initial three or four visits to the vet. Puppies get some immunity from their mothers, but the duration of the immunity is highly variable. Because maternal antibodies prevent the puppy from forming an immune response to the vaccine, puppies are vaccinated several times, with the last vaccine of the series usually occurring between 12 and 16 weeks of age. In addition to rabies, most pet owners will want to vaccinate their dogs at least once after the puppy series for the most common and deadly diseases, distemper and parvo.

The Booster-shot Dilemma

There is some controversy regarding booster vaccinations, both about what to vaccinate against, and how often to vaccinate. What most people don't understand is that it's not the vaccination that provides protection from disease; it's the dog's immune response to the vaccine. According to veterinarian Ronald Schultz, if a dog forms a proper immune response to the first vaccine, research has shown that he usually keeps that level of protection for a long period of time, perhaps the duration of his life. Revaccination doesn't improve his level of immunity. It's not like topping off your windshield washer fluid; you can't make your immune dog more immune.

Some dogs never form a good immune response and aren't protected, no matter how many times they are vaccinated. In addition, there is evidence that overvaccination, especially with killed vaccines and combination vaccines instead of modified live, single vaccines, can cause more problems than they prevent, particularly allergic reactions and autoimmune diseases. Owners of dogs that aren't vaccinated according to traditional schedules may want to do occasional titer tests, although they probably aren't necessary or even a 100 percent accurate portrayal of the dog's level of immunity. It never hurts to research the issue and discuss it frankly with your veterinarian to come up with the vaccination schedule that is most appropriate for your dog and lifestyle. Some training and boarding facilities require particular vaccines, but some will accept titers or waivers, so consider those factors, as well as your dog's health, when making your decision.

FACT

With the growing concern surrounding vaccinosis or vaccine-related health problems, many vet schools have changed their booster vaccine protocol from every year to every three years.

Rabies

Rabies is a public health issue and a zoonotic disease, which means it can pass from animals to people, with a near 100 percent fatality rate. It is required by law to vaccinate pets for rabies, although the frequency of vaccination varies from one to three years depending on the area you live in. If your dog ever bites or scratches someone and he doesn't have a current rabies vaccine, he will (at least) be quarantined, so make sure you know the laws in your area. Yearly vaccination is often required in areas where rabies is prevalent in wildlife like raccoons.

Parasites

There are a variety of internal and external bugs that, at best, make your dog miserable with itching, chewing, and scratching, and at worst, cause serious, even deadly disease.

Heartworms

Once common only in the southern states, heartworm disease is now common in most states. The heartworm larvae are carried and transmitted by mosquitoes, migrate to the heart, and grow up to 14 inches long, causing heart failure and eventual death, if untreated. The treatment itself can cause death in dogs with a heavy parasitic load or who were left untreated for so long that they were already ill before detection. The presence of heartworms is easily detected by a simple blood test, which should be part of your dog's annual checkup. Thankfully, heartworms are easily prevented with daily or monthly medication, but even dogs on heartworm preventative should be tested yearly.

External Parasites

External parasites, like fleas, ticks, and ear mites, are the bane of many dogs' (and their owners') existence. In addition to the annoying and skin-damaging chewing and scratching, external parasites can also transmit serious diseases, like Lyme disease. As mentioned previously, you should check your dog weekly for the presence of fleas and ticks by parting the hair or ruffling it against the grain. You will usually find evidence of fleas, if they're present, in the triangle above your dog's tail. If you see little black specks, put a few on a wet paper towel. If they dissolve and turn red, your dog has fleas. Ticks can be found anywhere on your dog's body, but they are particularly attracted to the face, neck, and ears. Some species of ticks are very tiny, about the size of the period at the end of this sentence. In areas where parasites are common, keeping your dog on some kind of repellant is a good idea. There are a multitude of choices, from herbal sprays that you apply every time your dog goes out to once-a-month chemical treatments.

Internal Parasites

Along with heartworms and external parasites, there is also a host of internal parasites that can infect your dog. The most common intestinal parasites are roundworms, hookworms, and whipworms. Most puppies are born with roundworms and are routinely dewormed several times before they are weaned and sent to their new homes. Hookworm and whipworm eggs are distributed in the feces and acquired often by accidental ingestion, e.g., licking the paws after coming home from the dog park. Some of the monthly heartworm medications deworm as well as prevent heartworm disease, but your dog should have a fecal test to check for the presence of parasites once a year with the annual check-up, as well as any time the dog loses weight or condition, or has persistent diarrhea. Some parasites aren't affected by the heartworm medications including common protzoans like coccidia and giardia. Tapeworms are another type of intestinal parasite that dogs get, usually from eating an infected flea or small animal. If your dog has fleas, there's a good chance he also has tapeworms.

ALERT!

Certain species of worm eggs can survive in the right environment for years, waiting for a host to walk by and pick them up. You can minimize your dog's chance of becoming infected by making sure you keep your yard scooped regularly, and walking him in areas that aren't filthy with feces. Don't let him drink from standing puddles, ponds, lakes, or rivers, which are often the source of protozoal infections.

Nutrition

Good nutrition is a vital part of your dog's health and longevity, and can even have an impact on behavior. From the big box store's cheapest kibble to home-prepared cooked or even raw meals, there is a wide range of options when it comes to feeding your dog. What you choose to feed him will depend on your dog, your budget, the amount of time you have to devote to preparing your dog's meals, and how much control you want over what goes into your dog.

Commercial Diets

Most people will choose to feed their dogs a commercial dog food, whether dry, canned, or frozen. When considering which dog food to purchase, completely disregard the advertisements you see on TV—after all, they're trying to sell dog food—and do your own research. Read the label. Is meat listed as the first ingredient? Is meat mentioned several times? Good! Are there several sources of grains, like rice, corn, wheat (or their parts) mentioned several times? Not so good. Food is one area of dog care where you pretty much get what you pay for. Cheap dog foods tend to be full of cheap ingredients, like an abundance of grains and starches, which while filling and cheap, are completely useless for a carnivore's specialized digestive system.

While you can't pick them up at the grocery store while you're doing your weekly shopping, premium quality and highly digestible kibbled diets are widely available in pet-supply stores, and are well worth the trip. There are even several dry, canned, and frozen foods that are completely grain free.

FACT

A fat dog is not a healthy dog. To reduce the chance of joint problems, keep your dog slim and trim. Your dog should look well muscled, but most breeds should have a defined waist when viewed from above. You should be able to fairly easily feel the spine and ribs.

Homemade Dog Food

There is a growing trend among dog enthusiasts and pet owners to prepare their dog's food at home from scratch. Some cook the food and include limited grains, while others feed a prey model diet in which the raw diet of a wild canine is mimicked. While there is little doubt that less processed, "real" food is healthier than heavily processed convenience food, the process of preparing meals is not to be taken lightly. In addition to the expense and effort involved, you also have to educate yourself about the nutritional needs of the animal you're feeding and create a balance over time. This is definitely a do it right, or don't do it at all situation, so if you do decide to try it, be prepared. You should also be prepared to defend your choice to skeptics and critics, and perhaps even your vet, but the devotees of home-prepared diets swear by them.

How Much to Feed

How much you feed depends on what kind of food you use, and the metabolism of your dog. You certainly cannot feed your dog according to the directions on the back of the bag. For one thing, they're in the business to sell dog food, so they want you going through this bag as fast as possible. And, the dogs the food is tested on aren't generally house pets; they're usually kennel dogs, under more stress than the average pet dog.

You're safe to start with about three-quarters of what the label recommends, then adjust up or down as needed to keep your dog in good condition. If you're feeding a homemade diet, the general guideline is to feed 3 percent of your dog's body weight, but you'll have to adjust it for your individual dog.

Grooming

Every dog requires some degree of grooming. For shorthaired breeds, grooming is relatively simple: regular nail trimming, ear cleaning, and brushing (of the teeth and the fur or hair), accompanied by an occasional bath. Double-coated breeds like German shepherds require more frequent brushing, as do drop-coated and curly-coated breeds, like Maltese and poodles, respectively. Many breeds require regular trimming to keep them looking and feeling their best. Understanding the grooming requirements of your dog is an important part of responsible dog ownership.

What You Can Do at Home

Most dog owners are able to brush and bathe their own dogs at home, and brush their teeth and clean their ears. Some owners can even clip their dog's nails, although it does require a bit of practice, and a cooperative dog is helpful, too. Some dogs will try to get you to stop brushing or nail trimming by crying or snapping, but it is important that they learn that such measures will not work to get you to stop. You can try smushing a little peanut butter, liverwurst, or canned dog food on the front of the fridge to keep your dog busy while you perform at least a small part of your grooming process; even trimming one nail is something. Securing your dog to something sturdy can also be helpful. Don't give her enough room to turn her head around to reach you, and brush gently, ignoring any protests. As soon as she relaxes and accepts what you're doing, praise, treat, and turn her loose. She'll learn quickly that calm acceptance, not hysterical protest, earns freedom. Do not try to soothe her out of her temper tantrum; the only attention she should get is for accepting handling.

You can teach your dog to tolerate, if not enjoy, grooming procedures at home using shaping in much the same way that you use it to teach your dog any number of behaviors. It helps a lot to start teaching your dog to accept grooming right from the start as part of the initial acclimation process when you bring her home. If your dog is really serious about protecting her "private parts"—and for most dogs the most private area tends to be the feet— call a professional trainer to help. Of course, you could always just take her to a professional groomer instead, and avoid the whole issue. Pet owners are often amazed that their little darling that is such a terror about grooming at home doesn't even give the groomer a sideways glance when she performs the same procedures.

ALERT!

If your groomer tells you that your dog needs to be shaved because of matting, believe her. The groomer generally wants to make you happy, but if you're not taking proper care of your dog or bringing her in for regular professional grooming, why make the groomer literally torture your dog with dematting for your vanity? Shave the matted hair—it is just hair, after all—and start over, with a firm resolve not to be negligent of your dog's grooming in the future.

Professional Grooming

If you have a bichon frise, poodle, spaniel, terrier, or a drop-coated breed like a Maltese, chances are you will have to have your dog professionally groomed on a regular basis. For most trimmed dogs, they should be groomed anywhere from every four to twelve weeks, depending on the breed and style. In general, the longer the owner wants to keep the hair, the more frequently the dog will need to be groomed—as often as once a week for drop-coated breeds in full coat. Unfortunately, most pet dog owners expect that they can keep their dogs looking like show dogs without frequent professional grooming or doing daily work at home, and the sad truth is, it just isn't possible in most cases.

For dogs that require regular trims, there is no substitute for the job an experienced professional does. Even shorthaired dogs can benefit from professional grooming, with the array of spa treatments and deshedding treatments that are now available. Double-coated breeds that blow their undercoats twice a year definitely benefit from the attention of a professional groomer who has the knowledge, products, and tools to remove the shedding hair more thoroughly. Ask friends, neighbors, and other pet professionals for a recommendation for a good groomer in your area.

Boarding, Doggie Day Care, and Pet Sitters

Because of a family emergency, business travel, or vacation, there's a good chance you will need to board your dog at some point in her life. You might be lucky enough to have a family member or friend that is willing to keep your dog (or stay at your home with her) while you're away, but it's a good idea to familiarize yourself with the facilities and services available in your area before you need them, just in case.

Kennels

Kennels provide overnight care for your pets. They vary widely in style, price, services, and accommodations, from the most basic outdoor runs to luxury suites. Before booking a reservation, visit the facilities. Make sure you call ahead to see when the kennel allows tours. Most kennels will have specific hours that you can visit during less hectic times of their day. If the kennel doesn't allow tours at all, you're better off going somewhere else, for your peace of mind if nothing else.

The type of kennel you choose depends as much on your dog as it does on your budget. Nervous or shy dogs will often benefit from a quieter, more private setting, while a gregarious or boisterous dog usually does better in a kennel that offers regular access to a run, or offers play time or walks as an additional service.

Doggie Day Care

Doggie day care has become very popular in the past decade or so, as more dog owners send their puppies off for a day of socializing and playing while they are at work. For some people, it's a guilt thing—they feel bad that the puppy would be crated otherwise—but for others, it's all about being practical, as they get to bring home an exhausted puppy at the end of the day.

Some centers offer training as well as playing, including potty breaks and "nap time," complete with snacks in crates. For most puppies, a more structured program is better than an all day free-for-all, especially if the facility is entirely indoors. No need to set your puppy up for housebreaking problems if he learns that he can relieve himself whenever and wherever it pleases him; he'll see no reason to do anything different at home.

For older, housebroken dogs, more play–oriented programs are generally fine. Observe for an hour or so one day to see if the program is right for your goals with your dog. Does the staff encourage polite behavior, or are they letting dogs jump all over them or playing with them in ways that aren't appropriate or safe? Are the dogs getting along? Does the number of dogs seem reasonable in comparison to the amount of space and number of staff caring for them? Is the facility relatively clean? It's basically a doggie playpen, so you shouldn't expect it to be completely spotless and free of loose hair, but there certainly shouldn't be multiple uncleaned potty spots, and water dishes should look reasonably clean. Are the toys and obstacles safe and supervised? It is possible for your dog to get injured in his romps with his pals, but the equipment itself should be sturdy.

Pet Sitters and Dog Walkers

As an alternative to taking your dog to a kennel or day-care facility, you might also consider using a dog walker or pet sitter. The services they offer vary a good bit, from simple walks one or more times a day to a complete vacation service, including overnight stays, checking the mail, and watering the plants. Some even offer field trips with multiple dogs, taking them to the park or beach to play off leash.

You should always take the time to personally interview a pet sitter with your dog to see if he handles your dog with confidence and kindness. You should also make sure that anyone who is going to have a key to your house is bonded and insured, and when it comes to pet sitters, having recommendations from other happy clients is a big plus. You can find out more about pet sitters at *www.petsitters.org*.

Appendix A
Resources for Dog Owners

Breed Registries

American Kennel Club

51 Madison Ave.
New York, NY 10010
(212) 696-8200
✑ *www.akc.org*

United Kennel Club

100 East Kilgore Rd.
Kalamazoo, MI 49001
(616) 343-9020
✑ *www.ukcdogs.com*

American Rare Breed Association

100 Nicholas St. NW
Washington, DC 20011
✑ *www.arba.org*

Canadian Kennel Club

Commerce Park
88 Skyway Ave., Suite 100
Etobicoke, ON M9W 6R4
✑ *www.ckc.ca*

American Mixed Breed Obedience Registry

Po Box 36
Springfield, WI 53176
✑ *www.amborusa.com*

Therapy Dog Organizations

Delta Society

PO Box 1080
Renton, WA 98057
✑ *www.deltasociety.org*

Therapy Dog International

6 Hilltop Rd.
Mendham, NJ 07945
(201) 548-0888
✑ *www.tdi-dog.org*

Therapy Dogs, Inc.

PO Box 20227
Cheyenne, WY 82003
(877) 843-7364
✑ *www.therapydogs.com*

Dog Supplies

Pet Edge
(800) 738-3343
✑ *www.petedge.com*

General dog supplies
Dog.com
(800) 367-3467
✑ *www.dog.com*

General dog supplies
SitStay.com
(800) SIT-STAY
✑ *www.sitstay.com*

Dog and training supplies

Canine Genius
✑ *www.caninegenius.com*

Leo food puzzle toys
Pet Expertise
✑ *www.petexpertise.com*

Health-Related Organizations

American Kennel Club Canine Health Foundation

251 W. Garfield Rd., Suite 160
Aurora, OH 44202
(888) 682-9696
✍ *www.akcchf.org*

ASPCA Animal Poison Control Center

1717 S. Philo, Suite 36
Urbana, IL 61802
(888) 426-4435
✍ *www.napcc.aspca.org*

American Veterinary Medical Association

1931 N Meacham Rd., Suite 100
Schaumberg, IL 60173
(800) 248-2862
✍ *www.avma.org*

American Holistic Veterinary Medical Association

2218 Old Emmorton Rd.
Bel Air, MD 21015
(410) 569-0795
✍ *www.ahvma.org*

Handicapped Dogs

SARAH, Inc

✍ *www.sarahandicaps.org*

Websites

✍ *www.deafdogs.org*
✍ *www.petswithdisabilities.org*

Training and Behavior

The Canine Connection Dog Training, LLC

✍ *www.canineconnectiondogtraining.com*

American Dog Trainers Network

✍ *www.inch.com/~dogs*

Campbell's Pet Behavior Resources

✍ *www.webtrail.com/petbehavior/index.html*

Dog Obedience and Training Page

✍ *www.dogpatch.org/obed/*

Dr. P's Dog Training Library

✍ *www.uwsp.edu/psych/dog/dog.htm*

Appendix B

Bibliography

Benjamin, Carol Lea. *Second Hand Dog: How to Turn Yours into a First Rate Pet* (New York: Howell Publishing, 1988).

———. *Mother Knows Best: The Natural Way to Train Your Dog.* (New York: Hungry Minds, 1985).

———. *Dog Problems* (New York: Hungry Minds, 1989).

Burnham, Patricia. *Playtraining Your Dog* (New York: St Martin's Press, 1980).

Campbell, William. *Behavior Problems in Dogs* (Grants Pass, OR: BehavioRx Systems, 1999).

Clothier, Suzanne. *Bones Would Rain from the Sky, Deepening Our Relationships with Dogs* (New York: Warner Books, Inc., 2002).

Coren, Stanley. *The Intelligence of Dogs: A Guide to the Thoughts, Emotions, and Inner Lives of Our Canine Companions* (New York: Simon & Schuster, 1994).

Dodman, Nicholas. *The Dog Who Loved Too Much: Tales Treatments and the Psychology of Dogs* (New York: Bantam Books, 1996).

Donaldson Jean. *The Culture Clash* (Berkeley, CA: James and Kenneth Publishers, 1998).

Dunbar, Ian. *How to Teach an Old Dog New Tricks* (Berkeley, CA: James and Kenneth Publishers, 1998).

Evans, Job Michael. *People, Pooches and Problems.* (New York: Howell Books, 1991).

———. *Training and Explaining: How to be the Dog Trainer You Want to Be* (New York: Hungry Minds, 1995).

Fogle, Bruce. *The Dog's Mind: Understanding Your Dog's Behavior* (New York: Howell Book House, 1991).

Lewis, Janet. *Smart Trainers, Brilliant Dog* (Ellicot City, MD: Canine Sports Productions, 1997).

McConnell, Patricia. *The Cautious Canine* (Black Earth, WI: Dog's Best Friend, Ltd., 1996).

———. *Puppy Primer* (Black Earth, WI: Dog's Best Friend, Ltd., 1996).

———. *Beginning Family Dog Training* (Black Earth, WI: Dog's Best Friend, Ltd., 1996).

Monks of New Skete. *The Art of Raising a Puppy.* (Boston: Little, Brown and Company, 1991).

———. *How to be Your Dog's Best Friend.* (Boston: Little, Brown and Company, 1978).

Pryor, Karen. *Don't Shoot the Dog: The New Art of Teaching and Training* (New York: Bantam Books, 1999).

Reid, Pamela. *Excel-Erated Learning: Explaining in Plain English How Dogs Learn and How Best to Teach Them* (Oakland, CA: James and Kenneth Publishers, 1996).

Rogerson, John. *The Instructor's Manual* (Toronto: Rogerson, 1994).

Rugaas, Turid. *On Talking Terms with Dogs* (Carlsborg, WA: Legacy by Mail, 1997).

Schultze, Kymythy. *Natural Nutrition for Dogs and Cats* (Carlsbad, CA: Hay House, 1998).

Volhard, Joachim, Gail Fisher, and Job Michael Evans. *Teaching Dog Obedience Classes: The Manual for Instructors* (New York: Howell Book House, 1986).

Volhard, Joachim, and Gail Fisher. *Training Your Dog: The Step-by-Step Manual* (New York: Howell Book House, 1983).

Index

The EVERYTHING Series!

BUSINESS & PERSONAL FINANCE

Everything® Accounting Book
Everything® Budgeting Book
Everything® Business Planning Book
Everything® Coaching and Mentoring Book
Everything® Fundraising Book
Everything® Get Out of Debt Book
Everything® Grant Writing Book
Everything® Guide to Personal Finance for Single Mothers
Everything® Home-Based Business Book, 2nd Ed.
Everything® Homebuying Book, 2nd Ed.
Everything® Homeselling Book, 2nd Ed.
Everything® Improve Your Credit Book
Everything® Investing Book, 2nd Ed.
Everything® Landlording Book
Everything® Leadership Book
Everything® Managing People Book, 2nd Ed.
Everything® Negotiating Book
Everything® Online Auctions Book
Everything® Online Business Book
Everything® Personal Finance Book
Everything® Personal Finance in Your 20s and 30s Book
Everything® Project Management Book
Everything® Real Estate Investing Book
Everything® Retirement Planning Book
Everything® Robert's Rules Book, $7.95
Everything® Selling Book
Everything® Start Your Own Business Book, 2nd Ed.
Everything® Wills & Estate Planning Book

COOKING

Everything® Barbecue Cookbook
Everything® Bartender's Book, $9.95
Everything® Cheese Book
Everything® Chinese Cookbook
Everything® Classic Recipes Book
Everything® Cocktail Parties and Drinks Book
Everything® College Cookbook
Everything® Cooking for Baby and Toddler Book
Everything® Cooking for Two Cookbook
Everything® Diabetes Cookbook
Everything® Easy Gourmet Cookbook
Everything® Fondue Cookbook
Everything® Fondue Party Book
Everything® Gluten-Free Cookbook
Everything® Glycemic Index Cookbook
Everything® Grilling Cookbook

Everything® Healthy Meals in Minutes Cookbook
Everything® Holiday Cookbook
Everything® Indian Cookbook
Everything® Italian Cookbook
Everything® Low-Carb Cookbook
Everything® Low-Fat High-Flavor Cookbook
Everything® Low-Salt Cookbook
Everything® Meals for a Month Cookbook
Everything® Mediterranean Cookbook
Everything® Mexican Cookbook
Everything® No Trans Fat Cookbook
Everything® One-Pot Cookbook
Everything® Pizza Cookbook
Everything® Quick and Easy 30-Minute, 5-Ingredient Cookbook
Everything® Quick Meals Cookbook
Everything® Slow Cooker Cookbook
Everything® Slow Cooking for a Crowd Cookbook
Everything® Soup Cookbook
Everything® Stir-Fry Cookbook
Everything® Tex-Mex Cookbook
Everything® Thai Cookbook
Everything® Vegetarian Cookbook
Everything® Wild Game Cookbook
Everything® Wine Book, 2nd Ed.

GAMES

Everything® 15-Minute Sudoku Book, $9.95
Everything® 30-Minute Sudoku Book, $9.95
Everything® Blackjack Strategy Book
Everything® Brain Strain Book, $9.95
Everything® Bridge Book
Everything® Card Games Book
Everything® Card Tricks Book, $9.95
Everything® Casino Gambling Book, 2nd Ed.
Everything® Chess Basics Book
Everything® Craps Strategy Book
Everything® Crossword and Puzzle Book
Everything® Crossword Challenge Book
Everything® Crosswords for the Beach Book, $9.95
Everything® Cryptograms Book, $9.95
Everything® Easy Crosswords Book
Everything® Easy Kakuro Book, $9.95
Everything® Easy Large Print Crosswords Book
Everything® Games Book, 2nd Ed.
Everything® Giant Sudoku Book, $9.95
Everything® Kakuro Challenge Book, $9.95
Everything® Large-Print Crossword Challenge Book

Everything® Large-Print Crosswords Book
Everything® Lateral Thinking Puzzles Book, $9.95
Everything® Mazes Book
Everything® Movie Crosswords Book, $9.95
Everything® Online Poker Book, $12.95
Everything® Pencil Puzzles Book, $9.95
Everything® Poker Strategy Book
Everything® Pool & Billiards Book
Everything® Sports Crosswords Book, $9.95
Everything® Test Your IQ Book, $9.95
Everything® Texas Hold 'Em Book, $9.95
Everything® Travel Crosswords Book, $9.95
Everything® Word Games Challenge Book
Everything® Word Scramble Book
Everything® Word Search Book

HEALTH

Everything® Alzheimer's Book
Everything® Diabetes Book
Everything® Health Guide to Adult Bipolar Disorder
Everything® Health Guide to Controlling Anxiety
Everything® Health Guide to Fibromyalgia
Everything® Health Guide to Postpartum Care
Everything® Health Guide to Thyroid Disease
Everything® Hypnosis Book
Everything® Low Cholesterol Book
Everything® Massage Book
Everything® Menopause Book
Everything® Nutrition Book
Everything® Reflexology Book
Everything® Stress Management Book

HISTORY

Everything® American Government Book
Everything® American History Book, 2nd Ed.
Everything® Civil War Book
Everything® Freemasons Book
Everything® Irish History & Heritage Book
Everything® Middle East Book

HOBBIES

Everything® Candlemaking Book
Everything® Cartooning Book
Everything® Coin Collecting Book
Everything® Drawing Book
Everything® Family Tree Book, 2nd Ed.
Everything® Knitting Book
Everything® Knots Book
Everything® Photography Book

Everything® Quilting Book
Everything® Scrapbooking Book
Everything® Sewing Book
Everything® Soapmaking Book, 2nd Ed.
Everything® Woodworking Book

HOME IMPROVEMENT

Everything® Feng Shui Book
Everything® Feng Shui Decluttering Book, $9.95
Everything® Fix-It Book
Everything® Home Decorating Book
Everything® Home Storage Solutions Book
Everything® Homebuilding Book
Everything® Organize Your Home Book

KIDS' BOOKS

All titles are $7.95
Everything® Kids' Animal Puzzle & Activity Book
Everything® Kids' Baseball Book, 4th Ed.
Everything® Kids' Bible Trivia Book
Everything® Kids' Bugs Book
Everything® Kids' Cars and Trucks Puzzle
& Activity Book
Everything® Kids' Christmas Puzzle
& Activity Book
Everything® Kids' Cookbook
Everything® Kids' Crazy Puzzles Book
Everything® Kids' Dinosaurs Book
Everything® Kids' First Spanish Puzzle and
Activity Book
Everything® Kids' Gross Cookbook
Everything® Kids' Gross Hidden Pictures Book
Everything® Kids' Gross Jokes Book
Everything® Kids' Gross Mazes Book
Everything® Kids' Gross Puzzle and
Activity Book
Everything® Kids' Halloween Puzzle
& Activity Book
Everything® Kids' Hidden Pictures Book
Everything® Kids' Horses Book
Everything® Kids' Joke Book
Everything® Kids' Knock Knock Book
Everything® Kids' Learning Spanish Book
Everything® Kids' Math Puzzles Book
Everything® Kids' Mazes Book
Everything® Kids' Money Book
Everything® Kids' Nature Book
Everything® Kids' Pirates Puzzle and Activity Book
Everything® Kids' Presidents Book
Everything® Kids' Princess Puzzle and Activity Book
Everything® Kids' Puzzle Book
Everything® Kids' Riddles & Brain Teasers Book
Everything® Kids' Science Experiments Book
Everything® Kids' Sharks Book
Everything® Kids' Soccer Book
Everything® Kids' States Book
Everything® Kids' Travel Activity Book

KIDS' STORY BOOKS

Everything® Fairy Tales Book

LANGUAGE

Everything® Conversational Japanese Book with
CD, $19.95
Everything® French Grammar Book
Everything® French Phrase Book, $9.95
Everything® French Verb Book, $9.95
Everything® German Practice Book with CD,
$19.95
Everything® Inglés Book
**Everything® Intermediate Spanish Book with
CD, $19.95**
**Everything® Learning Brazilian Portuguese
Book with CD, $19.95**
Everything® Learning French Book
Everything® Learning German Book
Everything® Learning Italian Book
Everything® Learning Latin Book
**Everything® Learning Spanish Book with
CD, 2nd Edition, $19.95**
Everything® Russian Practice Book with CD, $19.95
Everything® Sign Language Book
Everything® Spanish Grammar Book
Everything® Spanish Phrase Book, $9.95
Everything® Spanish Practice Book
with CD, $19.95
Everything® Spanish Verb Book, $9.95
Everything® Speaking Mandarin Chinese Book
with CD, $19.95

MUSIC

Everything® Drums Book with CD, $19.95
**Everything® Guitar Book with CD, 2nd
Edition, $19.95**
Everything® Guitar Chords Book with CD, $19.95
Everything® Home Recording Book
Everything® Music Theory Book with CD, $19.95
Everything® Reading Music Book with CD, $19.95
Everything® Rock & Blues Guitar Book
with CD, $19.95
**Everything® Rock and Blues Piano Book
with CD, $19.95**
Everything® Songwriting Book

NEW AGE

Everything® Astrology Book, 2nd Ed.
Everything® Birthday Personology Book
Everything® Dreams Book, 2nd Ed.
Everything® Love Signs Book, $9.95
Everything® Numerology Book
Everything® Paganism Book
Everything® Palmistry Book
Everything® Psychic Book
Everything® Reiki Book

Everything® Sex Signs Book, $9.95
Everything® Tarot Book, 2nd Ed.
Everything® Toltec Wisdom Book
Everything® Wicca and Witchcraft Book

PARENTING

Everything® Baby Names Book, 2nd Ed.
Everything® Baby Shower Book
Everything® Baby's First Year Book
Everything® Birthing Book
Everything® Breastfeeding Book
Everything® Father-to-Be Book
Everything® Father's First Year Book
Everything® Get Ready for Baby Book
Everything® Get Your Baby to Sleep Book, $9.95
Everything® Getting Pregnant Book
Everything® Guide to Raising a One-Year-Old
Everything® Guide to Raising a Two-Year-Old
Everything® Homeschooling Book
Everything® Mother's First Year Book
**Everything® Parent's Guide to Childhood
Illnesses**
Everything® Parent's Guide to Children
and Divorce
Everything® Parent's Guide to Children
with ADD/ADHD
Everything® Parent's Guide to Children
with Asperger's Syndrome
Everything® Parent's Guide to Children
with Autism
Everything® Parent's Guide to Children with
Bipolar Disorder
**Everything® Parent's Guide to Children with
Depression**
Everything® Parent's Guide to Children
with Dyslexia
**Everything® Parent's Guide to Children with
Juvenile Diabetes**
Everything® Parent's Guide to Positive Discipline
Everything® Parent's Guide to Raising a
Successful Child
Everything® Parent's Guide to Raising Boys
Everything® Parent's Guide to Raising Girls
Everything® Parent's Guide to Raising Siblings
Everything® Parent's Guide to Sensory
Integration Disorder
Everything® Parent's Guide to Tantrums
Everything® Parent's Guide to the Strong-Willed
Child
Everything® Parenting a Teenager Book
Everything® Potty Training Book, $9.95
Everything® Pregnancy Book, 3rd Ed.
Everything® Pregnancy Fitness Book
Everything® Pregnancy Nutrition Book
Everything® Pregnancy Organizer, 2nd Ed., $16.95
Everything® Toddler Activities Book
Everything® Toddler Book

Everything® Tween Book
Everything® Twins, Triplets, and More Book

PETS

Everything® Aquarium Book
Everything® Boxer Book
Everything® Cat Book, 2nd Ed.
Everything® Chihuahua Book
Everything® Dachshund Book
Everything® Dog Book
Everything® Dog Health Book
Everything® Dog Obedience Book
Everything® Dog Owner's Organizer, $16.95
Everything® Dog Training and Tricks Book
Everything® German Shepherd Book
Everything® Golden Retriever Book
Everything® Horse Book
Everything® Horse Care Book
Everything® Horseback Riding Book
Everything® Labrador Retriever Book
Everything® Poodle Book
Everything® Pug Book
Everything® Puppy Book
Everything® Rottweiler Book
Everything® Small Dogs Book
Everything® Tropical Fish Book
Everything® Yorkshire Terrier Book

REFERENCE

Everything® American Presidents Book
Everything® Blogging Book
Everything® Build Your Vocabulary Book
Everything® Car Care Book
Everything® Classical Mythology Book
Everything® Da Vinci Book
Everything® Divorce Book
Everything® Einstein Book
Everything® Enneagram Book
Everything® Etiquette Book, 2nd Ed.
Everything® Inventions and Patents Book
Everything® Mafia Book
Everything® Philosophy Book
Everything® Pirates Book
Everything® Psychology Book

RELIGION

Everything® Angels Book
Everything® Bible Book
Everything® Buddhism Book
Everything® Catholicism Book
Everything® Christianity Book
Everything® Gnostic Gospels Book
Everything® History of the Bible Book
Everything® Jesus Book

Everything® Jewish History & Heritage Book
Everything® Judaism Book
Everything® Kabbalah Book
Everything® Koran Book
Everything® Mary Book
Everything® Mary Magdalene Book
Everything® Prayer Book
Everything® Saints Book, 2nd Ed.
Everything® Torah Book
Everything® Understanding Islam Book
Everything® World's Religions Book
Everything® Zen Book

SCHOOL & CAREERS

Everything® Alternative Careers Book
Everything® Career Tests Book
Everything® College Major Test Book
Everything® College Survival Book, 2nd Ed.
Everything® Cover Letter Book, 2nd Ed.
Everything® Filmmaking Book
Everything® Get-a-Job Book, 2nd Ed.
Everything® Guide to Being a Paralegal
Everything® Guide to Being a Personal Trainer
Everything® Guide to Being a Real Estate Agent
Everything® Guide to Being a Sales Rep
Everything® Guide to Careers in Health Care
Everything® Guide to Careers in Law Enforcement
Everything® Guide to Government Jobs
Everything® Guide to Starting and Running a Restaurant
Everything® Job Interview Book
Everything® New Nurse Book
Everything® New Teacher Book
Everything® Paying for College Book
Everything® Practice Interview Book
Everything® Resume Book, 2nd Ed.
Everything® Study Book

SELF-HELP

Everything® Dating Book, 2nd Ed.
Everything® Great Sex Book
Everything® Self-Esteem Book
Everything® Tantric Sex Book

SPORTS & FITNESS

Everything® Easy Fitness Book
Everything® Running Book
Everything® Weight Training Book

TRAVEL

Everything® Family Guide to Cruise Vacations
Everything® Family Guide to Hawaii
Everything® Family Guide to Las Vegas, 2nd Ed.
Everything® Family Guide to Mexico
Everything® Family Guide to New York City, 2nd Ed.
Everything® Family Guide to RV Travel & Campgrounds
Everything® Family Guide to the Caribbean
Everything® Family Guide to the Walt Disney World Resort®, Universal Studios®, and Greater Orlando, 4th Ed.
Everything® Family Guide to Timeshares
Everything® Family Guide to Washington D.C., 2nd Ed.

WEDDINGS

Everything® Bachelorette Party Book, $9.95
Everything® Bridesmaid Book, $9.95
Everything® Destination Wedding Book
Everything® Elopement Book, $9.95
Everything® Father of the Bride Book, $9.95
Everything® Groom Book, $9.95
Everything® Mother of the Bride Book, $9.95
Everything® Outdoor Wedding Book
Everything® Wedding Book, 3rd Ed.
Everything® Wedding Checklist, $9.95
Everything® Wedding Etiquette Book, $9.95
Everything® Wedding Organizer, 2nd Ed., $16.95
Everything® Wedding Shower Book, $9.95
Everything® Wedding Vows Book, $9.95
Everything® Wedding Workout Book
Everything® Weddings on a Budget Book, $9.95

WRITING

Everything® Creative Writing Book
Everything® Get Published Book, 2nd Ed.
Everything® Grammar and Style Book
Everything® Guide to Magazine Writing
Everything® Guide to Writing a Book Proposal
Everything® Guide to Writing a Novel
Everything® Guide to Writing Children's Books
Everything® Guide to Writing Copy
Everything® Guide to Writing Research Papers
Everything® Screenwriting Book
Everything® Writing Poetry Book
Everything® Writing Well Book